FENG SHUI

— FOR —
2018

戊戌

狗
年運程
下卷

戊戌年

The Year of the Earth Dog

Feng Shui for 2018

All intellectual property rights including copyright in relation to this book belong to Joey Yap Research Group Sdn. Bhd.

No part of this book may be copied, used, subsumed, or exploited in fact, field of thought or general idea, by any other authors or persons, or be stored in a retrieval system, transmitted or reproduced in any way, including but not limited to digital copying and printing in any form whatsoever worldwide without the prior agreement and written permission of the copyright owner. Permission to use the content of this book or any part thereof must be obtained from the copyright owner. For more details, please contact:

JOEY YAP RESEARCH GROUP SDN BHD (944330-D)
19-3, The Boulevard, Mid Valley City,
59200 Kuala Lumpur, Malaysia.
Tel   : +603-2284 8080
Fax   : +603-2284 1218
Email   : info@masteryacademy.com
Website   : www.masteryacademy.com

DISCLAIMER:

The author, copyright owner, and the publishers respectively have made their best efforts to produce this high quality, informative and helpful book. They have verified the technical accuracy of the information and contents of this book. However, the information contained in this book cannot replace or substitute for the services of trained professionals in any field, including, but not limited to, mental, financial, medical, psychological, or legal fields. They do not offer any professional, personal, medical, financial or legal advice and none of the information contained in the book should be confused as such advice. Any information pertaining to the events, occurrences, dates and other details relating to the person or persons, dead or alive, and to the companies have been verified to the best of their abilities based on information obtained or extracted from various websites, newspaper clippings and other public media. However, they make no representation or warranties of any kind with regard to the contents of this book and accept no liability of any kind for any losses or damages caused or alleged to be caused directly or indirectly from using the information contained herein.

INDEX

PREFACE

With the recent wave of Feng Shui Renaissance, we find ourselves once again drenched in a newfound interest and respect for the historic art and science of Classical Feng Shui.

If you're a careful observer, you can certainly observe what this new wave of Feng Shui pushed in: an era of accessibility where F-I-Y or "Feng Shui-It Yourself" methods ubiquitously emerged left, right and centre. Everywhere, Feng Shui enthusiasts and amateurs can be seen dipping their hands and proclaiming the methods and applications of Feng Shui in ways never seen before. As a master trainer, consultant and practitioner of this field, I am of course more than glad to see this escalating trend and interest in the field of Feng Shui and its complementary studies, Chinese Astrology, Yi Jing and Face Reading taking off.

This book is produced as my call to answer the pressing demand from the masses seeking accessible Feng Shui information and knowledge, as well as to provide an avenue of learning to those who, for reasons of the time, or perhaps distance, are unable to attend my annual Feng Shui and Astrology seminars. Just treat this annual publication as your trusty go-to guidebook to foster a new layer of understanding on the Qi that will influence properties in 2018, and the correct know-how on how to best deploy these energies in your home and workplace to your advantage. The book you're holding also clarifies and draws a comprehensive overview for the year based on the Flying Stars chart and the Afflictions for 2018.

Together with the monthly Flying Stars outlook based on the Main Door and Bedroom locations for all Twelve Months of 2018, the section on the Flying Stars for all eight Houses for 2018 presents a clean and solid foundation to enable you to gain more direct and encompassing insights on how the Qi in 2018 will affect you, your family, or your business.

If you're unfamiliar with the methods of plotting a Flying Stars chart, don't worry, I'll make it more convenient for you. Just go to the link as indicated on Page 12 to obtain your individual access code and generate your own results with the online Flying Stars calculator there.

Those with a more thorough understanding of Chinese Metaphysics studies would know that luck is divided into Man Luck, Earth Luck and Heaven Luck – all collectively known as the Cosmic Trinity. Notably, Feng Shui makes up only one single component of the

Cosmic Trinity, so don't be exceedingly concerned if there is a presence of negative stars in your property. Remember, any view in Feng Shui is incomplete without taking into consideration the proportion and the bigger picture of the situations or structures. Hence, the full impact of the stars must also be viewed in light of the landforms in the surrounding area, which will trigger or activate the stars' negative or positive energies.

If you're interested and would like to know more about how to do simple assessments of forms, you may want to look into my Feng Shui for Homebuyers series.

Every once in a while, I would give some "words of wisdom" to my clients to let them view things in a bigger picture. Giving in to your fear and paranoia will succumb you to a state of inaction and thus, making you incapable of accepting changes. It is important for you to note that in Chinese Metaphysics, nothing is completely bad or purely good. For every Yin, there's a Yang, and vice versa. Worrying is essentially useless; the most important thing you need to do is to understand what the Feng Shui influences are, prioritise your actions and make informed decisions.

I hope you'll find this book supportive, practical and most importantly, informative. To wrap it up, I wish you a smooth sailing year ahead in the Year of the Earth Dog!

Warmest regards,

Dato' Joey Yap
July 2017

Connect with us:

www.joeyyap.com   JOEYYAP TV www.joeyyap.tv

@DatoJoeyYap   @DJoeyYap   @JoeyYap

Academy website:
www.masteryacademy.com l jya.masteryacademy.com l www.baziprofiling.com

BONUS CONTENT
FREE DOWNLOAD

Exclusive content available for download with your purchase of the Feng Shui for 2018 book.

Claim your FREE ONLINE ACCESS now at:
www.masteryacademy.com/bookbonus2018

FSR81AC7 *Expires 31st December 2018*

Introduction

Introduction

In order to fully utilise the information and material in this book, you need to have a basic understanding of how to derive certain information - for example, the location of your Main Door, the various directional sectors in your home and your personal Gua Number.

How to ascertain the Location of your Main Door

In order to tap into the beneficial Qi of the year and the kind of Qi that will influence your home in 2018, it is important to be able to identify the various directional sectors of your home and also to determine which sector your Main Door is located. This knowledge is particularly important for those who wish to make use of the information contained in the Eight Houses for 2018 chapter, which is based on the directional sector in where your house or office's Main Door is found.

The first step is to divide your house into Nine Grids. To do this, you just need a simple scout's compass and the plan of your house. On the plan of your house, draw the Nine Grids as illustrated in Step 1 and Step 2.

Step 1

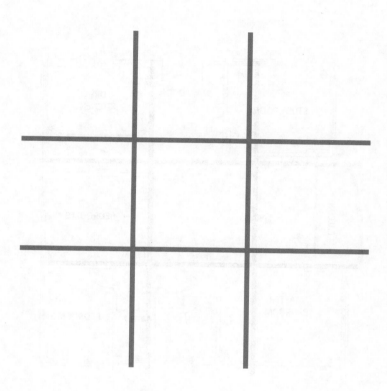

The Year of the Earth Dog

Step 2

Next, stand at the center point of your house and establish the North direction using the compass. On the plan of your house, mark out the sector in that direction as North and then identify all the other directions according to the directions of the compass.

Step 3

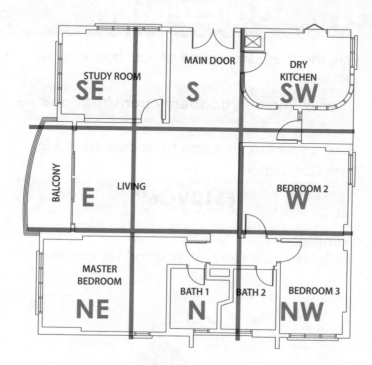

Using this simple Nine Grids, you will be able to identify the favourable and unfavourable sectors of your home and make less or more use of the corresponding rooms. You will also be able to ascertain the location of your Main Door and determine what kind of energies will influence your home in 2018.

Flying Stars Feng Shui Calculator

Print the Flying Stars chart of your house at the URL below:

www.masteryacademy.com/regbook

Here is your unique code to access the Flying Stars Calculator:

FS12VC69

Sample:
This is how your Flying Stars Chart will look like:

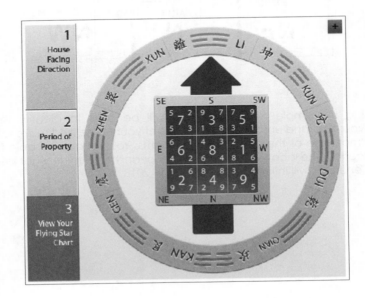

Find Your Gua Number and Animal Sign

Gua Numbers for Years 1912 - 2007

Year of Birth		Gua (M)	Gua (F)	Year of Birth		Gua (M)	Gua (F)	Year of Birth		Gua (M)	Gua (F)	Year of Birth		Gua (M)	Gua (F)
1912 壬子 Ren Zi	Water Rat	7	8	1936 丙子 Bing Zi	Fire Rat	1	8	1960 庚子 Geng Zi	Metal Rat	4	2	1984 甲子 Jia Zi	Wood Rat	7	8
1913 癸丑 Gui Chou	Water Ox	6	9	1937 丁丑 Ding Chou	Fire Ox	9	6	1961 辛丑 Xin Chou	Metal Ox	3	3	1985 乙丑 Yi Chou	Wood Ox	6	9
1914 甲寅 Jia Yin	Wood Tiger	2	1	1938 戊寅 Wu Yin	Earth Tiger	8	7	1962 壬寅 Ren Yin	Water Tiger	2	4	1986 丙寅 Bing Yin	Fire Tiger	2	1
1915 乙卯 Yi Mao	Wood Rabbit	4	2	1939 己卯 Ji Mao	Earth Rabbit	7	8	1963 癸卯 Gui Mao	Water Rabbit	1	8	1987 丁卯 Ding Mao	Fire Rabbit	4	2
1916 丙辰 Bing Chen	Fire Dragon	3	3	1940 庚辰 Geng Chen	Metal Dragon	6	9	1964 甲辰 Jia Chen	Wood Dragon	9	6	1988 戊辰 Wu Chen	Earth Dragon	3	3
1917 丁巳 Ding Si	Fire Snake	2	4	1941 辛巳 Xin Si	Metal Snake	2	1	1965 乙巳 Yi Si	Wood Snake	8	7	1989 己巳 Ji Si	Earth Snake	2	4
1918 戊午 Wu Wu	Earth Horse	1	8	1942 壬午 Ren Wu	Water Horse	4	2	1966 丙午 Bing Wu	Fire Horse	7	8	1990 庚午 Geng Wu	Metal Horse	1	8
1919 己未 Ji Wei	Earth Goat	9	6	1943 癸未 Gui Wei	Water Goat	3	3	1967 丁未 Ding Wei	Fire Goat	6	9	1991 辛未 Xin Wei	Metal Goat	9	6
1920 庚申 Geng Shen	Metal Monkey	8	7	1944 甲申 Jia Shen	Wood Monkey	2	4	1968 戊申 Wu Shen	Earth Monkey	2	1	1992 壬申 Ren Shen	Water Monkey	8	7
1921 辛酉 Xin You	Metal Rooster	7	8	1945 乙酉 Yi You	Wood Rooster	1	8	1969 己酉 Ji You	Earth Rooster	4	2	1993 癸酉 Gui You	Water Rooster	7	8
1922 壬戌 Ren Xu	Water Dog	6	9	1946 丙戌 Bing Xu	Fire Dog	9	6	1970 庚戌 Geng Xu	Metal Dog	3	3	1994 甲戌 Jia Xu	Wood Dog	6	9
1923 癸亥 Gui Hai	Water Pig	2	1	1947 丁亥 Ding Hai	Fire Pig	8	7	1971 辛亥 Xin Hai	Metal Pig	2	4	1995 乙亥 Yi Hai	Wood Pig	2	1
1924 甲子 Jia Zi	Wood Rat	4	2	1948 戊子 Wu Zi	Earth Rat	7	8	1972 壬子 Ren Zi	Water Rat	1	8	1996 丙子 Bing Zi	Fire Rat	4	2
1925 乙丑 Yi Chou	Wood Ox	3	3	1949 己丑 Ji Chou	Earth Ox	6	9	1973 癸丑 Gui Chou	Water Ox	9	6	1997 丁丑 Ding Chou	Fire Ox	3	3
1926 丙寅 Bing Yin	Fire Tiger	2	4	1950 庚寅 Geng Yin	Metal Tiger	2	1	1974 甲寅 Jia Yin	Wood Tiger	8	7	1998 戊寅 Wu Yin	Earth Tiger	2	4
1927 丁卯 Ding Mao	Fire Rabbit	1	8	1951 辛卯 Xin Mao	Metal Rabbit	4	2	1975 乙卯 Yi Mao	Wood Rabbit	7	8	1999 己卯 Ji Mao	Earth Rabbit	1	8
1928 戊辰 Wu Chen	Earth Dragon	9	6	1952 壬辰 Ren Chen	Water Dragon	3	3	1976 丙辰 Bing Chen	Fire Dragon	6	9	2000 庚辰 Geng Chen	Metal Dragon	9	6
1929 己巳 Ji Si	Earth Snake	8	7	1953 癸巳 Gui Si	Water Snake	2	4	1977 丁巳 Ding Si	Fire Snake	2	1	2001 辛巳 Xin Si	Metal Snake	8	7
1930 庚午 Geng Wu	Metal Horse	7	8	1954 甲午 Jia Wu	Wood Horse	1	8	1978 戊午 Wu Wu	Earth Horse	4	2	2002 壬午 Ren Wu	Water Horse	7	8
1931 辛未 Xin Wei	Metal Goat	6	9	1955 乙未 Yi Wei	Wood Goat	9	6	1979 己未 Ji Wei	Earth Goat	3	3	2003 癸未 Gui Wei	Water Goat	6	9
1932 壬申 Ren Shen	Water Monkey	2	1	1956 丙申 Bing Shen	Fire Monkey	8	7	1980 庚申 Geng Shen	Metal Monkey	2	4	2004 甲申 Jia Shen	Wood Monkey	2	1
1933 癸酉 Gui You	Water Rooster	4	2	1957 丁酉 Ding You	Fire Rooster	7	8	1981 辛酉 Xin You	Metal Rooster	1	8	2005 乙酉 Yi You	Wood Rooster	4	2
1934 甲戌 Jia Xu	Wood Dog	3	3	1958 戊戌 Wu Xu	Earth Dog	6	9	1982 壬戌 Ren Xu	Water Dog	9	6	2006 丙戌 Bing Xu	Fire Dog	3	3
1935 乙亥 Yi Hai	Wood Pig	2	4	1959 己亥 Ji Hai	Earth Pig	2	1	1983 癸亥 Gui Hai	Water Pig	8	7	2007 丁亥 Ding Hai	Fire Pig	2	4

• Please note that the date for the Chinese Solar Year starts on Feb 4. This means that if you were born in Feb 2 of 2002, you belong to the previous year of 2001.

Gua Numbers for Years 2008 - 2103

Year of Birth			Gua Number Male	Gua Number Female	Year of Birth			Gua Number Male	Gua Number Female	Year of Birth			Gua Number Male	Gua Number Female	Year of Birth			Gua Number Male	Gua Number Female
2008	戊子 Wu Zi	Earth Rat	1	8	2032	壬子 Ren Zi	Water Rat	4	2	2056	丙子 Bing Zi	Fire Rat	7	8	2080	庚子 Geng Zi	Metal Rat	1	8
2009	己丑 Ji Chou	Earth Ox	9	6	2033	癸丑 Gui Chou	Water Ox	3	3	2057	丁丑 Ding Chou	Fire Ox	6	9	2081	辛丑 Xin Chou	Metal Ox	9	6
2010	庚寅 Geng Yin	Metal Tiger	8	7	2034	甲寅 Jia Yin	Wood Tiger	2	4	2058	戊寅 Wu Yin	Earth Tiger	2	1	2082	壬寅 Ren Yin	Water Tiger	8	7
2011	辛卯 Xin Mao	Metal Rabbit	7	8	2035	乙卯 Yi Mao	Wood Rabbit	1	8	2059	己卯 Ji Mao	Earth Rabbit	4	2	2083	癸卯 Gui Mao	Water Rabbit	7	8
2012	壬辰 Ren Chen	Water Dragon	6	9	2036	丙辰 Bing Chen	Fire Dragon	9	6	2060	庚辰 Geng Chen	Metal Dragon	3	3	2084	甲辰 Jia Chen	Wood Dragon	6	9
2013	癸巳 Gui Si	Water Snake	2	1	2037	丁巳 Ding Si	Fire Snake	8	7	2061	辛巳 Xin Si	Metal Snake	2	4	2085	乙巳 Yi Si	Wood Snake	2	1
2014	甲午 Jia Wu	Wood Horse	4	2	2038	戊午 Wu Wu	Earth Horse	7	8	2062	壬午 Ren Wu	Water Horse	1	8	2086	丙午 Bing Wu	Fire Horse	4	2
2015	乙未 Yi Wei	Wood Goat	3	3	2039	己未 Ji Wei	Earth Goat	6	9	2063	癸未 Gui Wei	Water Goat	9	6	2087	丁未 Ding Wei	Fire Goat	3	3
2016	丙申 Bing Shen	Fire Monkey	2	4	2040	庚申 Geng Shen	Metal Monkey	2	1	2064	甲申 Jia Shen	Wood Monkey	8	7	2088	戊申 Wu Shen	Earth Monkey	2	4
2017	丁酉 Ding You	Fire Rooster	1	8	2041	辛酉 Xin You	Metal Rooster	4	2	2065	乙酉 Yi You	Wood Rooster	7	8	2089	己酉 Ji You	Earth Rooster	1	8
2018	戊戌 Wu Xu	Earth Dog	9	6	2042	壬戌 Ren Xu	Water Dog	3	3	2066	丙戌 Bing Xu	Fire Dog	6	9	2090	庚戌 Geng Xu	Metal Dog	9	6
2019	己亥 Ji Hai	Earth Pig	8	7	2043	癸亥 Gui Hai	Water Pig	2	4	2067	丁亥 Ding Hai	Fire Pig	2	1	2091	辛亥 Xin Hai	Metal Pig	8	7
2020	庚子 Geng Zi	Metal Rat	7	8	2044	甲子 Jia Zi	Wood Rat	1	8	2068	戊子 Wu Zi	Earth Rat	4	2	2092	壬子 Ren Zi	Water Rat	7	8
2021	辛丑 Xin Chou	Metal Ox	6	9	2045	乙丑 Yi Chou	Wood Ox	9	6	2069	己丑 Ji Chou	Earth Ox	3	3	2093	癸丑 Gui Chou	Water Ox	6	9
2022	壬寅 Ren Yin	Water Tiger	2	1	2046	丙寅 Bing Yin	Fire Tiger	8	7	2070	庚寅 Geng Yin	Metal Tiger	2	4	2094	甲寅 Jia Yin	Wood Tiger	2	1
2023	癸卯 Gui Mao	Water Rabbit	4	2	2047	丁卯 Ding Mao	Fire Rabbit	7	8	2071	辛卯 Xin Mao	Metal Rabbit	1	8	2095	乙卯 Yi Mao	Wood Rabbit	4	2
2024	甲辰 Jia Chen	Wood Dragon	3	3	2048	戊辰 Wu Chen	Earth Dragon	6	9	2072	壬辰 Ren Chen	Water Dragon	9	6	2096	丙辰 Bing Chen	Fire Dragon	3	3
2025	乙巳 Yi Si	Wood Snake	2	4	2049	己巳 Ji Si	Earth Snake	2	1	2073	癸巳 Gui Si	Water Snake	8	7	2097	丁巳 Ding Si	Fire Snake	2	4
2026	丙午 Bing Wu	Fire Horse	1	8	2050	庚午 Geng Wu	Metal Horse	4	2	2074	甲午 Jia Wu	Wood Horse	7	8	2098	戊午 Wu Wu	Earth Horse	1	8
2027	丁未 Ding Wei	Fire Goat	9	6	2051	辛未 Xin Wei	Metal Goat	3	3	2075	乙未 Yi Wei	Wood Goat	6	9	2099	己未 Ji Wei	Earth Goat	9	6
2028	戊申 Wu Shen	Earth Monkey	8	7	2052	壬申 Ren Shen	Water Monkey	2	4	2076	丙申 Bing Shen	Fire Monkey	2	1	2100	庚申 Geng Shen	Metal Monkey	8	7
2029	己酉 Ji You	Earth Rooster	7	8	2053	癸酉 Gui You	Water Rooster	1	8	2077	丁酉 Ding You	Fire Rooster	4	2	2101	辛酉 Xin You	Metal Rooster	7	8
2030	庚戌 Geng Xu	Metal Dog	6	9	2054	甲戌 Jia Xu	Wood Dog	9	6	2078	戊戌 Wu Xu	Earth Dog	3	3	2102	壬戌 Ren Xu	Water Dog	6	9
2031	辛亥 Xin Hai	Metal Pig	2	1	2055	乙亥 Yi Hai	Wood Pig	8	7	2079	己亥 Ji Hai	Earth Pig	2	4	2103	癸亥 Gui Hai	Water Pig	2	1

• Please note that the date for the Chinese Solar Year starts on Feb 4. This means that if you were born in Feb 2 of 2002, you belong to the previous year of 2001.

Using the 12-Month Outlook based on Bedroom Location Section

To use this section, you must know the location of your property's Main Door and the location of your bedroom. Note that your bedroom may be located on the Ground Floor or 1st or 2nd floor.

1. Identify the location of your Main Door.

In the example below, the Main Door is located in the West. So turn to page 153 for the section on the 12-month outlook for all 8 bedrooms for a West Sector Main Door.

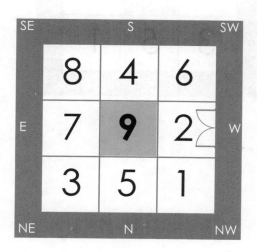

2. Identify the location of your bedroom.

In the example below, the bedroom is located in the South. So turn to page 162 and you will find the 12-month outlook for your bedroom, located in a West Sector Main Door.

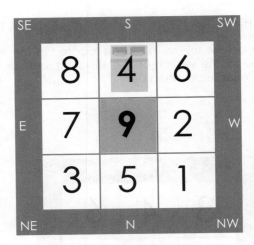

2018 Feng Shui Afflictions

2018 Feng Shui Afflictions

The Three Killings (三煞) – NORTH 337.6° - 22.5°

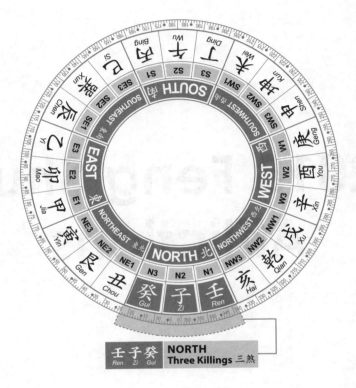

壬子癸	NORTH
Ren Zi Gui	Three Killings 三煞

The Three Killings takes up residence in the North sector, which is the "double jeopardy" sector of this year. Three Killings is one of the more inauspicious Stars you will need to wary of. This means you should keep this sector free from any activities or disturbances to ensure that it stays dormant.

Any activity which involves breakage of the walls or ground should be avoided for the rest of the year as these will definitely trigger the negative effects of the Star. Its unfavourable effects include disruptions in your endeavours and a host of seemingly endless problems. More serious issues could include serious health complications, loss of wealth and material possessions, accidents and mishaps, as well as robbery and theft.

The Five Yellow (五黄) – NORTH 337.6° - 22.5°

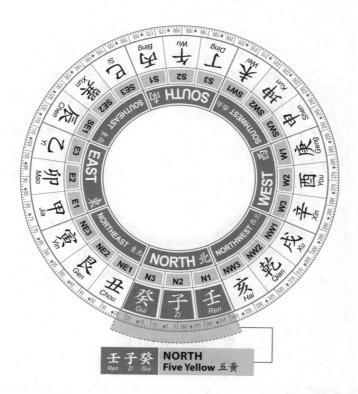

| 壬子癸 | NORTH |
| Ren Zi Gui | Five Yellow 五黄 |

Compounding to the problems afflicting the North sector this year is the Five Yellow, the most dangerous among the negative stars to watch out for. Hence, if the Three Killings is not bad enough, you should actively look to leaving the North sector well alone, lest you inadvertently activate its unpleasant effects. No renovations should be performed in this sector through the entire year – even something as minor as drilling or nailing the wall should be avoided. Keep it as quiet as possible and try to keep your activities here to a minimal.

If the sector is occupied or in use as a bedroom or a study room, it will be in the best interest of the occupant to relocate. Continuous usage of the affected sector could result in serious accidents and mishaps which could be life threatening in nature, aside from other issues and problems affecting your daily life. Together with the Three Killings, these problems may even be further amplified.

The Year Breaker (歲破) – SOUTHEAST 1 112.6° - 127.5°

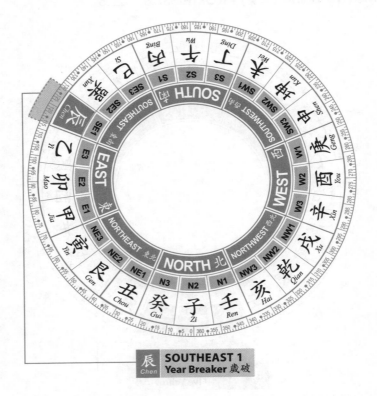

| 辰 Chen | **SOUTHEAST 1** |
| | **Year Breaker 歲破** |

Also known as the "Wrath of the Grand Duke", the Year Breaker occupies the sector directly opposite the Grand Duke, which is Southeast 1. Minimise all activity in this sector and keep it undisturbed whenever possible to avoid activating the negative effects of the Year Breaker.

If triggered, it may lead to serious issues which are more severe in nature compared to the Grand Duke itself. Hence, make every effort to avoid renovating this sector or moving furniture about as these activities could inadvertently trigger its effects.

The Grand Duke (太歲) – NORTHWEST 1 292.6° - 307.5°

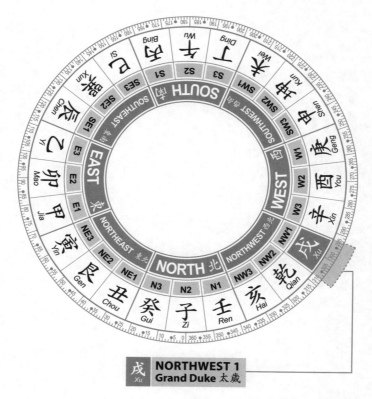

戌 Xu NORTHWEST 1
Grand Duke 太歲

Where the Grand Duke takes up residence, trouble is bound to follow if one is not careful in taking the necessary precautions. Northwest 1 is the sector where the Grand Duke makes it home this year and you will need to be mindful using it. Its negative effects include undesirable incidences such as accidents and misfortunes. It will be important to not conduct any activity that is important in nature, in the Northwest 1 sector. In fact, it may be better to just avoid using it altogether.

The same steps apply if the place in reference is the office. Spending long hours facing or working in the Northwest 1 sector may bring about unpleasant repercussions. However, if you are looking to exert more authority, you may look to placing your back against this direction.

Flying Stars Feng Shui for 2018

Flying Stars Feng Shui for 2018

Overview

Wealth Sectors : Southeast

Academic Sectors: South, Northwest

Negative Sectors : North, West

2018 Flying Stars by Sectors

Direction/ Location	Annual Star	Forecast
東南 Southeast	八白 Eight White	The Southeast sector would be the one to look out for if you are seeking prosperity and good fortune as it is the main Wealth sector for this year. Having your Main Door located in this sector would be especially beneficial as it will help usher in positive energies, which in turn will bring about great returns in the form of investments. The Eight White is also excellent for encouraging a career boost and enhancing one's reputation. If the Main Door is not found in this sector, you can still harness its benefits by activating it with water features or Yang-natured objects such as clocks, fans and televisions. You can also look to using the sector more often by using it as a family or activity room.
南 South	四綠 Four Green	Those who are studying or still in school may seek to utilise the South sector as the Four Green is conducive for endeavours associated with academic and intellectual pursuits. Similarly, those who are working in academic, creative, literary and artistic fields may also benefit from it. Look to using this sector for those aforementioned activities. If your Main Door is found in the South sector, travelling could have positive outcomes this year and your relationships will flourish.

飞星

2018 Flying Stars by Sectors

Direction/ Location	Annual Star	Forecast
西南 Southwest	六白 Six White	The Six White is especially encouraging if you are looking to seek career opportunities and this can be found in the Southwest sector this year. Using it can help you gain recognition for your efforts in the workplace, especially by those who will be able to help with your career advancement, such as your superiors or bosses. If the Main Door of the office is located here, frequently using it will elevate your status and enhance your influence professionally. Take heed however that the Star is not activated by negative forces or you may experience untoward incidences such as undesirable sudden changes at the workplace and health complications related to the kidney or legs.
西 West	二黑 Two Black	The Two Black is among one of the more inauspicious Stars which needs to be avoided, especially by those with a poor constitution. It is particularly well-known for provoking health problems and aggravating existing medical complications. Expectant mothers will do well to avoid using the West sector to avoid pregnancy issues. In order to lessen its negative effects, look to placing metal objects made of brass, copper, iron or bronze in this sector. On the positive side however, the Two Black can be conducive for property-related investments which will bring about positive outcomes.

2018 Flying Stars by Sectors

Direction/ Location	Annual Star	Forecast
西北 Northwest	一白 One White	Those utilising the One White which is found in the Northwest sector this year can experience positive outcomes for career advancement. Opportunities for travel and wealth accumulation will be enhanced. Academic pursuits will similarly see positive improvements as the One White is conducive for activities related to literature or the written word. Additionally, the usage of this sector will promote relationships and social skills. As such, those seeking to get married may benefit from this. However, ne forwarded that one may have to be wary of emotional troubles and instability.
北 North	五黃 Five Yellow	The Five Yellow is the most dangerous and inauspicious sector to be aware of. If it is triggered, you may experience an endless parade of bad fortunes, mishaps and accidents. Leave the sector as quiet as possible to avoid activating its negative effects. This means avoiding or postponing any renovation work for this sector for the rest of the year. To mitigate its effects, place objects made of metals such as iron, brass, copper, bronze or even pewter, in this sector.

2018 Flying Stars by Sectors

Direction/ Location	Annual Star	Forecast
東北 Northeast	三碧 Three Jade	To avoid unpleasant conflicts, take care to avoid the Three Jade which resides in the Northeast sector. The Three Jade is particularly known to cause arguments, conflict and disagreements. At worst, it can result in legal entanglements and lawsuits which can leave one mentally and emotionally drained. To mitigate the effects, place an oil or red lamp in this sector.
東 East	七赤 Seven Red	If you find that your bedroom is located in the East sector, it will be best to relocate this year due to the effects of the Seven Red. It is known to affect one's emotional and physical well-being as you will constantly find yourself dealing with spats and chronic health issues. Marital problems such as constant arguments may also occur if the marital bed happens to be found in this sector. Additionally, houses with the Main Door in this sector will experience higher risk of being burgled and the occupants will also be prone to robbery and theft.

The Eight Types of Houses in 2018

North Sector Main Door

Overview

The North sector is the sector you have to be extremely careful about in 2018 as the star occupying it this year is the 5 Yellow Star. An omen of dangerous and inauspicious times, it brings with it the high possibility of all kinds of unfortunate accidents and undesirable outcomes. Out of all the stars, this is the one you do not want to trigger even by accident as doing so will most likely lead to you experiencing some kind of mishap or other.

In order to avoid falling victim to the effects of this star, you are strongly advised to leave this sector alone as much as possible. On that note, it would be for the best if you avoid doing anything here that has even the smallest chance of activating it. Just to be on the safe side, you should see if you can designate this area for something that requires little activity or discourages it outright such as a storeroom. If your Main Door happens to be located here, you may want to try and use a different entrance to go in and out of your house.

Aside from keeping your usage of this space to a minimum, you should especially avoid doing any renovations to this space for the entirety of these 12 months. If you already drew up plans to renovate this part of your home last year, it would be in your best interest to postpone them until 2019 comes around. This is because as far as activities which trigger sectors go, renovation works are one of the most capable of accomplishing just that.

On the off chance that you absolutely have no choice but to use this sector or have some renovations done to it, do not fret as there are steps you can take to help mitigate the impact this star will have on your life. The easiest way to accomplish this is to place metal objects in this sector. There are no rules when it comes to what you should put as the items can be made of iron, brass, copper, bronze or even pewter and it can be either a practical choice or an aesthetic one.

Northwest Sector Main Door

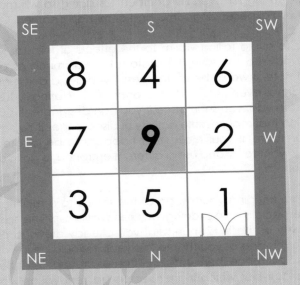

Overview

The general luck of occupants living in a house with its Main Door in the Northwest sector will be on the rise this year due to the presence of the 1 White Star. The star is also known as the Nobleman Star, for it helps to bring noble assistance to you and occupants of your house, which will most likely foster positive outcomes for career advancement and wealth accumulation.

If you have your Main Door in the Northwest sector, the auspicious star will make it seem almost effortless to get help from people at higher and important positions this year. Whether it's seeking approval from your bosses or getting assistance from your colleagues, having this Nobleman Star activated at your house will help you open doors and gain specific access to complete your tasks perfectly. A job promotion is highly possible as your work will gain acknowledgement much more easily. Therefore, if you do a wonderful job, your superiors will give you the credits you deserve and you may well be the next on the list to be promoted.

The 1 White Star will also enhance opportunities for travel and wealth accumulation. Having a Main Door in the Northwest sector will help you to tap into otherwise hidden opportunities to increase your financial standing. The presence of the Nobleman Star will see people with valuable and useful insights coming to your aid should you seek for it. Following these people's advice, you will most possibly increase your wealth by making the right investments or leading your projects to the right path.

Starting a family of your own is also favourable with the presence of the 1 White Star as it promotes relationships. However, to make the most of this positive star, this sector has to be supported by good features such as a mountain or a hill visible in the surroundings, which indicates noble help from people with authority; a Main Door should also be free from the influences of any water bodies or highways nearby. If your Main Door in the Northwest sector is affected by the presence of water bodies or highways, beware of psychological complications such as depression and emotional issues arising in the household this year.

West Sector Main Door

Overview

This year, the West sector will see the presence of the 2 Black Star, which is also known as the Sickness Star. This star is one of the more inauspicious stars, so it is advisable not to move into a new house with its Main Door located in the West sector this year, for its negative influence to the occupants' health will last throughout the year.

If you have your Main Door in the West sector, the Sickness Star will be activated and all occupants of your house will have to pay extra attention to their own well-being. Constant exposure to the negative influence of the Sickness Star will increase the risk of falling sick, especially having skin and stomach-related health issues. Be careful of what and where you eat, and make sure you get adequate rest. Scheduling for a full medical check-up this year is also advisable, so if there is anything amiss, early detection will ensure better chances of recovering sooner. Expectant women should avoid using the West sector this year.

As the 2 Black Star will aggravate existing medical complications, having a Main Door in the West sector this year is not favourable for those with pre-existing medical conditions. Besides placing items made of iron, bronze, copper, pewter or brass to minimise the negative effect of the star, it's best to go for check-ups regularly and immediately get professional consultation from a doctor should you feel any discomfort. If you are on medication, be mindful not to skip taking your medication. Keep your medications and emergency kit handy so you could reach them easily when needed. Put the phone number of your family doctor or anyone you could trust on speed dial, so when there's any emergency you could get help instantly.

Although unfavourable for the occupants' health, the 2 Black Star can be conducive for real estate and investment endeavours, and can help to increase financial gains in these areas. You could tap into the Indirect Wealth Luck the star brings by having a Bright Hall free from any negative features outside your Main Door. This way, you can better collect the positive Qi in your surroundings.

Southwest Sector Main Door

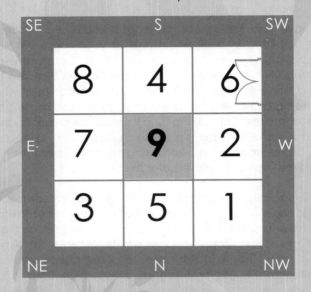

SE	S	SW
8	4	6
E 7	**9**	2 W
3	5	1
NE	N	NW

Overview

The 6 White Star, also known as the Power and Authority Star, resides in the Southwest sector in the year 2018. Having a Main Door in the Southwest sector will give you the advantage of having this star activated by default this year, since the occupants are frequently using this sector. It's definitely good news to see this star at your Main Door due to its auspicious significance.

The Power and Authority Star is extremely helpful in gaining power, authority and career success. Having this star at the Main Door of your house will bring opportunities for you to showcase your capabilities and talents at your workplace, helping you to win your superiors' hearts and recognition. If you are seeking career advancement, with this star at your Main Door, this year will most likely be the year you could get the job promotion you deserve. You will find your superiors more open to your suggestions and ideas. If your ideas are good, you will most probably get to lead the execution. Brilliant execution of your plans will prove your worth to your bosses. This star is especially favourable for those in the military, academic and sports fields.

The 6 White Star residing in the sector where a Main Door is located is also favourable for leaders and managers. A Main Door in the Southwest sector of an office will allow those in the managerial or leadership positions to present their strengths and gain the respect they deserve. Frequent usage of the Main Door in this sector will boost one's status and influence professionally. Besides, with the presence of this star, tourism, printing and freight-related businesses will benefit the most this year.

However, take note of any negative features visible from the Southwest sector, as any negative forces activating the star will turn its positive influence negative. Negative features include pylon and sharp corners outside a Main Door. When activated by negative forces, the 6 White Star may bring about disruptions at the workplace and health complications, especially health issues related to the kidneys and legs.

South Sector Main Door

SE	S	SW
8	4	6
7	**9**	2
3	5	1
NE	N	NW

E — W

Overview

In 2018, the star occupying the South sector will be none other than the 4 Green Star which should please you if you are involved in the world of academia in any way. This is because this star is linked to each and every kind of intellectual activity there is and bodes well for those involved in them.

As such, it is very good to have your Main Door located here, especially if you happen to be studying at this point in your life. It does not matter if you are still in school, which stage of your education you are currently at or that you are a working adult taking night classes. If you choose to use this sector especially as your study area, you will find that you are able to comprehend and remember what you are studying. This should prove particularly useful for when you have to sit for an examination.

You should also find this sector to be perfect for fields and activities that are driven more by creativity than the pursuit of knowledge. If you happen to work in a field or industry which requires imagination and ingenuity, you should consider doing any work-related tasks you might bring home here. This is especially true if your job involves literature or writing in general as getting the inspiration you need will be a piece of cake.

Additionally, this is a good place to use if you happen to have any hobbies of the artistic variety. This includes everything from drawing and painting to knitting and even assembling model kits. As long as you are creating something with your own two hands, you are encouraged to do it in this sector as your handiwork will likely turn out just the way you like it or perhaps even better.

Aside from all that, there are additional benefits to be enjoyed if you happen to have your Main Door located in this sector. Because this combination encourages positive outcomes when travelling is involved, you should take every opportunity to hit the road or visit far-off places that comes your way. Additionally, the relationships that you have with others will be able to flourish and become stronger this year.

Southeast Sector Main Door

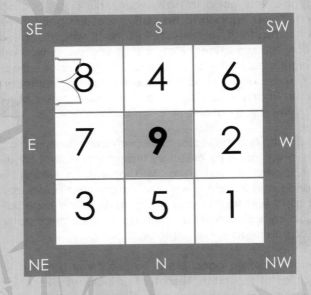

SE	S	SW
8	4	6
7	**9**	2
3	5	1
NE	N	NW

Overview

The 8 White Star will be taking up residence in the Southeast sector in 2018, making it the Wealth sector for this year. This is extremely good news for those of you who have their Main Door located here as good luck and prosperity are sure to be constant elements in your life for the next 12 months.

If your Main Door is located in this sector, it is safe to say that this will allow the year's positive energies to flow into your house and bring about good tidings. These energies will be immensely beneficial to your financial status in particular as you will be able to see a significant boost to your income on more than one front. On that note, you should pay close attention to your investment portfolio and make wise decisions about how to manage it as that is where you will likely see the most drastic uptick in activity.

Aside from that, the 8 White Star is also ideal for individuals who wish to experience an upwards trajectory in regards to their career advancement plans. If you are a corporate employee and happen to be eyeing a promotion or pay raise, a golden opportunity will cross your path. All you have to do is keep an eye out for it and seize it at the right time. Those of you seeking greater recognition in your respective fields will also have your chance to shine and get the credit you have long deserved.

On the off chance that your Main Door is not located in this sector, there is no reason for you to despair as you can still benefit from its presence. Activating it by placing water features in this location will allow you to tap into the positive energies present here and achieve almost the exact same effect. Should that kind of decorative item not be to your liking, you can opt to use Yang-natured objects such as clocks, fans and televisions. Alternatively, the same result can also be obtained if you simply use this sector more frequently. An easy way to accomplish this would be to designate it as a family or activity room.

East Sector Main Door

Overview

In 2018, the star occupying the East sector will be none other than the 7 Red Star which is considered inauspicious due to its negative associations with arguments and breakdown in communication. Hence, occupants of this sector will likely experience the deterioration of emotions and relationships, especially if they happen to use it as a bedroom.

Where the 7 Red Star resides, there is also the heightened risk of robberies, burglaries and thefts. This is especially true for properties with the Main Door located in the same place as the 7 Red Star. So if this scenario affects your property this year, investing in security features may be something worth looking at. Aside from that however, it would be advisable to be constantly vigilant of one's surroundings and personal safety.

Those with health issues should avoid using this sector as there may be a possibility that any pre-existing conditions may be worsened from its negative effects, resulting in frequent hospitalisation and visits to the doctor. At its worst, it may even result in conditions where surgeries are required and chronic illnesses may also flare up.

Be especially wary if the sector is aggravated by the presence of negative features such as lamp posts and sharp roof corners. These may result in extremely inauspicious occurrences ranging from injuries to the possibility of losing one's job. Not all is bad however if a notable hill is found in this direction, as this would instead bring positive implications such as the availability of noble people throughout the year who will be ever ready to lend a helping hand.

Northeast Sector Main Door

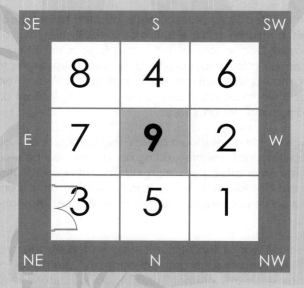

SE	S	SW
8	4	6
E 7	9	2 W
3	5	1
NE	N	NW

Overview

While it is not particularly dangerous, it would still be for the best if you avoid using the Northeast sector as much as possible in 2018. This is because the star which will be residing here for the year is the 3 Jade Star and its presence does not bode well for you where your relationships with others are concerned.

To be more precise, this star has a negative effect on the usually harmonious bonds you have with the people in your life. This disruption to your social network will manifest in the form of arguments, quarrels and disagreements both big and small. You may find yourself being subjected to misunderstandings and maybe even false accusations which could cause lasting damage to your relationships if you do not do your best to salvage the situation as quickly as possible.

If you are particularly unlucky, this star's influence on your life could take a more serious turn and embroil you in something far more severe than just a dispute between friends or family. You may end up getting into legal trouble of some kind whether it is in your personal life or your professional one. In the worst case scenario, you could even find yourself becoming dragged into a lawsuit either by proxy or where you are the primary target yourself.

As it would of course be difficult for you to avoid this sector outright especially if your Main Door is located here, you can take comfort in the fact that there are still ways for you to minimise this star's effect on your life. What you can do is place an oil or red lamp in this sector as this will help supress the negative energies that the star attracts. Nevertheless, sparing use of this space would be the most effective way of keeping its influence on your relationships to a bare minimum.

12-Month Room-by-Room Analysis for the Eight Types of Houses

INDEX

Using the 12-Month Outlook based on Bedroom Location Section

To use this section, you must know the location of your property's Main Door, and the location of your bedroom. Note that your bedroom may be located on the Ground Floor or 1st or 2nd floor.

1. Identify the location of your Main Door.

In the example below, the Main Door is located in the West. So, turn to page 153 for the section on the 12-month outlook for all 8 bedrooms for a West Sector Main Door.

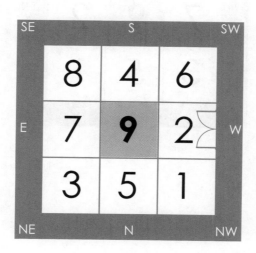

2. Identify the location of your bedroom.

In the example below, the Bedroom is located in the South. So turn to page 162 and you will find the 12-month outlook for your bedroom, located in a West Sector Main Door.

Note: Instead of the bedroom, you can also use the same analysis for your office or study room located in that sector.

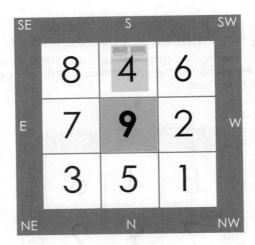

North Sector
Main Door

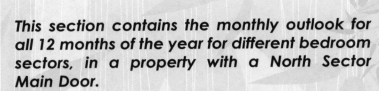

This section contains the monthly outlook for all 12 months of the year for different bedroom sectors, in a property with a North Sector Main Door.

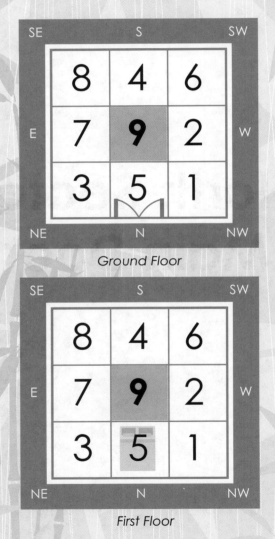

Ground Floor

First Floor

農曆正月 (February 4th - March 4th) 甲寅

Females who are pregnant should be cautious this month, as there might be problems with your pregnancy – especially if you're using this room. As a precaution (if possible), you are advised to change to a different room. There will be other health problems affecting individuals in this room as well. This include liver infections and skin diseases. Try to get adequate amounts of rest and give yourself plenty of breathing space, so you do not overstrain your body. Be prepared for an aggressive competition put up by your rivals and competitors this month. Consider yourself warned that this battle will likely leave you feeling quite drained.

農曆二月 (March 5th - April 4th) 乙卯

Marketing and public relations industries will take a hit this month as things will begin to slow down. Be ready for a sharp decline on clients and high turnovers. This is a good month to take stock of things and plan ahead. Remember, action without thought will not get you very far this month. For entrepreneurs, you might encounter business issues which arise this month and you'll find it difficult to solve. Try to persevere and be ready to face the music. Pay extra attention to your health, as there are signs of sexually-transmitted diseases.

農曆三月 (April 5th - May 4th) 丙辰

Try not to spend too much this month. You are also advised not to gamble or invest unnecessarily. If these activities are carried out, you may find yourself not profiting at all. The best thing for you to do is avoid all forms of risky financial endeavours. Your Romance Luck is not too favourable for this month, and as boring as this may sound, you will be better off focusing on your career at this point! Elderly ladies using this room should be careful of any stomach problems that might occur.

農曆四月 (May 5th - June 5th) 丁巳

Individuals who are blessed with the gift of the gab and possess great communication skills might find it difficult to get things done (or said) this month. You'll have problems articulating yourself and you might end up saying the wrong things. Always think before you speak. Pending legal matters should be put to bed this month and make sure it's really done! Otherwise, this could end up draining your finances.

Main Door	North	Bedroom Sector	North

農曆五月 (June 6th - July 6th) 戊午

For this month, things are about to get real nasty at work. Beware of backstabbers around you, and always get your armour on before it occurs. Do not fight it with the similar tactic. You should be the bigger person and let it slide like water off a duck's back. There is no sense in getting involved with office politics because it will only bring you down and increase stress levels. While you may be pressured at work, don't forget to ensure that the pressure doesn't affect your relationships and social life.

農曆六月 (July 7th - August 6th) 己未

When it comes to relationship matters, be it professional or personal, you should definitely avoid causing any troubles, whenever you can. This is definitely not the month to make a stand or forcing your opinion on others. Try to lay low and stay out of the firing line until things take a turn for the better. Do not pay attention to property deals that could be risky for you, as this could lead to big losses. Always be careful with your finances and save for rainy days ahead. In terms of health, there may be injuries related to your nerves or tendons.

農曆七月 (August 7th - September 7th) 庚申

Individuals using this room for this particular month will need to be careful, especially when engaging in public speaking or delivering presentations. It will be especially challenging this month for lawyers because individuals in this profession may find themselves having to face obstacles when presenting their cases. Individuals using this room will also find the competition heating up from professional and personal rivals, resulting in emotional situations filled with manipulation and confrontations.

農曆八月 (September 8th - October 7th) 辛酉

Individuals in this room will encounter bad Wealth Luck this month. All investment deals should be avoided. This is also not the month to be particularly soft-hearted, especially when people come by asking you for loans, as you're unlikely to see your money back if you lend it out. Health-wise, be careful of any physical injuries that could result in head or bone injuries. If any minor health ailments occur, it would be best for you to see the doctor at the first chance possible to avoid serious complications in the future.

農曆九月 (October 8th - November 6th) 壬戌

This month, when it comes to your professional and work life, you should maintain a low profile. Lay low and do not get involved in anything too ambitious this month. This is because the chances of a backfire is likely. As for new projects and endeavours – it is best for you to embark on it at a more favourable time in the future. Health-wise, you should take care of yourself and get minor issues checked out. Otherwise, you might encounter serious problems. Whenever possible, try to avoid long-distance travel by car or automobile this month, because accidents are very likely. It goes without saying that you should also not break traffic laws.

農曆十月 (November 7th - December 6th) 癸亥

Females who are pregnant should be careful this month because problems with your pregnancy could occur if this room is used. Whenever possible, you should change rooms. Health-wise, individuals in this room will likely develop liver infections and skin diseases. Try to get as much rest as possible and rest whenever you can – do not stress your body out. Alas, be prepared to fight for yourself among competitors and rivals this month.

農曆十一月 (December 7th 2018 - January 4th 2019) 甲子

This month, be careful when handling things or situations which involve fire. There is a high risk of fire hazards, so make sure you're taking extra precautions when it comes to your stove, kitchen gas outlets and always check your electrical wiring. In regards to your work schedule, you will need to take some time to plan and organise your projects carefully. If you find that your plate is full, then make your opinion known and demand for a more reasonable timeline.

農曆十二月 (January 5th - February 3rd 2019) 乙丑

This is a good month for individuals in this room to dabble in property dealings. Take it step by step though, you wouldn't want to dive in head first and get into deep trouble. Besides, it's always better to be careful with your finances than to splurge all-out this month. Any problems that come up in your relationships and marriages at this point in time should be handled with maturity, diplomacy and tact. Young children and toddlers are at risk of muscle, tendon and ligament problems and injuries this month, so pay extra attention to their movements.

農曆正月 (February 4th - March 4th) 甲寅

Matters regarding relationships that began this month or in the past, will not likely lead to something long term. You're advised to not invest your body and soul into it. Look towards a better long-term investment instead. It's high time to focus on your career and work on building up your professional life. Medical problems that start off as minor and unimportant could become more serious in the future, so get medical treatment even if it seems like a minor issue at this point. If you work in the entertainment industry, exercise extreme care and deliberation when signing contracts, and don't put pen to paper if even the smallest thing seems amiss.

農曆二月 (March 5th - April 4th) 乙卯

For those who are married, you will need to pay more attention to your partner because you might've been spending too much time focused on your career. If you've inadvertently neglected your loved one, then make your feelings known instead of letting it fester inside. For those of you in real estate, or with property deals and investments, you will find it to be profitable month but you'll need to be quick enough to make the most out of opportunities as they arise. Health problems involving the lungs might crop up this month, so take extra care.

農曆三月 (April 5th - May 4th) 丙辰

Your health continues to be somewhat weak this month, so make an effort to put your physical health first and foremost. Ulcers could cause some problems if you're not careful. This is not a month to stick your nose into other people's problems and affairs, as you could get dragged into some sticky messes, and will only have to bear the brunt of other people's resentments as your reward. Relationships will be distracting you from more important matters at hand, so keep your concentration focused on what is of higher priority.

農曆四月 (May 5th - June 5th) 丁巳

Your personal reputation takes centre stage this month, and not in a way you might have imagined! In fact, it could be that your name and character are being called into question, so don't provide fuel to the fire in any way by making missteps. Pay close attention to your words and actions, being careful not to do or say anything in a fit of anger or carelessness. If you're a professional sportsperson, you will do well this month. However, it will be best to be wary of competitors.

Main Door	North	Bedroom Sector	Northwest

農曆五月 (June 6th - July 6th) 戊午

Those of you in the property and real estate industries will find this a particularly tough and challenging month. This is mainly due to the fact that you have trouble organising your thoughts and achieving some form of clarity in your analytical processes. This might cause you unnecessary problems when it comes to making decisions, so it might be better off for you in the long run to delay those decisions, if possible, to a better time in the future.

農曆六月 (July 7th - August 6th) 己未

In this particular month, there will be health issues for individuals in this room. Kidney problems might befall individuals in this room, so watch out for signs of those and seek medical opinion early, if necessary. Children or students who need to sit for important exams should be careful about using this room for revision and study, as any negative structures or landforms outside this sector could cause some problems. If you have any offshore deals in the making, it's best for you to wait for a more favourable time in the future before finalising them.

農曆七月 (August 7th - September 7th) 庚申

Individuals in this room could get caught up in fights and arguments this month. For couples, they will be constantly bickering with each other, if the room is used. Try to switch rooms in the house and always be careful with the things you say to each other. Think before you speak. Legal problems rear their head again this month, and possible betrayals and about-faces are likely. People might turn against you, threatening the reputation of your business. This will no doubt bring about its fair share of stress and anxiety, and the rumours are likely to affect your business relationships – but keep your head low and endure it, as it will blow over very soon.

農曆八月 (September 8th - October 7th) 辛酉

Individuals in this room who are elderly males will need to get their health problems checked this month. Individuals in the real estate industry will be able to secure good deals. However, you will need to exercise your analytical skills to choose the right deals and score a jackpot! It will be worth your time to be completely thorough in checking out credentials. In fact, it is particularly important that you sift through all the information you come across this month, because other individuals are out to pull the wool over your eyes.

農曆九月 (October 8th - November 6th) 壬戌

Temptation is your weakness this month. Individuals in this room, this month, will be particularly tested if they are newly-recovering alcoholics. The best way to deal with this situation is to put yourself out of the way from all forms of temptation. Romance Luck is poor, in general. Affairs are likely, and if tempted – it will cause a strain to your relationship. Be careful how you proceed, as the consequences are serious and break-ups and separations are likely.

農曆十月 (November 7th - December 6th) 癸亥

Relationships cultivated this month or started in the past will not have long-term potential. Don't invest your heart and soul into it. Build a solid long-term career instead. Focus on your professional life. You might encounter medical problems which should be looked into before it gets ugly. If you work in the entertainment industry, proceed with extreme care and deliberation when signing contracts, and don't sign anything if it seems too good to be true or shady.

農曆十一月 (December 7th 2018 - January 4th 2019) 甲子

Entrepreneurs or businessmen should be grateful as this is a particularly good month for business expansion. The future looks bright and you'll receive support from your employees. However, in the midst of the success expansion, do be careful of any legal wrangles. There could be legal issues cropping up so you're advised to check documents carefully before signing them. Additionally, if you're using this sector's bedroom, your health will be under attack, so pay more attention to your physical well-being and don't ignore the warning signs.

農曆十二月 (January 5th - February 3rd 2019) 乙丑

This room will bring about problems for matters related to the heart. This is especially so for individuals who are in relationships. You should make it a point not to put your nose in other people's affairs and arguments as resentment will result. This is a time to lay low and maintain distance in problems that are not your own, or you will be dragged into messy situations which will be hard to extricate yourself from. Health is weak this month with mouth ulcers causing some problems.

| Main Door | North | Bedroom Sector | West |

農曆正月 (February 4th - March 4th) 甲寅

You will need to avoid signing important documents or contracts this month. This is due to the fact that sometimes, things are not what they seem to be. Make sure that you're paying attention to the fine print and always understand each and every word mentioned in the contracts or agreements. Also, if you're sitting for a major exam this month, avoid using this room, if possible. In general, arguments could plague domestic harmony this month, causing family members to exchange heated words with each other. If you can't exactly prevent every argument, then keep your cool throughout each and every one to avoid saying anything you might regret later.

農曆二月 (March 5th - April 4th) 乙卯

Individuals using this room will suffer from depression and stress-related mental anxiety this month. Manage your lifestyle carefully or you'll run the risk of paying a huge price for emotional disturbance. The plus point is that it will generally be a problem-free month for individuals using this room, so if you're committed to finding peace of mind, you're likely to find it! Make an effort to streamline your life according to your desires, and you're likely to feel rested, peaceful, balanced and well-adjusted.

農曆三月 (April 5th - May 4th) 丙辰

If you're someone who works in the legal field, you will be able to live positively this month. Your contribution at work will earn you the well-deserved respect from others, securing your reputation and status as one of the top figures in the field. Health-wise, the presence of any negative landforms outside this sector could cause some serious health implications, which can include diseases as severe as cancer. There are substantial financial gains to be made from all your business dealings, but make sure you know exactly what to do in order to actually see these profits.

農曆四月 (May 5th - June 5th) 丁巳

Things looks good from the investment front and there's money to be made. Individuals in this room are advised to use their knowledge in this field to make it for them, this month! For those who are married, however, things might not be going as smoothly as you might like it to be. The issues boil down to your in-laws, in particular. Smooth over these problems as best as you can, as there is no point in fanning the flames with more anger. Where your physical health is concerned, be careful of any illnesses that could affect your spleen or internal organs, or you're likely to be seeing the interior of a hospital more often than you'd like.

| Main Door | North | Bedroom Sector | West |

農曆五月 (June 6th - July 6th) 戊午

This sector will be particularly suitable for activities related to spiritual or religious knowledge and pursuits. However, using it as a bedroom may cause some emotional turbulence or instability, and in some extreme cases, depression. Be on guard against this and sleep in another room for the time being, if possible. At work, you'll find yourself putting your nose to the grindstone but the likelihood of seeing any rewards for that is slim – try to stay strong.

農曆六月 (July 7th - August 6th) 己未

For those of you in the medical industry, or work as a medical professional, you're likely to perform well this month. However, females who are pregnant are advised not to use this room, because the risk of complications and miscarriage is high. If you're in doubt, it would be best to seek the advice of your doctor at the first sign of trouble. The same applies to elderly females using this room – if something seems amiss, seek professional medical advice to avoid worsening complications. For those of you sitting for examinations, avoid using this sector for this month, or you might not pass with flying colours.

農曆七月 (August 7th - September 7th) 庚申

Individuals this month will experience immense stress at the workplace. If they're not careful, it could also lead to health problems, such as gastrointestinal issues and ulcers. If you can't avoid the stress, you will do well to learn how to manage it. There is no point in sacrificing your health for work! There is also a strong likelihood that you'll be able to make money from investment in the property industries, but ensure that you take the time and effort to do your homework and analyse the deal from every angle. The worst thing you can do for yourself is to rush into something blindly just because the opportunity presents itself.

農曆八月 (September 8th - October 7th) 辛酉

Couples will find this to be a difficult month. Be tolerant and forgiving towards each other. There's no point hurling words of insult at each other – you'll only do your relationship a disservice and bring about unnecessary emotional pain. Those of you who are writers – or wishing to be one – should stop dreaming about doing it and actually do it, as the energies are conducive for your literary pursuits. So get those journals and notebooks out and start writing.

農曆九月 (October 8th - November 6th) 壬戌

For those of you who are on a spiritual journey or are inclined towards religious pursuits, the energies found in this sector, this month, could precipitate the inclinations further. In terms of health, however, you might want to get a professional medical opinion if some particular situation is troubling you. Otherwise, it could become a persistent illness or symptom. It's also a favourable month for those of you dealing in real estate and property, and it'll be a good time for you to acquire new portfolios, even if you have to start accepting small ones.

農曆十月 (November 7th - December 6th) 癸亥

Do not sign documents or contracts this month. Things might not be what it seems. Always read between the lines and pay extra attention to terms. Students should avoid using this sector as a study room, especially if they are facing important examinations this month. There will be lots of arguments, particularly within the family, if you're using this sector's room. If arguments cannot be avoided, then choose your battles with care to avoid fighting over trivial matters – let sleeping dogs lie.

農曆十一月 (December 7th 2018 - January 4th 2019) 甲子

Be careful when making new property deals, as these could result in financial losses. It will be better to be safe than sorry, so spend that extra bit of time verifying credentials. This month, be wary of who you socialise and mingle with – and be careful not to overindulge too much in good times. Also, it will be wise for you to steer clear of risky investments and financial gambles.

農曆十二月 (January 5th - February 3rd 2019) 乙丑

Do not get yourself involved with shady dealings as they could end up turning sour and could cost you a lot of money to ensure they are all above board. The bottom line is, try not to be a hero and attempt any "under the table" dealings. Rivals, subordinates and colleagues are looking to undermine your authority this month, so you will want to keep your eyes open and your ears peeled. Those in real estate will make money on property deals this month but just make sure that all the legal issues are well taken care of as well.

| Main Door | North | Bedroom Sector | Southwest |

農曆正月 (February 4th - March 4th) 甲寅

Love is in the air! The pursuits for love and romance will be fruitful for you – so if you're single, this is the time to meet your potential soulmate. In terms of health, there are possible eye ailments or infections, so you would need to take extra care when it comes to that particular area. If your line of work falls under state security and defense, this month requires you to do your homework before you invest in any new technology. Knowing exactly what you're doing will help you increase your profits.

農曆二月 (March 5th - April 4th) 乙卯

This month, those of you in the printing, courier and logistics industries will need to travel overseas to find new markets for your products and services. These opportunities to travel will rake in profits for your companies. Individuals using this room will suffer from mental stress and emotional instability, so be prepared to remain mentally and emotionally sound when handling these issues. It also seems to be a good month to reach out and forge a new alliance with another party or person, as it will likely lead to a profitable future.

農曆三月 (April 5th - May 4th) 丙辰

Family members who are fathers and sons will face problems with each other in this room, this month. You're advised to stay away from this sector as much as possible. There could be minor health issues occurring and it will bother you, but always remember to take the time to treat it, otherwise it will turn into more problems for you. Avoid all forms of speculative investments this month, unless you're in the engineering industry – in which case you should expand and actively seek out new clients and customers.

農曆四月 (May 5th - June 5th) 丁巳

For couples, you will be able to cultivate a positive and peaceful relationship with your partner, this month. Take advantage of the time spent together and build closer bonds with each other. For your wealth, you'll be able to gain some money from investments previously made in the real estate and property industries. In general, this month brings about some happy tidings for you – so don't be afraid to indulge in a few celebrations!

Main Door	North	Bedroom Sector	Southwest

農曆五月 (June 6th - July 6th) 戊午

Although your health issues will be minimised this month, you will still need to take extra care when it comes to potential headaches and migraines. Always ensure that you get enough rest, especially when facing stressful situations. If your job role involves strategic thinking and analysis, this will be a good month for you. You'll see chances to advance your career and build a reputation for yourself. Use your talents and skills to your best advantage and plan carefully on how you can let others see the best of your true abilities.

農曆六月 (July 7th - August 6th) 己未

There will be great dividends this month, and this is due to your long-term investments. Remember to always avoid false confidence by trying to continue your winning streak the wrong way. Don't get into any short-term investments at this point hoping to make a quick buck, because the opposite is likely to occur. Sons who use this room may be particularly defiant towards their fathers, and some discord could be likely on the home front. But otherwise, health and relationships are both good for most people using this room, and you'll definitely feel a sense of rest and relaxation seeping into your life.

農曆七月 (August 7th - September 7th) 庚申

Ask and you shall receive. This is the month to ask for help if you need it. There is absolutely no shame in being sincere and upfront about your needs. This may be particularly relevant where your business projects are concerned. Consider asking the opinion of an older or wiser mentor, and you just might see the negative transforming into the positive faster than you expected! Stress and mental pressure affect you quite strongly this month, and that in turn will play havoc with your ability to think clearly and reason things out. Always make sure that you have some time-out for relaxation, and don't overstrain yourself.

農曆八月 (September 8th - October 7th) 辛酉

Individuals in the legal and advertising industries will notice an increased demand for their respective skills. This is good for them to increase their finances and client base. However, for most people, jealousy and competition will start to heat up at the workplace, causing some messy legal issues if it escalates out of control. If possible, try to play the role of a peacemaker and smooth over ruffled feathers, lest the situation explodes into something that no one can handle. Always remember to keep your expectations in check!

農曆九月 (October 8th - November 6th) 壬戌

For entrepreneurs and business owners, this is not a good time for you to expand your businesses. This month shows that this move will not work in your favour. Instead, you should spend your time concentrating on your core products or services. Take a step back and wait for a better time in the future to consider your next move. High-risk investments should be avoided this month at all costs, because it could bring about some potentially severe legal problems. Individuals who work in the engineering industries will be well-supported by their bosses and superiors, leading to some nice financial remunerations!

農曆十月 (November 7th - December 6th) 癸亥

This is not the month for corporate retrenchment due to the predicted legal issues resulting from this move. If you have elder family members who are using this room, you should be careful of their health as they may face lung problems in this sector. You should also be prepared for losses during this month. Your employees could also betray and lie to you – so if you're a business owner, always be on the ready and ensure that your employees are not out to get you.

農曆十一月 (December 7th 2018 - January 4th 2019) 甲子

All signs point to a positive outcome for business and leisure travels. So, if you're an academician, you can travel anywhere you want to attend seminars and conferences overseas. For those who are in speculative investments or stocks and equities, you will make a great profit this month, if you use this sector's room, but you must first be thorough with your decisions. As for couples using this room, they will enjoy a harmonious relationship this month. This is due to the decrease in petty arguments and quarrels.

農曆十二月 (January 5th - February 3rd 2019) 乙丑

You should stay away from speculative investments this month. But for those of you in the engineering industry, this is the month to venture into new markets and seek fresh clients. There will also be minor health issues this month. Do not consider these unimportant, as it could lead to more serious conditions requiring greater medical treatment and care further down the road, so you should get it sorted out early.

North Sector Main Door

農曆正月 (February 4th - March 4th) 甲寅

There will be last minute changes out of your control in your travels this month. These changes could turn into problems for your trip – so you should be prepared for this. Always buy insurance for your travels. For those of you in the fashion and cosmetic industries, this is a good month because of increased exposure and revenue. As for your professional life, things are looking good, as recognition comes your way and a promotion and advancement are in store for you. But you will need to bear in mind that these come with its own set of responsibilities and issues.

農曆二月 (March 5th - April 4th) 乙卯

You should be careful this month as you could find yourself trapped in a sticky situation with female subordinates at work. Ensure that all your communication is clear and direct. You'll have good opportunities to make a profit from property dealings abroad, and this will work out even better if you're required to travel to sign the documents! If you're interested in meditation and reading, this room will be conducive for those activities as well.

農曆三月 (April 5th - May 4th) 丙辰

Those who are single will be in good standing when it comes to seeking a partner, this month. But this will only happen if there are no natural water formations located in this particular sector. For business owners, you should consider expanding your business or building a bigger network with your international partners. At the same time, do consider revisiting business connections made in the past as these will bode well for you. Also, individuals in the mining and engineering industries will find that their businesses doing well this month, with profits increased.

農曆四月 (May 5th - June 5th) 丁巳

You're advised not to invest in speculative or high-risk investments. It's for your own good to just keep a low profile and your money safe. If not, you'll most probably end up with less than what you have! This is a good month to concentrate on building a good rapport with your colleagues, business affiliates, partner and loved ones. Your relationships will be fruitful and they could turn into long-term bonds. If there is work-related travel for you this month, you should accept it because it will bring about greater influence and higher status at work.

| Main Door | North | Bedroom Sector | South |

農曆五月 (June 6th - July 6th) 戊午

For those of you in the forestry and dairy farming industries, you will find business demands increasing this month, which is good news for you, because revenues and profits could only get higher in return! Generally, it's a good month for you to make a property-related investment or venture into property deals. Elderly women using this room might have migraines, or in worst-case scenarios, a stroke. Always pay attention to any signs that indicate something's amiss.

農曆六月 (July 7th - August 6th) 己未

For those of you in the legal field (be it a lawyer, or a legal advisor etc.), your knowledge and services are in demand this month. Be prepared to be productive and on standby for a busy month! If you're using this room as well, it is best for you to avoid conflicts, arguments or quarrels this month. This is because these situations or negative behaviours might actually lead to violence. Always practice extra caution when working with sharp tools and implements this month, like knives and scissors.

農曆七月 (August 7th - September 7th) 庚申

Competitiveness is the key word this month. For those of you who are in competitive sports or an all-rounded athlete or sportsperson – this is the time to make a name for yourself. Get the medal and seal the deal as one of the best in your field. But be prepared for this elevated status not equating to financial rewards for you. Romantic relationships will start to take on a whole new level of intensity and commitment this month. For couples, it will also be a good time to make important decisions together or to have that talk you've both been putting off for awhile now. Good luck!

農曆八月 (September 8th - October 7th) 辛酉

Individuals in this room should refrain from making business deals, ventures or investments this month. This is because the outcome might not be in your favour and there will be more chances of losses than gains. Married couples will have to endure strained, tense relations this month as well. Instead of sweeping issues under the rug, simply give each other more space and things will return to normal. This is also not a good month to continue playing in the stock market as there could be potential losses as well.

農曆九月 (October 8th - November 6th) 壬戌

For professional females with female bosses or superiors – kudos to you, as this will be the month where you will be recognised for your efforts at work! You'll be finally appreciated for your diligence and hard work that you've given to the company. This is also a good month to feed your inner wanderlust, so get on that plane and fly off to your dream destination. And for those of you in the management and consulting field, there will be good financial benefits and profits. To summarise, this will be the month that you'll see a substantial increase in your wealth standing.

農曆十月 (November 7th - December 6th) 癸亥

For those of you who are travelling this month, make sure you purchase travel insurance because there could be unexpected twists and turns taking place. Always be on the alert for your travel-related plans and keep your personal documents safe. For those of you in the fashion apparel and cosmetics industries, you will find that this month brings more business contacts that result in increased turnover for you.

農曆十一月 (December 7th 2018 - January 4th 2019) 甲子

Individuals using this room should be ready for problems at the workplace caused by female superiors or bosses. There will be benefits and opportunities to make considerable profits from properties abroad – therefore you'll need to make your way there through your business travels and seal the deal. If meditation and reading are some your interests, then this will also be a good room for you this month, because it's actually favourable for those particular interests.

農曆十二月 (January 5th - February 3rd 2019) 乙丑

For those of you who are single and utilising this sector's bedroom, you're likely to have your fairy tale come true this month. Auspicious Romantic Luck is in the air this month and you'll just be smiling from ear to ear because of that special someone or other potential romantic partners. This is also a good month to engage in business expansion or to build new networks with potential partners overseas. This move will be worthwhile to pursue any previous business connections made in the past. If you're in the mining and engineering industries, you will also find that your business excels this month. Things will look good continuously as there are financial profits and benefits to be gained.

| Main Door | North | Bedroom Sector | Southeast |

農曆正月 (February 4th - March 4th) 甲寅

Health-wise, there will be liver problems that could afflict you if this sector's bedroom is used, especially if there are negative features or structures outside the room. Property deals will be financially worthwhile this month, but it will take some effort to close these deals. You'll need to summon up your power of persuasion in order to bring the deals to a conclusion.

農曆二月 (March 5th - April 4th) 乙卯

The progress on projects looks good, thus resulting in the employees being recognised for their success and being rewarded accordingly. This creates a general sense of well-being in the workplace as well. As for couples using this room, they will find their relationship to be extremely harmonious this month. One can also expect to enjoy closer ties and a heightened sense of intimacy. Mentors, life coaches and those in the self-help and motivational businesses will see success in their endeavours this month, especially if they make changes in their personal lives that reflect their advice to others.

農曆三月 (April 5th - May 4th) 丙辰

This month, it will be wise for you to stay out of others' affairs or it could backfire on you. It will be a good month in terms of recognition and reward, especially if you work in the banking or finance industries. This will spur you on to create more good work, and the motivation factor at the workplace will be high. Your relationships will take a back seat this month, and this is not necessarily a bad thing as this gives you and your partner a chance to catch up on your individual lives.

農曆四月 (May 5th - June 5th) 丁巳

Do not overwork and overexert yourself, as you will only be prone to bladder or kidney problems at the end of the day. And know that no matter how successful you may be, there will always be jealous parties out there plotting your downfall. Hence, it's important that you learn how to manage your stress levels wisely. The energies of the month augur well for short-term gains from speculative investments, but be reasonable in your expectations and don't succumb to greed.

| Main Door | North | Bedroom Sector | Southeast |

農曆五月 (June 6th - July 6th) 戊午

Expect your ventures to gain a fresh and new start. There will also be big changes taking place. These changes will help you revive a stagnant career or a business this month. If you use the West bedroom, you will also feel a need to develop self-cultivation and improvement this month. However, children using this room will be somewhat rambunctious.

農曆六月 (July 7th - August 6th) 己未

Despite a slightly rocky start to the month, your relationship with your spouse will flourish and remain harmonious. You need to be aware of jealous co-workers, who are only plotting your downfall. Nevertheless, this is a favourable month to launch a new development, as any such real estate or property investments will yield handsome benefits, in due time.

農曆七月 (August 7th - September 7th) 庚申

If you're in the entertainment or food and beverage industry, this will be a profitable month for you in terms of relationships and finances. Generally, this will also be a good month for relationships, which indicates happy and harmonious outcomes, unless there is a water feature close to the Southeast sector. If this is so, you can expect some acrimonious moments that can mar the peace in your relations with others.

農曆八月 (September 8th - October 7th) 辛酉

This is a month for happy times. There will be an abundance of celebrations and joyous activities taking place. There will also be good news for those using the West bedroom this month. Positive outcomes such as a recognition, a promotion and an advancement will take place this month. These rewards and positive outcomes are attained in the business environment. Individuals in the workplace will finally see their hard work appreciated as well. If you're in a relationship, it will be happy and carefree and it can be formalised this month with positive outcomes too!

農曆九月 (October 8th - November 6th) 壬戌

There will be plenty of financial opportunities coming your way this month, but you will find that you are unable to make use of most of them. This could lead to some frustration and disappointment on your part. This is also a good month to consolidate both professional and personal relationships, although in the beginning, they may be a little rocky. The long-term outlook, however, seems stable. Health-wise, you should be careful of gallstone problems and kidney-related ailments this month if you are using this bedroom.

農曆十月 (November 7th - December 6th) 癸亥

You will need to practice patience this month, especially when it comes to matters involving property deals. This is because things may be moving rather slowly for you. With time, your patience will prove to be worthwhile with the benefits that you will receive at the end of the day. Because of the energies in this sector, it is also likely that your relationship will take a rough turn this month due to jealousy. Keep your jealously in check by practicing openness and frankness in your communication with your partner.

農曆十一月 (December 7th 2018 - January 4th 2019) 甲子

Your hard work will be recognised this month, especially when it comes to specific projects that you might be handling. You'll enjoy working at your current office. As for couples, this room will be harmonious for the both of you. There will be an increased amount of intimacy between the two of you. And if you are a mentor, either a life coach or a self-help guru, there will be success in what you do this month. You'll be touching the lives of many and inspire change in them.

農曆十二月 (January 5th - February 3rd 2019) 乙丑

Individuals using this sector's bedroom, will be able to enjoy positive Wealth Luck this month. And if there's a water feature present in this room as well, one can expect gains from speculative investments – bringing about great results! If you're working for others, you'll need to be prepared for stressful situations at work. This is because of pressure brought on by your superiors. Find some time to relax to bring down your stress levels. Try not to worry too much because it might just throw you off your game.

Main Door	North	Bedroom Sector	East

農曆正月 (February 4th - March 4th) 甲寅

If you're a lawyer or a solicitor, you'll enjoy a good month! There will be a lot of business prospects coming your way and you'll be reaping the benefits from them. You should always enjoy the results of your hard work. Elderly women who use this room should be prepared for possible limb-related injuries or health problems – so don't take any warning signs lightly. Individuals in the cellphone and telecommunications device industries will enjoy a good month too, as financial profits come rolling in.

農曆二月 (March 5th - April 4th) 乙卯

For athletes, sportsmen or those who are just starting out professionally in the sports field, they will find this to be a good month to focus on a specific sport they're interested in. Work hard and develop your talent. The results from this will be good for you. Women involved in business ventures, especially those in the medical field, will do swimmingly. This is provided if they are smart enough and embark on clever business deals that could bring in some huge gains. In the workplace, you should keep an eye on your competition or you could find yourself caught in a messy argument or lawsuit.

農曆三月 (April 5th - May 4th) 丙辰

Individuals in the mobile devices industry will have to face technical problems and glitches occurring this month. This will undoubtedly take all of your time and energy, especially when trying to make things right. If you're an actor or a doctor, you'll find yourself being the flavor of the month for the media. This is a good thing as the boost in your reputation will only bring about further accolades and benefits. This month, err on the side of caution and try to be conservative, because you'll find yourself trapped in some sticky legal complications if you don't – it's time to lawyer up!

農曆四月 (May 5th - June 5th) 丁巳

You might be overwhelmed by the demands of your relationship this month, but it's not an excuse to run away from the issue at hand. In fact, don't try to dance or party your sorrows away in clubs and bars as you'll be mired deeper in unwanted problems. This is a good month to look on the brighter side of things, and failing that, do some soul searching instead. You might just be able to find the solutions to your problems if you look hard enough. Career-wise, you will be recognised for your efforts at work, but you will need to be wise enough to find the avenues to carve out a good name for yourself.

Main Door	North	Bedroom Sector	East

農曆五月 (June 6th - July 6th) 戊午

Expectant ladies who use this room could suffer a possible miscarriage, so it might be better for you to consider using a different room. Generally, individuals who use this room will be prone to stomach-related illnesses and trouble, especially elderly women. Take proper precautions and don't neglect your health. Fire-related accidents and hazards are very likely this month, especially if there are negative landforms or structures outside this sector.

農曆六月 (July 7th - August 6th) 己未

If you've been thinking about starting new ventures in the communications industry this month, think again – because there are many hurdles along the way that will slow you down. They will also lead to unnecessary delays and losses. It will be best for you to attempt this at a more favourable time in the future. Those seeking some short-term romantic pleasure will find that flings will bring their fair share of problems. You don't need more trouble at this point, so don't go looking for any, either. Women who invest in business deals and ventures in another country are likely to enjoy good profits.

農曆七月 (August 7th - September 7th) 庚申

There will be fire hazards cropping up this month, so you should be careful with your electrical appliances at home and everywhere else. Always remember to double check all electrical wiring and gas valves and openings thoroughly. Don't be negligent and careless, as the risk is high. Avoid getting into any joint ventures at this point, because they could bring you financial losses instead of success. If you're an entrepreneur or a businessperson, let your wildest, most innovative idea take root – it will bode well in terms of promoting you and your career, and you will gain the admiration and acclaim that you deserve.

農曆八月 (September 8th - October 7th) 辛酉

There are plenty of opportunities for you to smile this month, as you are likely to enjoy good Wealth Luck – with opportunities to make a sizeable mark in the property and real estate industries. Additionally, your personal relationships are enjoying some positive vibes, so make an effort to spend more time with the individuals you care about as this emotional investment will bring about its own rewards for you. If you own a business, this is the right time to attract new customers and clients that could lead to solid financial returns, so make a concentrated effort to reel them in. Always try out new ideas and techniques that could give you a different response.

農曆九月 (October 8th - November 6th) 壬戌

Always be careful with your personal belongings, money, and valuables, as there is an increased risk of robbery and theft this month. At the same time, professional rivalry will heat up this month as well. You'll need to protect your material and intellectual properties equally, so it'll be a balancing act for sure! Married men should steer clear of temptation, and avoid doing anything that will compromise the sanctity of your marriage vows. Otherwise, you might risk causing some serious damage to your relationship. Generally, people using this room should be careful of potential injuries to the limbs.

農曆十月 (November 7th - December 6th) 癸亥

For those of you in the legal and judicial fields, you will do well this month, as the demand for your services increases. You might also find yourself bombarded with offers for work, and while it might increase stress levels, it is also be a good sign of future benefits and gains. However, you will need to watch out for arguments becoming violent and physical as competition and rivalry increases this month. Whenever you're really angry, it will be good to step aside and take a few deep breaths (or counting to 100, do whatever works for you best!). Relationships are plagued by disagreements and conflicts caused by jealousy and suspicion – don't feed into your paranoia.

農曆十一月 (December 7th 2018 - January 4th 2019) 甲子

In your personal life, watch out for arguments with your spouse or other half if you use the East room. For those of you in the mining and engineering industries, you should take care with new deals, as these could result in a breakdown in negotiations, thus resulting in negative outcomes. All official deals should be concluded in writing as miscommunication will arise this month. It will be good and extremely useful for you to get all terms and conditions noted down in black and white.

農曆十二月 (January 5th - February 3rd 2019) 乙丑

If you are in the mobile phone industry, there will be many technical problems and glitches cropping up this month. You will be kept on your toes trying to resolve the various issues faced! Fret not, it's a good month for those of you who are in the entertainment or medical fields, as you will enjoy increased stature. A conservative approach will be best adopted this month, if not, complications may arise, with lawyers getting involved and things becoming progressively messy for you.

| Main Door | North | Bedroom Sector | Northeast |

農曆正月 (February 4th - March 4th) 甲寅

For those of you in the real estate and property investment industries, this is a good month to give your portfolios a boost. All signs point to great results. As for those of you who are married, this month will bring about tension and stress – causing discord between the two of you. Speak to each other and have an open dialogue. If you let things or issues fester, it could only lead to separation and even divorce. As much as possible, avoid fighting over anything as well, as these are likely to end badly.

農曆二月 (March 5th - April 4th) 乙卯

In terms of health, there will be liver-related problems and illnesses for the individuals in this room, this month. Watch out for the signs and get minor issues checked out. For those of you who work in the travel industry, you can expect sudden changes and advances which will work in your favour. This could lead to increased profits. As for all matters related to negotiations this month, beware of having the rug being pulled out from under you. Always be careful of who you trust and try to keep your expectations low.

農曆三月 (April 5th - May 4th) 丙辰

In terms of career, your future looks bright! Rest assured that all the hard work and effort that you've put into your work will not go unrecognised. There is a promotion in the horizon, which comes with a raise. In terms of physical health, it's a good month for you to get moving and head to the gym! If you've ever wanted to lose some weight, there's no better time to start than now. However, the possibility of car accidents is very strong, so be carefully when you're behind the wheel and limit long-distance travel.

農曆四月 (May 5th - June 5th) 丁巳

For those of you who have been feeling under the weather and somewhat physically weak, you should avoid using this sector as much as possible. If any of your illnesses become worse, it would be best to consult a doctor as soon as possible. Decisions involving your business deals should be postponed to a later time. Otherwise, the risk of disputes or slander is high, and this is the kind of trouble you don't need at this point. You'll need to be a little more eagle-eyed with your staff than normal, as there are a few of them defecting to the other side or just attempting to get away with fraud.

| Main Door | North | Bedroom Sector | Northeast |

農曆五月 (June 6th - July 6th) 戊午

For those of you who have business deals or connections with partners abroad, there will be unexpected financial gains this month. In terms of health, individuals who are already battling infections and illnesses should be extra careful this month, as internal injuries are likely. Be especially vigilant and don't take your physical well-being for granted. There is also the unfortunate chance for robberies and thefts to occur this month, so be cautious with your belongings, cash, and assets. Hide all of your valuables as much as you possibly can.

農曆六月 (July 7th - August 6th) 己未

Elderly males who are using this room will have to be careful with their health this month, as potential lung problems can develop into something serious. Take all proper precautions and visit the doctor as soon as something seems slightly amiss. As for male teens who are using this room, they will be a lot more rebellious and insolent than normal, so it would be a wise idea to consider using a different month to cool that defiant spirit. Those of you who are due for some form of progress in your career are likely to see a possible new position that brings with it greater power and authority for you.

農曆七月 (August 7th - September 7th) 庚申

For those of you working in the service industry, you'll be enjoying relatively good business this month. But bear in mind that you must keep on top of your taxes, or otherwise all that good effect will be negated! Individuals in the real estate or property industries will have to push a little harder this month to see any form of revenue. Don't be afraid to try new things, instead of sticking to the tried and tested formulas. Things at home will be less than rosy, especially in families where mothers and sons are living together. Arguments and conflicts are likely between these two members of the family, so the best way to overcome it is to give each other space and room to breathe.

農曆八月 (September 8th - October 7th) 辛酉

For the individuals who sleep in this sector as a bedroom, there will be emotional and psychological problems. They might feel edgy and anxious. As for those in the marketing and media fields, they will find this month to be tough. This is because despite all your pushing and prodding, not much results or gains are likely to materialize. In terms of striking business deals, this is the month to play it safe. Go with your gut instinct to trust people you've dealt with before instead of going down a whole new path.

農曆九月 (October 8th - November 6th) 壬戌

Be careful when it comes to your words this month, as words said in the heat of the moment or in anger will get you into trouble. This is trouble you don't need, so you're much better off remaining silent when you can't think of anything nice to say. In terms of romance, any new encounters this month should be kept casual and light, as the chances of those becoming serious and long-term are slim to none. Fraudsters and conmen are still out to make a killing, so go into any deals or professional negotiations with your eyes wide open and your guard up.

農曆十月 (November 7th - December 6th) 癸亥

This month points to all things being beneficial when it comes to closing property-related deals. Remember to be very concise on the details, as legal issues will raise their head if you are not careful. Always pay attention to the fine print! Relationships will, however, come under fire this month. It will be best to let things slide for the time being. Taxes and outstanding fines should be put in order this month as problems with authorities is a real threat, and will pose a real hindrance in the future if not addressed now.

農曆十一月 (December 7th 2018 - January 4th 2019) 甲子

For those of you working in the travel industry, be prepared for sudden changes which will result in additional profits. Work that power of persuasion and negotiation skills that you have to secure deals for your own benefit. But always remember to keep your expectations low and try not to have too much riding on these deals. In terms of health, liver problems are expected for those using the Northeast room this month.

農曆十二月 (January 5th - February 3rd 2018) 乙丑

Embark on your travels because if you're using the Southwest room this month, because it will only bring you rewards! There are also positive outcomes for students or those pursuing further education – all signs to point to you passing in flying colours! Clarity of thought will favour those who need to make important decisions this month, so attempt to think things through and decide now instead of postponing decision-making to another time.

East Sector
Main Door

Main Door	East	Bedroom Sector	East

This section contains the monthly outlook for all 12 months of the year for different bedroom sectors, in a property with an East Sector Main Door.

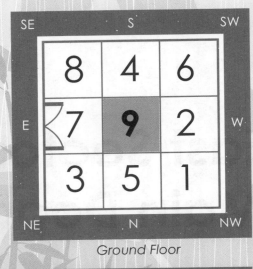

Ground Floor

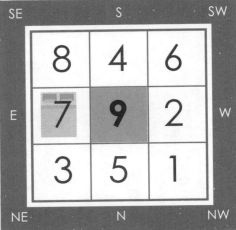

First Floor

農曆正月 (February 4th - March 4th) 甲寅

Power struggles for authority at work will intensify this month and you can expect unpleasant outcomes. Avoid unhealthy rivalry by refusing to play the dirty game yourself. This is a good month for those in competitive sports, as you will have the edge over your rivals. You will benefit if there are any competitions scheduled for the month. Your personal relationships will be plagued by disagreements and conflicts caused by jealousy, so you will need to exercise caution on how you proceed.

農曆二月 (March 5th - April 4th) 乙卯

If there are negative features outside this sector, it would be very unwise to embark on any business dealings at all this month. This is because, most of them will lead to financial losses, especially for people in the engineering and construction industries. Do not become involved in any property deals because these deals will bring about legal problems to you. You might even wrangle with conmen who will cheat you out of your money. For couples, your relationship will continue to be strained.

農曆三月 (April 5th - May 4th) 丙辰

If you are in the communications or publishing industries, then this is the month to make some good financial investments. If you're unsure about how to proceed, it will be ideal to gather the resources and intelligence of those in the know so that you can make the most of the auspicious energies of this month. Professional and personal relationships are on a good standing this month, and you will enjoy smooth communication unhampered by misunderstandings.

農曆四月 (May 5th - June 5th) 丁巳

You may come into some money, but do not advertise your wealth this month, as there is an increased risk of robbery and burglary. Be discreet with whom you share information with. There is an increased risk of occupational injury, especially for people involved in hazardous jobs. Be extra careful when handling heavy and dangerous machineries. This is a good month to start a new relationship, most probably with someone from your circle of friends.

Main Door	East	Bedroom Sector	East

農曆五月 (June 6th - July 6th) 戊午

If you're in the medical field, you'll notice an increase in the demand for your services this month. Women who own businesses will have an opportunity to make money this month, especially if they are in the medical or finance fields. There is also a good chance to make side income this month, even if you are already employed. Seek out some of these opportunities and see where they lead.

農曆六月 (July 7th - August 6th) 己未

Your relationships will be tense due to your heightened emotions this month. Think with your head; not your heart. If you're a business owner, refrain from undertaking any new ventures or attempting to expand your business this month. You'll do well to monitor your employees closely instead, as there's a possibility that dishonest staff may try to deceive or defraud you.

農曆七月 (August 7th - September 7th) 庚申

If your work involves invention and research, this is a good month to share your findings with the public. This is a good month for travel so those who enjoy it should take advantage of the good energies of this sector. There is a fire hazard this month, so be careful when using electrical appliances which are in need of attention. Be especially careful and refrain from attempting any reckless moves.

農曆八月 (September 8th - October 7th) 辛酉

This is a month to have a go at the lotto as windfall gains are a possibility. It's also a good time to attract new customers and clients to your business which will in turn give good financial returns and profits. Relationships will be smooth sailing this month and to make up for the earlier months of tension, it might be a good idea for the two of you to go away on a short vacation and enjoy this newfound peace.

農曆九月 (October 8th - November 6th) 壬戌

Be mindful of what you say as you'll be prone to saying the wrong thing and causing some hurt towards others, this month. In terms of your career, if you're in the media and publishing industries, you may consider expanding your business this month – but seek professional legal advice before you embark on any such venture. The energies of the East are also good for those with scholarly pursuits.

農曆十月 (November 7th - December 6th) 癸亥

Love comes to those who go out and seek it, so if you're single and searching, then this is the month for you to enter the game of love! You never know when you might meet the love of your life, but even if you don't, you can chalk it all up to experience – which is invaluable. There is a heightened risk of theft and burglary this month, so it would be in your best interests to install a secure alarm and security system in your home and workplace. Lawyers and legal professionals will find that their services are much sought-after at this point in time, leading to profitable financial gains.

農曆十一月 (December 7th 2018 - January 4th 2019) 甲子

If there are negative features outside this sector, it would be very unwise to embark on any business dealings at all this month, as these will lead to financial losses. This is especially true for people in the engineering and construction industries. Do not become involved in any property deals because these will end up in legal problems. At its worst, you might even wrangle with conmen who are out to cheat you of your money. Personal relationships will be strained this month, so make sure that you do not end up drinking too much as a solution to all of life's woes. If you've continually drank too much, this could result in a serious addiction.

農曆十二月 (January 5th - February 3rd 2019) 乙丑

Fatigue and exhaustion may overwhelm you this month, primarily if you've been occupied with countering opposition or intense competition at work. But remember that no job should be held at the expense of your personal health and contentment, so give yourself time to rest and recuperate to get back your energy again. Avoid embarking on all-new ventures or enterprises this month, because you're likely to come across a few serious stumbling blocks that will put your plans on hold and invite needless legal complications.

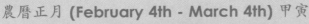

農曆正月 (February 4th - March 4th) 甲寅

New ventures need to be analysed correctly as financial loss is possible from negligent decision-making. Do your homework and research and the results will be in your favour. If you are in the real estate and property development industries, you should invest in clearly thought-out deals in your field of work because this is a time to make beneficial returns. In your marriage, be open with your spouse this month and discuss all important decisions with each other. Keeping things from each other will only lead to problems.

農曆二月 (March 5th - April 4th) 乙卯

Employees should keep away from gossip or slander because it could easily turn into heated arguments or even aggressive behaviour this month. Refrain from indulging in rumour-mongering and keep office politics to a minimum. You'll find that deals which need to be concluded will do well, so long as your negotiator is able to use his or her powers of persuasion and argument. If you're handling it on your own, be sure to up the charm and work on your persuasive skills!

農曆三月 (April 5th - May 4th) 丙辰

Be careful of possible fraudsters this month because there is an increased risk of betrayal and deceit at this point in time. This could possibly result in legal issues, so you will need to be especially vigilant. Do not give unsolicited advice this month, as it will not be favourably received. If there are negative structures outside this sector's bedroom, there is a risk of liver problems or injuries to the legs.

農曆四月 (May 5th - June 5th) 丁巳

Young boys should be careful of injury to their limbs from sharp metal objects and implements. Military men and strategists will find this a rewarding combination, as they will find increased wisdom when planning for the future. This is a good month for accumulating profits from property, especially using your past experience and superior knowledge to your best advantage.

Main Door	East	Bedroom Sector	Northeast

農曆五月 (June 6th - July 6th) 戊午

Be mindful of your feelings this month, because the energies of this bedroom can lead to emotional turbulence. Bosses and business owners might also want to initiate special audits or spot-checks this month, as the risk of being defrauded or cheated by your employees is quite likely. That aside, those in the media and marketing industries will find this to be a positive month, as far as achievements and accolades are concerned.

農曆六月 (July 7th - August 6th) 己未

Analysts and scientific researchers will find the energies of this room to be conducive to their work this month. But in interpersonal relations, you will certainly want to keep out of any disputes, gossips or quarrels this month, as they will most likely result in legal entanglements ultimately. Mind your own business and take good care of yourself, and your own safety this month, as you run the risk of being robbed – especially if you happen to notice the presence of negative features outside this sector's bedroom.

農曆七月 (August 7th - September 7th) 庚申

Speculative investments and gambling should be avoided this month as these will end in losses. However, if the investment is in real estate and you are astute with your knowledge, then a certain amount of profits can be made. Couples using this bedroom must be patient and tolerant, as both parties will listen to other people instead of each other. Don't let the words of others influence you. It's important to always remember that you know each other best. If you're using this room, there is an increased risk of accidents while driving – so be warned!

農曆八月 (September 8th - October 7th) 辛酉

If you're a single man, the energies of the Northeast bode well for you. You'll be able to meet a suitable partner this month if you set your mind to it! Take advantage of the good financial advice given to you and invest it in research and development. People in the media and travel industries may find this to be a month of achievements and great honour, and you will find your reputation enjoying a good boost.

農曆九月 (October 8th - November 6th) 壬戌

If you use this sector's bedroom, you are likely to prosper and enjoy good Wealth Luck, as well as possessing the wisdom to safeguard and retain your wealth! But bear in mind that the presence of negative structures outside this sector may lead to the possibility of occupants being involved in underhand dealings or illegal matters. Be mindful of this. This is also a good sector to be utilised by students preparing for important examinations.

農曆十月 (November 7th - December 6th) 癸亥

New ventures need to be checked thoroughly as financial loss is possible from negligent decision-making. Do your homework and research, and the results will be in your favour. All you need to do is put in a couple hours of extra legwork now to reap its dividends way into the future. People who are in real estate and property development should invest in clearly researched deals in their field of work, as this is a time to make beneficial returns. Those of you who are married should be frank, direct, and open with your spouse this month. Remember to discuss all important decisions with each other, as neglecting to do so could lead to stressful relations with your partner.

農曆十一月 (December 7th 2018 - January 4th 2019) 甲子

People in the legal fields will do well this month, as persuasive powers and the ability to argue constructively will result in positive features this month. Those of you who are able to articulate your arguments well should make the most of the positive energies of this room. Travel brings positive outcomes for you and could result in an increase in status this month, especially if you are in the construction or architecture business. But in general, all senior personnel should be on their guard against thieves and unscrupulous third parties who will end up extorting large sums of money from you.

農曆十二月 (January 5th - February 3rd 2019) 乙丑

If you're a contractor who has been working hard to land that 'deal of a century' that could change your life, then watch out for any potential tenders. Don't hesitate to submit your bid accordingly. Don't be too cautious that you miss out on a good opportunity! However, those working on construction sites should prioritise their safety and keep their helmets on at all times while on-site. This should be practiced so you could minimise the risk of a head injury, especially if it proves to be a significant risk at this point in time. Parents may also find their sons rebellious and prone to questioning their authority and advice this month, so it may be wise to temporarily relocate them to another bedroom.

Main Door	East	Bedroom Sector	North

農曆正月 (February 4th - March 4th) 甲寅

You should avoid gambling this month because there is a high chance that you could lose your property or even your entire fortune. Even casual gambling should best be avoided. If you have made profits from investments it would be a good idea to cash in on these gains this month. In terms of health, this is not the time to indulge in flings or casual relationships because these will result in sexually-transmitted diseases.

農曆二月 (March 5th - April 4th) 乙卯

Those who are establishing new businesses in the property development or real estate field will find that they will gain success relatively quickly. Ensure that you make headway by utilising your network. People in the legal and arbitration business should use the good energies of this sector to advance their cause. If you have children using this bedroom this month, they may be rebellious and difficult to control, and you will have to be more authoritative.

農曆三月 (April 5th - May 4th) 丙辰

Profits may be realised from conservative property or real estate investments, as long as you're well aware and cognisant of prevalent market trends. Don't rush into anything without thought. There's also the possibility of a mismanagement of your family's assets, so be vigilant at the workplace and look out for any traces of foul play or sheer negligence.

農曆四月 (May 5th - June 5th) 丁巳

Communicate more coherently and openly with your partner or spouse this month, as miscommunication will mar your harmonious ties. You need to be extra sensitive to your partner's feelings as well. If you're a lawyer, you may find it harder to put your points across this month and argue your case convincingly. This is particularly the case if you use the North room, as the energies are not conducive for communication and speech.

Main Door	East	Bedroom Sector	North

農曆五月 (June 6th - July 6th) 戊午

This will be a trying month, especially for those in authority. You might want to monitor your employees or staff just a little more closely this month, as there's a possibility of disloyal (and overly ambitious) subordinates who will cause significant problems. If you happened to have just established a new relationship – be it personal or professional – remember to give your partner some space and room to negotiate or otherwise you may find the strength of your partnership eroding over time.

農曆六月 (July 7th - August 6th) 己未

Good profits can be made from conservative property deals but to benefit, you will need to watch the markets carefully and be cautious. Relationships are not good this month and people using these rooms should be patient with their loved ones. Emotional and mental instability may be exacerbated by monetary and relationship problems this month, so you will need to maintain strength in the face of adversity.

農曆七月 (August 7th - September 7th) 庚申

Miscommunication will be a problem this month. For those of you who have to give speeches or have speaking engagements in public, you may find that things get in your way or hamper your ability to do so! If you work in the cell phone and IT industries, you will find that losses may be incurred. If you are involved in disputes, you should either delay or settle because the chance of winning is minimal.

農曆八月 (September 8th - October 7th) 辛酉

If you're involved in competitive sports, you will find that competitions are an uphill battle this month. Don't waste too much energy on competing, work harder on your training instead. This will also be a difficult month for those who travel to gain income. This affects those in positions of authority, especially. If you use the North room for studies or scholarly activities, always bear in mind that your concentration will be weak.

East Sector Main Door

農曆九月 (October 8th - November 6th) 壬戌

Refrain from embarking on anything new this month, as your ventures could encounter stumbling blocks that will cause these ventures to fail miserably. Likewise, those involved in the real estate or property businesses should go about their dealings carefully and shrewdly. This is to avoid running into substantial financial losses, as a result of negligence or disputes. Women using this room should watch out for their health, as possible lumps or irregularities in the breast could be cause for concern.

農曆十月 (November 7th - December 6th) 癸亥

Expectant mothers are advised not to use this bedroom for the month and to also go for a thorough medical checkup. This is done to prevent the risk of pregnancy complications or a possible miscarriage. In fact, those who have been suffering from chronic or persistent health problems should consult their physician without delay. Otherwise, you are likely to end up with kidney problems or diabetes as the result of poor health coupled with negligence. Pay special attention while on the roads this month or you risk meeting with an accident.

農曆十一月 (December 7th 2018 - January 4th 2019) 甲子

The good energies of this room for this month should help those among you involved in the legal and arbitration fields. Therefore, use it to advance your cause and career. If you're establishing a new business in the field of property development or real estate, you will gain success relatively quickly. Parents will find that regarding their children using this room, this month will be a lot more defiant, rebellious and difficult to control – so make sure you take the reins, instead of letting your children control you!

農曆十二月 (January 5th - February 3rd 2019) 乙丑

As much as possible, new romantic relationships should be avoided this month. This is because the outcomes will be less than happy and they will also fall far below your expectations. It might be a better idea for you to concentrate on some other aspect of your life. If you're looking to expand your business, get some advice from mentors or seasoned professionals in your field – otherwise, you risk making incorrect choices that will cost you quite a bit, financially.

農曆正月 (February 4th - March 4th) 甲寅

Married couples should consider going on a holiday together this month. Your ties can be strengthened by some time together, apart from everyone else. In terms of your career, this is a good month to apply for the promotion you require, as your superior will see that you are a talented and capable person and be inclined to reward you accordingly. If there are negative features in the Northwest, there is a chance of spine or bladder problems for the inhabitants of the room.

農曆二月 (March 5th - April 4th) 乙卯

This is an excellent bedroom for those in the printing and media fields, as financial gains are ripe and plentiful this month! You should close business deals at this point in time, especially if it is in the property sector because the terms are likely to be in your favour. Your spouse may feel a little neglected this month if you place too much importance and attention into your work obligations and focus on money-making excessively.

農曆三月 (April 5th - May 4th) 丙辰

Academics as well as people in research and development have a chance to commercialise their research and ideas but they will need to be careful so that they're not taken advantage of by shady individuals. In other words, be wary of those who might try to steal your ideas and pass them off as their own. You should be able to enjoy an improvement in interpersonal relationships amongst family and friends this month. If you need to travel this month, consider getting travel insurance as there is a chance of injury to your limbs.

農曆四月 (May 5th - June 5th) 丁巳

People in competitive sports will find this to be a productive month, especially when competing abroad or in foreign countries. This is a month to spend time networking, as new contacts and connections will be made. There will be a Nobleman Star to help you achieve your aims this month, but you need to bear in mind that there will still be people who are out to sabotage you. You will still need to watch your back and spend more time cultivating ties with those who are willing to help.

Main Door	East	Bedroom Sector	Northwest

農曆五月 (June 6th - July 6th) 戊午

If you own a business, it will be difficult for you to make progress in anything, so it would be better to consolidate your position this month and not try to be too ambitious. Couples using this room will need to communicate more with each other, as suspicion may cause trouble in the relationship. If you work for or own a business in the logistics, courier or travel fields, you will need to be prepared for a tough month ahead, as you could face some financial challenges.

農曆六月 (July 7th - August 6th) 己未

Those in the construction industry will have a good month as they receive increased media attention – thus bringing in more customers. Fame, recognition and publicity will come to those in the marketing and public relations industries, resulting in increased profits and revenue. It's a good month to use this bedroom to deepen marital or relationship ties, as you'll enjoy greater intimacy and closeness.

農曆七月 (August 7th - September 7th) 庚申

Try to settle disputes amicably this month, as these may then end up in the law courts which will cost you dearly. In general, it's not a good month for relationships and partnerships which may come under fire from people with different agendas and opinions. Where possible find the middle path of reconciliation, instead of going at it with guns blazing.

農曆八月 (September 8th - October 7th) 辛酉

The energies of this sector are favourable for those who are in the real estate business. This is because deals will be profitable. You should strive to make connections that can help you further your opportunities, as this could mean a significant increase in finances. No matter what happens this month, be sure to double check and confirm information before acting on it.

農曆九月 (October 8th - November 6th) 壬戌

Lawsuits and people talking behind your back could prove to be expensive and time-consuming, so watch your behaviour this month. Where possible, try to alleviate the problem and see if it can be settled outside of the courts. Partnerships and new alliances will become strained for those using this bedroom this month. Try to settle disputes amicably, as these may then end up in the law courts which will cost you dearly.

農曆十月 (November 7th - December 6th) 癸亥

It's a good month for married couples to consider going on a holiday together. All you need to do to improve your relationship is to get away from the daily stresses of the 'real world' and find a way to reconnect deeply. For those of you applying for a promotion, it's a good month to go ahead and do it. Your superiors have likely recognised your talents and abilities, and will be very inclined to reward you accordingly. Health-wise, watch out for spine or bladder problems, if you are using this room.

農曆十一月 (December 7th 2018 - January 4th 2019) 甲子

This is an excellent bedroom for those in the printing and media fields, as financial gains are ripe and plentiful this month! You should ensure that you close all business deals at this point in time, especially those in the property sector. This is because the terms are likely to be in your favour, so don't hesitate to do it if the timing is right! Spouses may feel a little neglected, as one partner is busy making money and has no time for the other half. Endeavour to pencil in more time together in your schedule, as relationships are like growing plants and also need tending to!

農曆十二月 (January 5th - February 3rd 2019) 乙丑

Avoid taking on your rivals this month or getting involved in office politics, as you are sure to come off second best and this will add on to your frustration. Refrain from getting involved at all and use this month to recapitulate your talents and strengths. Do not get involved in casual relationships this month as these may end up tarnishing your reputation or just causing general problems. What may seem to be a harmless distraction could turn out to be anything but! Couples using this bedroom should be wary of issues that could cause jealousy and lead to marital discord. It will be best to address these directly and openly as they come up.

| Main Door | East | Bedroom Sector | West |

農曆正月 (February 4th - March 4th) 甲寅

There is a possibility of discord, arguments and family disharmony for those using this bedroom this month. If you're married, you must strive to keep the situation from escalating. In your professional life, evaluate all new deals conclusively otherwise these could end up costing you money. Alternatively, these deals could end up in the law courts! Abdominal problems will be a concern for older people using this bedroom, so they need to be more vigilant of their health.

農曆二月 (March 5th - April 4th) 乙卯

People involved in businesses which require logic and deduction to produce their income will find this a particularly difficult month. Avoid employing new staff members, as you will tend to recruit stubborn and less intelligent people who will make your work harder in the long run. You should also avoid making important decisions this month, because you will find that you're not particularly clear-headed and may end up making some ill-fated choices.

農曆三月 (April 5th - May 4th) 丙辰

It's a good month for you if you're a salaried employee. If you want to gain a foothold in terms of status and authority, you will find it to be smooth sailing this month. Underhanded deals may end up turning sour and costing you money, so make sure that these are all above board and vetted by legal experts. This is the month to invest in real estate but make sure that all the legal issues are taken care of.

農曆四月 (May 5th - June 5th) 丁巳

Manage your stress levels properly; otherwise you could very well end up with gastrointestinal problems or ulcers. This is due to increased stress at work. Still, those dabbling in the property or real estate business stand to gain financially, as long as they have worked through their deals diligently and carefully. Try to minimise contact with your in-laws this month, lest such interaction results in domestic discord between you and your spouse.

Main Door	East	Bedroom Sector	West

農曆五月 (June 6th - July 6th) 戊午

Using this bedroom, this month may bring about some emotional turbulence. Employees will find that no matter how hard they work, they will have difficulty making money this month. Someone will always be undercutting you and causing you unexpected trouble and stress. If there are negative features outside this sector, bear in mind that there is a chance for you to lose money in the stock market.

農曆六月 (July 7th - August 6th) 己未

There is a chance of gambling losses this month, so people who enjoy this particular activity should abstain from it until a more favourable time comes along. Unforeseen problems are prevalent this month so you will need to be sure to have a contingency plan or be adaptive where your business is concerned. This is especially the case if you are in the risk fields and industries. If there are negative features outside the West, then there could be serious risk of illness later on.

農曆七月 (August 7th - September 7th) 庚申

There will be a chance for growth this month. This is a time for self-cultivation and if the opportunity arises, you should take a course in self-development. You will find the results to be beneficial in the long run. The spleen and internal organs will cause illness and health troubles, so even minor problems should be taken seriously. See your doctor without trying to delay it.

農曆八月 (September 8th - October 7th) 辛酉

Employees in the financial sector should keep a low profile this month because there will be disputes, arguments and legal problems arising at work. If you're in a relationship, this will be a good month to give each other more space. This is also a good sector for those who want to be involved in religious endeavours and embark on spiritual pursuits.

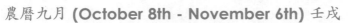

農曆九月 (October 8th - November 6th) 壬戌

This is a good month to avoid running afoul of the law. Err on the side of caution and be careful of your actions and words with others. If you're involved in research and development, you might want to refrain from making any important decisions, as your ability to think rationally and logically may not be at its best, this month. Elderly men should go for a full medical check-up at the first sign of trouble. This is in order to prevent minor ailments from developing into a more serious condition.

農曆十月 (November 7th - December 6th) 癸亥

Where possible, avoid engaging your female co-workers in unhealthy competition this month. This should be practiced to sidestep the possibility of ending up with a dispute or even legal issue in your hands. It will be best to simply hunker down and focus on your own work, instead. Get a qualified expert to check for any fire hazards in your home and office this month, especially if you notice any negative external features located outside this sector. If you are an experienced lawyer, you could be pleasantly surprised by a promotion to a position of status and authority this month.

農曆十一月 (December 7th 2018 - January 4th 2019) 甲子

This is not the month to bite off more than you can chew, especially when it comes to property investments. Things could easily take a turn for the worse, no matter how promising they may look initially. Try not to spread yourself too thin where your finances are concerned. While this room is a good one to use to gain spiritual knowledge, you should definitely watch out for any negative structures outside this sector, as you could end up feeling quite disturbed by the negative energy instead. In general, if you have a tendency towards emotional or mental instability, avoid using this room this month to prevent further exacerbating the situation.

農曆十二月 (January 5th - February 3rd 2019) 乙丑

Students or candidates who are bound to sit for examinations soon' should refrain from using this bedroom for revision and learning purposes. If you do, you will find your results to be less than stellar! Any unexpected business issues that arise this month should be dealt with carefully and swiftly, with the help of legal professionals if necessary – to prevent these problems from becoming much worse, with long-term implications. Those of you in the chemical and mechanical industries, however, will find this to be a smooth-sailing, hassle-free month.

Main Door	East	Bedroom Sector	Southwest

農曆正月 (February 4th - March 4th) 甲寅

Couples looking to conceive should try to use this bedroom, this month. This is the best way to get your endeavours to bear fruit, so to speak! Meanwhile, metaphysics professionals should also venture forth and expand their businesses, as this is a good time to do so. And if you happen to have a portfolio of several properties under your wings, it will be the right time to divest some of these off and pocket the profits from your investments. You might find yourself laughing all the way to the bank.

農曆二月 (March 5th - April 4th) 乙卯

This will be a fairly good month to engage in long-term investments, so do your homework and research, and get cracking! Those of you who are analysts will also find your career taking off quite nicely as a result of positive developments in the equities and financial markets. Ensure that you strike while the iron is hot. Similarly, academics, scholars and those involved in the literary, creative or artistic fields will find their skills and efforts recognised and possibly even celebrated, thereby bringing them a good measure of fame and brighter career prospects.

農曆三月 (April 5th - May 4th) 丙辰

This month, you will need to be aware of travel-related problems that could result in injury to the limbs. Be careful when you're out on one of your travel adventures, and invest in a good form of insurance. Injuries are also especially prevalent for those of you involved in extreme sports. And for those among you who are working as salaried employees, you should watch out for competition at work and keep out of any arguments. Reason being, these situations could escalate and end up in legal issues and troubles. For those in the engineering industry, this is generally a good month, because there could be unexpected recognition and financial rewards coming your way if you use this bedroom.

農曆四月 (May 5th - June 5th) 丁巳

Traders deeply immersed in the precious metals or metal futures market will derive beneficial spin-offs from their investments in these industries this month. Therefore, pursue any new leads with vigour and don't be afraid to take some bold risks. Newly-married couples who wish to enjoy a good start to your new life and relationship should also use this bedroom for positive results. For those of you attempting to invest in the stock market, you will do well to heed the advice of your mentors and financial advisors and act on their suggestions accordingly. There is no reason for you to stumble about if you're unsure – ask for advice from the right people and you're bound to receive it.

| Main Door | East | Bedroom Sector | Southwest |

農曆五月 (June 6th - July 6th) 戊午

Your reputation and efforts at your job will finally be acknowledged this month, and your superiors will be inclined to reward you with substantial financial benefits. In general, relationships will run smoothly at this point in time, so if you wish to finalise the partnership, this is the month to take that big step! If you're an analyst, you will find this to be an exciting month for you, as your career is liable to take off due to strategic positioning in the equities market.

農曆六月 (July 7th - August 6th) 己未

Those of you aiming for the #1 spot in a professional sports tournament or competition should use this room. This is because all signs point to it being beneficial in your endeavours. Similarly, employees and workers in the courier, logistics and printing industries should double their efforts this month. This is because you are likely to be rewarded with that promotion and salary increment you've been seeking all along! Married couples, however, are in a spot of trouble. Both partners will need to be more mindful of each other's feelings and emotions this month – this will preserve the harmony in the relationship.

農曆七月 (August 7th - September 7th) 庚申

This is not a very favorable month for most – if not all – endeavours, to say the least. Elderly males using this bedroom may find themselves especially susceptible to lung problems this month, so extra care and attention must be paid to their health. Employers might find it necessary to keep a tighter rein on their company's finances, as employees will be disloyal and even dishonest at work. Keep an eagle eye out for all fraudulent activities. If you're a salaried worker, however, you may also find your efforts going unnoticed by your superiors – so be patient and continue to work diligently.

農曆八月 (September 8th - October 7th) 辛酉

Couples using this bedroom will find their relationship harmonious and thriving this month. Communication flows smoothly and it will lead to an increased sense of contentment and happiness! Use this room if you will be sitting for an important examination soon or if you happen to be involved in the academic and scholarly fields. Meanwhile, those of you in the marketing, consultancy and strategic-planning businesses will find your services and expertise much sought-after this month – so go ahead and show them what you're made of!

農曆九月 (October 8th - November 6th) 壬戌

Stay away from any form of speculative investments this month, although you may most certainly use this time of the year to expand your business and widen your client base. This will be especially pertinent if you're involved in the engineering business. And do not neglect any seemingly minor ailments or they might develop into more serious conditions. Therefore, seek the advice of your doctor at the first sign of trouble or irregularity. If you're going to be travelling this month, be extra cautious and ensure that you've the necessary insurance policies in place. This is because the risk of meeting with an accident while travelling is somewhat high.

農曆十月 (November 7th - December 6th) 癸亥

For professional athletes utilizing this room, this month – you'll need to take note of potential leg injuries occurring. If not avoided and treated, it could lead to serious repercussions. Hostile takeovers are possible this month as well. So be more proactive and not be taken aback by such developments. As for those of you in banking, equity and financial industries, you will go through some tough times this month. As such, you should stop taking and signing on any new/major business deals – the outcome could only increase your stress levels.

農曆十一月 (December 7th 2018 - January 4th 2019) 甲子

For those of you in relationships, this is the time to settle down and start a family, this month. And if you're in the business of metal or equity trading, you should expect great rewards and returns this month. This comes in the form of good deals and financial gains. For those in the marketing, consulting and research and development fields, you should find that things are looking good and picking up this month. There will also be promotion for employees and recognition for the owners.

農曆十二月 (January 5th - February 3rd 2019) 乙丑

This month, the energies in this room could cause arguments and conflicts at home. These negative situations will affect fathers and sons of the household. Do not invest this month, as the results may not be in your favour. There will also be legal issues, so you'll need lawyer up. For athletes and professional sportspersons, be cautious of possible sprains and tendon injuries, especially when there is negative Sha outside of this sector.

| Main Door | East | Bedroom Sector | South |

農曆正月 (February 4th - March 4th) 甲寅

Domestic disputes and family issues are likely this month; however, it will affect the females using the South bedroom more than the males. If you're travelling this month, you should be prepared for slight delays to your plans or schedule. Be careful with your personal documents and your own personal safety. If you're an artist or author, you're likely to have professional success this month.

農曆二月 (March 5th - April 4th) 乙卯

This is a good month if you're in the property field, as there are good opportunities for property investments. Profits are likely to be rather high. Individuals in the metaphysical disciplines will find opportunities opening up for them to pursue further studies in this field. Female employees will have an excellent month, bringing in an increased turnover – especially if they are in the real estate industry.

農曆三月 (April 5th - May 4th) 丙辰

This is a month where you'll be saying the wrong thing quite frequently and this could have disastrous results! Quarrels and disputes could be rife this month and must be settled amicably as quickly as possible. If you work in the media, marketing and public relations industries, you should also ensure that all legal documents are carefully scrutinised before committing to them or legal complications will ensue.

農曆四月 (May 5th - June 5th) 丁巳

This is a good month to strengthen the ties that bind you to your business affiliates, co-workers, and loved ones – and where necessary, formalise them. It's also a profitable month for dealings in shares and equities, although you will need to exercise patience, diligence and care in concluding them. However, this is not an ideal time for pregnant women to move around or embark on any travels, as they risk meeting with an accident if they do so, particularly if they use this bedroom.

Main Door	East	Bedroom Sector	South

農曆五月 (June 6th - July 6th) 戊午

This is a good month for property acquisitions, but these will produce even better financial rewards if you are required to travel to conclude the deal. If you work in the real estate field, promote yourself this month in order to reap the rewards, in terms of recognition and promotion. Joint ventures, especially in the property industry, will do particularly well this month and more benefits will be gained if these alliances are consolidated abroad.

農曆六月 (July 7th - August 6th) 己未

There will be serious disagreements between you and your partner this month. This is something to watch out for, especially if you're married. Otherwise, the consequences could be quite serious. People who work on industrial worksites should be careful of injuring their limbs with sharp metal objects or machinery. If meditation or spiritual development is your interest then using this room, this month, will be favourable.

農曆七月 (August 7th - September 7th) 庚申

In general, this is a beneficial time to consolidate personal and professional relationships, and maybe even formalising these ties where necessary. This is also a good month for professional sportsmen to excel and receive recognition, but unfortunately this will not bring great wealth. But don't worry too much, as the added recognition and acclaim will bode well for your future pursuits! Those working in the mining industry or trade in financial instruments will find that trading this month will bring about positive outcomes and increased profits.

農曆八月 (September 8th - October 7th) 辛酉

Couples will find that giving each other more space this month will benefit their relationship. Give each other room to breathe instead of placing too many demands on each other. You should avoid gambling and speculative investments this month, particularly in property, as the outcome is unlikely to be in your favour. If you own a business, steer clear of illegal deals as the long arm of the law will catch up to you!

農曆九月 (October 8th - November 6th) 壬戌

Financial benefits will come to you this month, especially if you're in management and financial consulting. It is a good time to draw attention to your accomplishments and fulfilled goals. If you're an artist, you also stand to enjoy a good month, as some measure of recognition and fame will come your way. Others will also start to appreciate your work and are keen to let you know!

農曆十月 (November 7th - December 6th) 癸亥

You'll have to be on the lookout for backstabbing and underhanded dealings at the workplace this month. Keep your guard up and be wary of the resentful few around you who are unhappy as their career path seems to be on a descent. As a result, they're likely to cause troubles for those around them. In general, the sense of unfriendly competition, coupled with deception, will also affect professionals in the entertainment industry. Those of you working in the food and beverage industry should be careful of possible health laws, because you will do well with the exception of a few run-ins with the law for this reason. If you're not careful, it could lead to financial losses.

農曆十一月 (December 7th 2018 - January 4th 2019) 甲子

If you have property deals abroad, this will be a very good month to make some financial profits. Don't be afraid to travel quite a bit to sign a few documents, as the results will be so good – outweighing that little bit of trouble. For most of you, consider this to be a month of self-improvement, as all endeavours begun along these lines will have extensive benefits. Consider taking up that class or new hobby that you've always dreamed about. Married females, however, will have face troubles with their mothers-in-law this month, so be sure to bite your tongue whenever you are angry. Don't be too emotionally reactive or the situation will only get worse for you.

農曆十二月 (January 5th - February 3rd 2019) 乙丑

Sticks and stones may break their bones, and words will find a way to hurt them! So be mindful of the words that come out of your mouth this month, as if you say something hasty in anger or heightened emotion, it will likely cause some trouble and rear its ugly head for some time after. Quarrels will begin at the drop of a hat this month, so bear this in mind and avoid getting enmeshed in one for trivial reasons. Try to resolve all conflicts as swiftly as possible. Individuals working in the media or in marketing and publicity will have to vet through all legal documents with care before putting pen to paper.

Main Door	East	Bedroom Sector	Southeast

SE	S	SW
8	4	6
E 7	9	2 W
3	5	1
NE	N	NW

農曆正月 (February 4th - March 4th) 甲寅

Entrepreneurs and businessmen will find that their employees will go the extra mile to produce what is needed. This is due to strong loyalty from the staff, and this is something that you should focus on this month. A cohesive work strategy will result in increased production and a subsequent improvement in profits and revenues. There is a possibility of moving home this month, as property investments are good and a change is needed for your general well-being.

農曆二月 (March 5th - April 4th) 乙卯

This is a stressful month for relationships, so do not make any important decisions about the future until a more suitable time. Big changes will be needed to revive stagnant careers and floundering ventures. Go all out and brainstorm for new ideas, as a fresh outlook is just what is needed. This is a good room to use for children sitting for important examinations this month, as the results are likely to be favourable. It will also be useful for scholars and academics preparing for important projects (i.e. thesis writing, etc.).

農曆三月 (April 5th - May 4th) 丙辰

Speculative investments in real estate will provide handsome profits this month, but make sure that all the details have been taken care of by lawyers. Individuals in positions of power and authority or of high social status will find that things are likely to be in your favour this month. It will be best to take advantage of any opportunity that comes your way without having to postpone it to a later time. If you've been in a long-term relationship and are ready to take the step towards marriage, this is an auspicious month to do so.

農曆四月 (May 5th - June 5th) 丁巳

Personal relationships come under strain this month, and you'll find yourself arguing quite a bit with your partner. If you're still single and searching, concentrate on your career as the energies of the month do not augur well for relationships. In fact, you should take advantage of the support from your superiors, by voicing out to them the fresh ideas and new projects that are your brainchild. Good news for investment and fund managers: Your portfolios will bring you substantial gains this month!

| Main Door | East | Bedroom Sector | Southeast |

農曆五月 (June 6th - July 6th) 戊午

If you are considering a new project, this is the month to launch it as the reception and outcome will be highly favourable. Recognition comes to those who have excelled in their chosen field or for people who have been responsible for initiating or driving something to a close. Couples looking to start a family should use this bedroom this month. In addition, good news and celebrations await those using this room. This is the time for new beginnings or new start-up ventures.

農曆六月 (July 7th - August 6th) 己未

If you're a salaried employee and want to make a breakthrough in the workplace, you'll do well to study and brush up on your skills. This is a good month to consolidate both personal and professional relationships although the start may be a little rocky and on unstable ground. Consider this is your month to go out and have a good time! Long-term relationships will not be on the cards this month for those who are single.

農曆七月 (August 7th - September 7th) 庚申

Your investments will flourish this month, especially for those in the communications industry – as long as you use your trusted networks of contacts instead of relying on new acquaintances. Individuals who have children will find that they become more independent and responsible, thus resulting in better academic achievements without the need for scolding or nagging! If you are in the share and equity markets, this month should show substantial profit if you cash in your shares. It is also important that you bank in the money rather than letting it slip through your fingers.

農曆八月 (September 8th - October 7th) 辛酉

People involved in the financial stocks and equities markets will have an opportunity to make good profits for either their companies or themselves, this month. However, you need to be aware of unscrupulous people who will try to bully you during negotiations. If you're in the family business or enterprise, there will be a surge of options that will allow you to move the business in different directions. There will also be a lot of room for financial growth and improvement, if you think wisely about your next move.

農曆九月 (October 8th - November 6th) 壬戌

Property deals abound, but you should be careful when entering into new deals. Make sure that you are completely happy with all the details and have read and understood the fine print before you sign on the dotted line. Athletes and long-distance runners should take care of their joints this month, as injuries are possible. Couples using this bedroom will find this to be a good room, and can expect to enjoy harmonious and close relationship ties.

農曆十月 (November 7th - December 6th) 癸亥

This room is recommended for those who are embarking on scholarly pursuits – such as exams. You will be able to tap into the auspicious energy of this sector's bedroom as a study and pass with flying colours! In terms of investments, it is imperative that you tailor your strategy and cash in some of the previous investments. In terms of relationships, couples who have been sleeping in this sector's bedroom, may also find their relationships improving significantly.

農曆十一月 (December 7th 2018 - January 4th 2019) 甲子

This month will not be a good month to make any major decisions in relation to your future. This is because your mental capacity will be overwhelmed by stress. Don't be afraid to make big changes that will revive stagnant careers and struggling ventures. This is the perfect time to go all out and live it up to your role and go beyond expectations. Gather new ideas and have a fresh outlook. This is also a good room to use for children facing important exams this month, as the results are likely to be favorable.

農曆十二月 (January 5th - February 3rd 2019) 乙丑

Great profits can be earned from investments in the property market this month. You just need to make sure that every single detail is thought over and get your legal counsels to go through everything. For those of you in positions of power, authority and general influencers – you will see things working in your favour swimmingly well this month. It would be best for you to grab the bull by the horns and seize every opportunity coming your way. For couples, this will be a good month for both of you to make things official by capitalising on the favourable energies of this sector.

Northeast Sector
Main Door

Main Door	Northeast	Bedroom Sector	Northeast

This section contains the monthly outlook for all 12 months of the year for different bedroom sectors, in a property with a Northeast Sector Main Door.

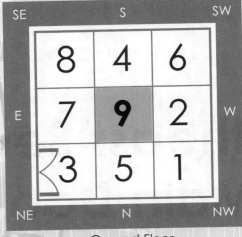

Ground Floor

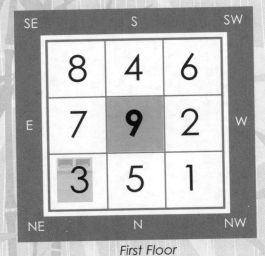

First Floor

農曆正月 (February 4th - March 4th) 甲寅

This will not be the ideal month for you to ponder upon your relationship or spend endless hours musing about 'where it's going' and 'what does it all mean.' If you do this, it could backfire on you and prolong any necessary actions you need to take. At this point in time, you will need to be more action-oriented. It's a good time to conclude any of your property deals, but be specific on the details – or otherwise, messy legal issues will rear their ugly head! If you fall ill this month, don't ignore the signs – what may seem trivial and minor could lead to something a lot more serious, especially if you're not careful.

農曆二月 (March 5th - April 4th) 乙卯

There is a strong likelihood that you will have to battle rumours and gossip, which could lead to conflicts, while using this room this month. It might be best for you to switch to another if this is affecting your peace of mind. Those of you working in the publishing or printing industries, you will find this to be a good month in terms of financial profits, especially when it comes from sales abroad. If you're involved in any arbitration work, you are likely to see good results as your skills are very much needed.

農曆三月 (April 5th - May 4th) 丙辰

Elderly males who use this room or sector will be susceptible to certain health problems and conditions, so it will be best to seek medical treatment immediately instead of pushing it forward to another time. Where relationships are concerned, it will be an exhausting month for those using this room. Your partner may suspect you of dishonesty and infidelity, so nip those jealous symptoms in the bud by being straightforward, or it could grow into something quite ugly. If possible, avoid going on any business trips this month!

農曆四月 (May 5th - June 5th) 丁巳

Possible injuries are likely this month, especially those brought on by driving accidents. So be extra careful and don't be negligent in your safety habits, for example, choosing not to wear your safety belt and suchlike. Your health isn't looking too rosy this month, either. You'll have to battle ulcers, gallstones and possible liver diseases. This is also a bad month to indulge in your gambling instincts, because any risks you take with your finances will only end in severe losses. All speculative, high-risk investments should also be avoided – as it might result in lawsuits, in addition to losses.

Main Door	Northeast	Bedroom Sector	Northeast

農曆五月 (June 6th - July 6th) 戊午

If you're sitting for exams at this point in time, this will be a good room to use for your exam studies and preparations. But those of you in the business world, you will have to be extra cautious, because there is a likelihood of fraud and embezzlement. Put all your business transactions and legal documents under the magnifying glass to ensure you catch all the details in the fine print! If you're looking to make more money, listen to the financial advice given to you by mentors or experts. This is the type of advice you can use for a long time and into the future.

農曆六月 (July 7th - August 6th) 己未

At the workplace, you will need to keep an eye out on your competitors. This is because they will be going all out to keep you down. If you let them get away with it, they could keep a possible promotion out of your path. If you work with heavy machinery and dangerous tools, be extra careful this month. Don't be careless and negligent, or an accident could happen. In general, you're also at risk for car accidents and travel-related mishaps.

農曆七月 (August 7th - September 7th) 庚申

Avoid all forms of gambling this month, as the only things likely to greet you are heavy losses. You are somewhat reckless this month and far from being able to make good judgment calls! Even speculative investments are a no-no at this point, as financial losses are not the worst that can happen – legal troubles are! Employees and subordinates are likely to be defiant and rebellious at this point, and a confrontation might take you aback, so be ready to act to prevent things from getting worse.

農曆八月 (September 8th - October 7th) 辛酉

Individuals in the media and marketing industries will enjoy the fruits of this month, as it brings great achievements and high honour. You should enjoy what comes your way without worrying too much about the future. But for those of you who suffer from depression, it might be best to move away from this room for the month. Bear in mind that covert, underhanded schemes by your competitors will only lead to financial loss and possible legal problems through fraud or embezzlement.

農曆九月 (October 8th - November 6th) 壬戌

Those of you who work in analytical or scientific fields, you will enjoy the positive energies of this sector and may find this affecting your work in good ways. You'll have clear breakthroughs in projects or tasks that you were working on. If you're in politics, going on a campaign for this month will bring about high chances of success, but it depends on how aggressive you are! If you're in the communications and construction industries, you will be able to make good headway into your competitors' markets this month.

農曆十月 (November 7th - December 6th) 癸亥

This is a good month to conclude property deals but you will need to be specific on the details, as legal issues will crop up if you are not extra careful with the fine print. If you're using this room this month, you should take illnesses seriously, because what may seem to be very minor can quickly change into something more serious. In terms of relationships, do not over-analyse or overthink. If action needs to be taken, you should get on it quick.

農曆十一月 (December 7th 2018 - January 4th 2019) 甲子

If you're a senior personnel in a business or in your firm, you will need to watch out for theft and backstabbing this month. Keep information of your finances and private matters discreet and undisclosed. It will not pay to reveal too much too soon. The artistically inclined, especially sculptors and carvers, will find that they attract increased commission for their work this month.

農曆十二月 (January 5th - February 3rd 2019) 乙丑

Scams, confidence tricksters and conmen are out to catch you this month, so you will need to be on your guard when conducting business. Do not meddle in other people's affairs, as you will get no gratitude for your advice, especially if it was unsolicited. If you have children using this sector's room, you will need to be on the lookout for their behaviours – which will largely be uncontrolled and a tad rebellious!

Northeast Sector Main Door

農曆正月 (February 4th - March 4th) 甲寅

For those of you in the publishing industry, success and career advancement will come at the end – but only after slogging through some serious hard work! Also, be wary of a certain someone who will go all out to undermine your position and point of view. You're likely to experience minor fallouts in your professional and personal relationships this month, so be prepared. It will also be a generally difficult month for lawyers, as you will face problems putting your case across in an effective manner.

農曆二月 (March 5th - April 4th) 乙卯

Romantic relationships continue to falter under stress and extreme pressure, resulting in tense relations and frazzled nerves. It will be imperative for both parties to be more understanding and considerate to each other. People working in the IT industry will have a very good month, primarily due to new business opportunities springing up from connections and recommendations.

農曆三月 (April 5th - May 4th) 丙辰

It's not a good month for your finances and this is largely in due part to disloyal subordinates undermining your moves. Be careful of potential accidents that could be caused by careless individuals. There will be possible muscles or tendon injuries faced, as a result of this. In general, using this room will aggravate any existing health problems and create potential new ones as well. This is especially the case with eye diseases or head injuries.

農曆四月 (May 5th - June 5th) 丁巳

Where your health is concerned this month, try to avoid eating out. You might have to battle some indigestion and stomach troubles. It will be best to prepare the food at home, for the sake of your physical well-being. Lawyers will find their number of clients increasing this month, so make the most of your extra uptake! Avoid making any significant financial investments this month, especially if you're in the communications industry – as the risk of losses is very high.

農曆五月 (June 6th - July 6th) 戊午

Individuals who have to sit for important examinations soon will have trouble focusing their attention and will find their mind wandering. Try to reign in your concentration, or else it could bear repercussions in your exam results. Isolation and loneliness will plague the people using this room, this month, so try to prevent it by seeking out the company of your good friends and family members. This is especially true if you wish to unburden some of the heavy burdens of your soul. If you're involved in professional sports, it will be best to concentrate on improving your fitness level instead of participating in competitions.

農曆六月 (July 7th - August 6th) 己未

This month, you'll have to pay careful attention to your health. Any symptoms that seem minor should be checked out thoroughly, in order to prevent any serious illnesses from developing. In general, where work is concerned, you'll do best to lay low and avoid ambitious projects this month. Things are not likely to progress smoothly, so it will be to your benefit to keep a low profile. Even in real estate and property transactions, you will do best to steer clear of major deals until a better time in the future.

農曆七月 (August 7th - September 7th) 庚申

Females using this room should be careful of potential cancer risks, especially breast cancer. Avoid succumbing to the temptation to engage in speculative or high-risk investments, including gambling. The chances of losses are higher than the potential gains. Problems come to the fore this month, both professional and personal. There are no easy solutions to solve them, as the source of most of it are also quite obscured. Be careful of potential enemies and rivals looking to take advantage of your situation, as well.

農曆八月 (September 8th - October 7th) 辛酉

There is trouble brewing in your work situation, and it will not be right to wholly depend on or rely on your employees. You might find that they tend to create more trouble than what's worth. It will be best to postpone any projects that require sustained teamwork and the collective support of all your staff. Males might have to face off some lawsuits this month, especially those that involve car or vehicle accidents. Individuals in serious relationships will find this a trying month of many arguments, disrupting the general peace.

農曆九月 (October 8th - November 6th) 壬戌

It would be best for pregnant women to avoid sleeping in this sector for the month, as complications could arise, leading to serious problems later on. In general, people using this room should focus more on their careers than on their romantic lives, as Cupid's arrow is not headed in your direction at this point in time. Hold off on making important decisions, especially if you're trying to expand your business – otherwise you could risk making some seriously dodgy ones that will cost you quite a bit in terms of finances.

農曆十月 (November 7th - December 6th) 癸亥

Success and promotion may be on your plate, if you're in the publishing field. This is obviously achieved through hard work but be warned that there is always someone in the background who will try to undermine you from an intellectual point of view. Therefore, be circumspect with whom you share your thoughts with. Professional and personal relationships will be difficult this month – with business partners and loved ones experiencing a falling out. If you work in the legal field, you'll have a particularly hard time putting your cases across.

農曆十一月 (December 7th 2018 - January 4th 2019) 甲子

Niggling health issues will be your main problem, especially if you use this sector's bedroom this month. You will be plagued with troubles involving your eyes and possibly your heart, as well. Fire hazards are also a risk this month and electrical wiring should be checked, especially where it is old and in need of replacement. Those in the political arena will find that friends and acquaintances will be around to help them with their political aspirations, and much of their goals can be accomplished.

農曆十二月 (January 5th - February 3rd 2019) 乙丑

Your finances may suffer from a drawback this month. If you run or manage a company or business, this will be due to employees or subordinates undermining your goals by backstabbing or being disloyal to you. Furthermore, using this sector's bedroom this month may aggravate health problems or could result in eye or head injuries, or injuries to your muscles and tendons, as well, if you're not careful.

Northeast Sector Main Door

農曆正月 (February 4th - March 4th) 甲寅

For individuals who are in the food and beverage or entertainment industries – this will be a relatively profitable month for you. Go all out to make the most of the deals headed your way! If there are any romantic interludes to look forward to this month, they are likely to be short-lived. It will be better for you not to put too much of yourself into it and to focus on other aspects of your life instead. Health-wise, be careful of heart and eye ailments, as these are likely to develop into something more serious.

農曆二月 (March 5th - April 4th) 乙卯

Those of you dabbling in the property field will be astounded by the many spectacular deals that come up. Keep an eagle eye out on possible good ones, but remember that you will need to close on your deals this month. This is a favourable month for all business deals in general. Where matters of the heart are concerned, bear in mind that your spouse will feel neglected this month, as your focus on your career could sideline intimacy and connection.

農曆三月 (April 5th - May 4th) 丙辰

There's a time to be nosey and there's a time to keep your nose strictly out of other people's affairs – and this is one of those times to do the latter! If you become enmeshed in the lives of others, you're likely to see resentment and brickbats being flung your way, as opposed to gratitude and bouquets. Where your physical health is concerned, get your travel and health insurance updated, especially if by chance you're going to be going out of town.

農曆四月 (May 5th - June 5th) 丁巳

For most of us, networking forms a big part of our day-to-day jobs. This month will prove beneficial for networking attempts, especially if you're out to corral in new clients and customers. Things are on a roll, so make sure you get on the wheel! If you're facing important examinations of any sort this month, it would be favourable for you to use this room to get your preparations and studying done. If you're in politics and looking to move ahead, it's a good month for you to solicit support from within your party or constituency.

| Main Door | Northeast | Bedroom Sector | Northwest |

農曆五月 (June 6th - July 6th) 戊午

This month doesn't bode well for your work projects and endeavours. Don't worry too much if progress seems to grind to a halt. It just means you need to take some time out to consolidate your position and make the most of the downtime that you have. Romantic relationships are going to be less rosy and more green this month – in terms of the green-eyed monster, that is! Try to keep rampant suspicion and jealousy at bay, or it will cause some serious damage to relationships.

農曆六月 (July 7th - August 6th) 己未

Any form of speculative investments, especially in asset acquisitions, will bring about a surfeit of profits. This is particularly true if it involves travelling abroad in order to gain something from it. If you have to sit for important examinations this month, you will do well to use this room – because it bodes well for scholarly pursuits. In general, you'll be able to enjoy favourable relationship conditions, but be careful of the presence of Water in this sector. It could result in possible relationship scandals that will cause a significant amount of stress and anxiety.

農曆七月 (August 7th - September 7th) 庚申

Where your business relationships or partnerships are concerned, you will have to be careful of possible tensions and problems that could cause a strain. It will be best to avoid forming new alliances at this point in time, because it's not likely to work in your favour. You should also be prepared for possible rumours plaguing you and your business endeavours this month. While it may seem trivial, it could cause you some problems with wealth and result in some messy legal issues. Relationships could also come under pressure this month, so you'll have to be more tolerant and less apt to losing your cool.

農曆八月 (September 8th - October 7th) 辛酉

Gossip arising out of third-party interference will cause tensions in your marriage and relationships this month, so be careful to what you listen to and to whom you put your trust in. Otherwise, you'll have to endure certain problems that will have some long-term repercussions and consequences. If you choose to make investments in property this month, you are likely to enjoy some profitable results.

Northeast Sector Main Door

農曆九月 (October 8th - November 6th) 壬戌

It's a month to take on significant and ambitious projects, as there are plenty of mentors and advisors around who will help you do what you need to do. Don't be afraid to ask for help when you need it, because you are likely to get the assistance that you need. For people involved in creative industries, you'll need to be ready to step into the limelight because you're likely to get the attention you need and make a name for yourself. Where your career is concerned, you need to make the right changes to ignite what is stagnant.

農曆十月 (November 7th - December 6th) 癸亥

Avoid working with people you do not know very well, as they may let you down, especially when you need to rely on them the most. This is a month to ask for the promotion you require as superiors will recognise your talents this month and are willing to show their appreciation! If you are involved in competitive sports, you will do well in international competitions this month, so make an effort to work and train hard in order to achieve your goals.

農曆十一月 (December 7th 2018 - January 4th 2019) 甲子

If you're in travel and logistics, you will find the opportunity to conclude new deals and build up alliances abroad. Therefore, make the most of your network of contacts in order to get some negotiations going! If you're in the real estate and property business, you'll find that your profits will be quite lucrative this month. Your relationship outlook with your partner and spouse will also be good, if you're using this bedroom.

農曆十二月 (January 5th - February 3rd 2019) 乙丑

Do not meddle in other people's affairs, as arguments and ill will, rather than gratitude, are likely to be the result. It will be best to refrain from getting involved. If you travel this month it would be advisable to have your health and travel insurance up to date, as there is a chance of slight ill-health or mishaps. Updated auditing provisions should be in place this month, as fraud and theft are possible.

| Main Door | Northeast | Bedroom Sector | West |

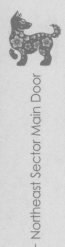

農曆正月 (February 4th - March 4th) 甲寅

Married couples should watch out for discords in marriage, resulting in arguments and general family disharmony. Make an effort not to let your emotions get the best of you. Endeavour to deal with the arguments and quarrels with a sense of proportion, and be patient and tolerant because it will go a long way! If you're a property developer, or involved in real estate, you will be able to make good and sound investments in property – but first you will need to ensure that you read the fine print or have the documents vetted by a skillful lawyer, in order to catch any irregularities.

農曆二月 (March 5th - April 4th) 乙卯

Love is likely to bloom for singles who are available and on the lookout! You will find this to be a good month to meet a person who will capture your interest and send your pulse racing, so don't waste the opportunities that present themselves! However, those of you involved in business ventures that require you to engage in plenty of logic and deduction in order to produce your income will run into difficulties. But to improve your business opportunities, most of you should consider focusing on networking, as meeting new people could be the ticket to more profits.

農曆三月 (April 5th - May 4th) 丙辰

Unfortunately, a month of unforeseen and unexpected problems is in store for you, so you will need to be quick on the uptake to be able to respond to these last-minute problems. It will be an ideal time to figure out a Plan B, and a Plan C too... for good measure! Your relationships will be plagued by misunderstandings, largely caused by tumultuous thoughts and emotions. It will also be better for you to lay low and avoid pressing the issue or engaging too closely with others. What you and everyone else needs right now are more breathing space and time to let things simmer down.

農曆四月 (May 5th - June 5th) 丁巳

Health problems and troubles are likely to crop up this month, resulting in colonic or gastrointestinal illnesses. Seek medical treatment as soon as something is amiss, as neglecting the symptoms will only make you feel worse in the long run. Those of you bitten by the literary bug or who are blessed with talents and interests in the area, will find this to be a month of recognition and rewards. Married women who are using this room and living in the same home as their in-laws will find that relations are testy and strained this month – so keep a low profile and try not to engage too closely with them.

Main Door	Northeast	Bedroom Sector	West

農曆五月 (June 6th - July 6th) 戊午

Those of you who have an accumulated store of unpaid fines, summonses and taxes – you will do well to attend to these matters this month! Otherwise, you risk paying a heavier penalty in the form of legal problems. Elderly women who use this room or sector, and who drive vehicles, should be careful of potential car accidents this month. Try not to drive for too long, or for further distances, unless it is absolutely necessary. For most of you, personal and professional relationships come under fire as arguments and disputes, including backbiting, are rife. Keep a cool head throughout it all and avoid dragging your emotions into the matter – as the results are likely to be ugly!

農曆六月 (July 7th - August 6th) 己未

Sudden business opportunities and deals that come up this month should be carefully considered and dealt with. You may want to enlist the help of experienced, skillful lawyers to help you weed out any irregularities before you get entangled in something messy. Haphazard thoughts and emotions could send relationships spiraling out of control this month, so most of you will do well to maintain a low profile and give each other more breathing space. It's not a good time to force any issue. Professionals in the legal field, especially judges and lawyers, will enjoy recognition and praise for your efforts.

農曆七月 (August 7th - September 7th) 庚申

Those among you working in the media, publicity, and journalism industries and fields will find money pouring into your pockets quite easily this month! Make the most of it, as you have worked hard for these rewards. Individuals involved in real estate will have ample opportunities to dabble in property-related speculative investments at this point in time. Most of you using this sector will find it a good time to immerse yourself in self-improvement and self-cultivation, so grab any chances that arise that enable you to take a course or program to improve your knowledge or skills.

農曆八月 (September 8th - October 7th) 辛酉

Relationships come under fire this month for people using this room or sector, and constant arguments and quarrels are very likely. Try your very best not to contribute to the tension. Instead, aim to alleviate the situation by approaching it calmly, and without reacting to everything in an emotional manner. People working for others should be careful not to get too drawn into workplace politics and gossip, or to take sides in any disputes. Otherwise, these could erupt into large-scale problems that no one will be interested to clean up in the end.

農曆九月 (October 8th - November 6th) 壬戌

The situation at work is a little tense for you this month, because there are plenty jealous subordinates and co-workers who will be ever-ready and willing to chip away at your efforts and hard work. Try not to pay attention to them, and instead focus on your work – this will blow over quite swiftly! Avoid getting into any deals that promise short-cuts or even underhanded methods of obtaining swift results. In the long run, it could turn out very sour and could cost you quite a bit of fortune. However, your personal relationships are likely to do quite well this month.

農曆十月 (November 7th - December 6th) 癸亥

Be careful in your business dealings as things are not what they seem and rivals are out to deceive you into deals that will not be financially sound. Be cautious and sceptical of what people try to convince you of. There are financial gains to be made from the property market this month but care must be exercised when doing so, otherwise you could just as easily sustain financial losses instead. Also, there is a risk of car accidents this month, so be on guard.

農曆十一月 (December 7th 2018 - January 4th 2019) 甲子

You will want to use this sector for spiritual and religious pursuits, if you wish to delve deeper into your area of interest. Keep a sharp look out, however, for the presence of any negative structures or features outside this sector, as they could cause health problems such as bone aches and joint pains. On the financial side of things, there will be possibilities to make a profit through property and real estate.

農曆十二月 (January 5th - February 3rd 2019) 乙丑

This is a good month to invest in property or property developments, as returns in that field will yield some beneficial income. If you need to make changes to your home, this is a good month to enter the market because you are likely to receive favourable returns as well. At work, if you're hoping to be promoted or even to enjoy an elevated sense of authority or status, this could be a good month for you!

SE	S	SW
8	4	6
7	**9**	2
3	5	1
NE	N	NW

E — left side, W — right side

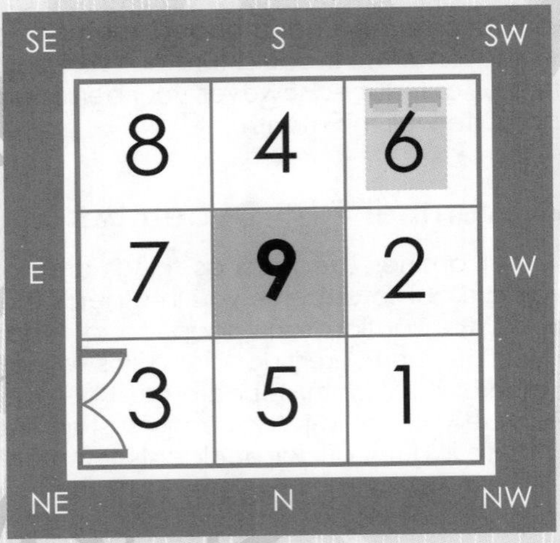

農曆正月 (February 4th - March 4th) 甲寅

In general, the situation at work will be less than ideal. Employees and subordinates are feeling disgruntled and defiant, and they are liable to betray their employers and their companies. At the very least, they may fall into behaviour and actions that could cost their company a significant amount of money. Also, hostile takeovers are very much likely this month – it would be better to take the appropriate action and have the initiative to right the situation, rather than be taken by surprise by the consequences. Individuals using this room might also suffer from headaches and migraines, largely brought upon by stress.

農曆二月 (March 5th - April 4th) 乙卯

For individuals who work in the research industry, you will enjoy a heightened status. You will also find it to be a good month to make money through smart and well-planned deals, but beware of the negative aspects to the situation, as well. Some unfortunate accidents could result as a result of earning this money. Spend a considerable amount of time improving both your personal and professional relationships, as these will bear fruit in the later months. This is a good month to focus on intensifying your connections.

農曆三月 (April 5th - May 4th) 丙辰

Tensions between fathers and sons are further heightened this month, especially if both of them use this room, and this will be further exacerbated if there are negative structures and forms outside this sector. For the elderly members of the household using this room, don't neglect the signs of any minor ailments. Delaying medical treatment could result in further complications down the road. Professionals in the engineering industry will glean unexpected recognition and possible financial rewards, only if they choose to use this particular room.

農曆四月 (May 5th - June 5th) 丁巳

In general, for most individuals using this bedroom, there is plenty to smile about as there is quite a bit of good news awaiting. Those among you who have put in your fair share of effort into your work, projects, and activities thus far, will find it to be a good month to reap the benefits. It's also an ideal time of the year to take up some property or gilt investments, but it requires you to occasionally enter unchartered territories and take some risks. There are several ill-intentioned souls out to put a dent in your plans, so be on the alert for that.

農曆五月 (June 6th - July 6th) 戊午

Legal professionals and academics will find your skills much sought-after this month, especially as others become aware of your expertise and are keen to utilise your abilities. Any relationships begun this month, whether personal or for professional purpose, will be fleeting in duration. Don't put in effort and expectations like you would for long-term ones, and you should be fine. The green-eyed monsters in all its forms will rear their ugly heads this month, which could cause a fair bit of trouble for you. Step away from the limelight and maintain a low profile and things will likely blow over.

農曆六月 (July 7th - August 6th) 己未

Individuals working in the entertainment and electrical industries should be careful, as possible bad business could lead to some serious financial losses. You might have to make more of an effort than usual in order to keep things going at an even keel. As for individuals holding positions of power and authority, they should be aware that there may be rumblings of dissent below you, creating various forms of challenges. At the home, this can be seen through disputes between sons and father or sons defiantly challenging their father figures. Employers should be careful with labour relations and arbitration, because employees are likely to be rebellious and difficult to manage.

農曆七月 (August 7th - September 7th) 庚申

Good financial gains can be made by taking some risks and really making an effort to put yourself out on a limb; but focus on property or gilt investments because these are likely to give you high profits. Investment and merchant bankers engaging in stock and corporate deals will find that their bottom lines are well on the way to increasing. Elderly people using this bedroom for the month should try using a different room, as there is a possibility of the risk of heart ailments.

農曆八月 (September 8th - October 7th) 辛酉

At the workplace, you should be prepared for competition starting to heat up. Rivalry increases and jealousy comes to the mix, but extreme care needs to be taken not to allow this situation to escalate into hostility. If you're not careful, legal issues could be the ramifications. The best thing to do at this point would be to keep your head down and concentrate solely on your work. Those of you who are embarking on a relationship this month will find these new relationships to be fleeting, short-term affairs. Avoid investing too much of your time or emotions into it.

農曆九月 (October 8th - November 6th) 壬戌

It's quite a good month for people in the engineering industry to realise their aspirations and fulfill their dreams and goals. It will bode well for you at this point in time, especially if you have worked hard to gain these financial rewards and acquire some recognition. Fathers or sons using this room are likely to experience tense and strained relations. To ease the situation and make the relationship smoother, both should (preferably) be using rooms in other sectors. Negative formations located outside this sector could result in headaches or leg injuries for the occupants.

農曆十月 (November 7th - December 6th) 癸亥

If you're a business owner, you should be careful of your finances this month, as there is a high possibility that your employees could betray you. While opportunities and projects may be slowing down, as a business owner, you should be more strategic in your pursuits, in order to remain profitable. Health-wise, you will feel stressed out, mentally pressured and anxiety encountered along the way. These issues will take its toll on those of you who are using this sector's bedroom, this month.

農曆十一月 (December 7th 2018 - January 4th 2019) 甲子

Individuals in positions of power will be blessed with good financial opportunities and lucrative investment deals. But they should always be cautious of possible mishaps that could occur as the result of the financial move. As for those in the civil service or academic industry, they will gain recognition and an elevated status in their respective field – and this is of course, a result of their hard work. This is also a good month to give your personal and professional relationships a boost – therefore, you might just want to spend some time building strong bonds with people.

農曆十二月 (January 5th - February 3rd 2019) 乙丑

There will be high chances of getting into injuries during travelling, this month. Always avoid making investments based on pure speculation, as well. For those of you in the engineering sector, you could benefit from expanding your network and seeking new clients. As for those of you in the competitive sports field, be very careful of sprains and tendon injuries, especially if there is a Negative Sha found outside this sector.

| Main Door | Northeast | Bedroom Sector | South |

SE	S	SW
8	4	6
7	**9**	2
3	5	1
NE	N	NW

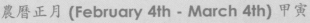
農曆正月 (February 4th - March 4th) 甲寅

You can expect to see some positive changes at your workplace that directly involve you, if you're using this room. It's bound to come in the form of promotions and advancements, or some form of major recognition. For individuals in the fashion and beauty industries, this is a month of increased business connections. This will only lead to increased profits! It will be a good month to go out and cultivate more of these connections. Where matters of the heart are concerned, single people in search of love will have a good opportunity to find it.

農曆二月 (March 5th - April 4th) 乙卯

Literary types or those of you who work in the literary and media industries, you will be happy to know that this month bodes well for you! Financial gains and profits are very much possible, so it if there was ever a time to double your efforts – this would be it! As for those of you who are purchasing new properties, there are good financial benefits in store as well, but you will have to be willing to travel to close those deals. Senior citizens using this room, however, need to be careful where their health is concerned. Be on guard against arterial blockages, blood circulation problems or even a possible stroke. If you're able to move to another room, this would be so much the better.

農曆三月 (April 5th - May 4th) 丙辰

This is a month to be careful with the handling of all sharp instruments, because the chances of an injury at the hands of a knife or metal tool are high. Also, be extra careful and keep a deliberate pace. You should also be careful when signing legal documents and important papers this month – remember to double-check everything on the pages thoroughly and pay attention to the fine print. You may also be prone to having serious arguments and conflicts that could turn violent, so you will need to be more or less argumentative and reactive, and more invested in maintaining your peace of mind. Keep a tight lid over your more explosive emotions and you will do a world of good in making yourself feel better.

農曆四月 (May 5th - June 5th) 丁巳

Ladies who are pregnant will have to be particularly careful this month, especially when they are embarking on long distance travel. There is a possibility that this could result in possible accidents or even pregnancy complications. Those of you who have to regularly deal with or face difficult clients or customers, or even business partners, will find it to be a good month to exercise diplomacy and patience – there are many rewards to be reaped from equities or shared deals. If you're required to travel for work or business, consider it a lucky break – as you'll be able to enhance your reputation and status too!

Main Door	Northeast	Bedroom Sector	South

農曆五月 (June 6th - July 6th) 戊午

Women need to be extra careful this month, as there is an increased risk of breast cancer. If something seems amiss, or if you notice any untoward signs, schedule an appointment with your doctor. You might also want to consider undergoing a mammogram. Everyone in general, should avoid gambling or engaging in speculative, high-risk investments – unless they have an express purpose in having less money than what they started out with! They should also avoid becoming involved in any business ventures or investments – as profits will be hard to obtain.

農曆六月 (July 7th - August 6th) 己未

If you've been bitten by the travelling bug, then this is the month to let it take full control! It is the ideal time for you to take a vacation or consider travelling to distant shores. In addition to boosting your spirits, you just might encounter some holiday romance while you're travelling! However, keep your expectations in proportion and don't assume that it will lead to anything long-lasting. There will be no lack of ideas and inspiration for those of you working in the artistic and creative fields, and plenty of brainwaves are bound to strike! Make the most of this time to generate new work.

農曆七月 (August 7th - September 7th) 庚申

There is further tension this month for married couples, so they'll have to be less apt to losing their temper or patience, and invest more of their energy in being understanding – even when it seems particularly difficult! Domestic disagreements could cause some serious disruptions in your home, and it will affect you in particular, especially if you're female. Cultivate your inner sense of calm so you're less likely to be blown about by every wind, and react emotionally. If you have children, especially those who are in school – keep a closer eye on them. Don't neglect paying attention to their needs or they may be adversely influenced by peer pressure and trouble.

農曆八月 (September 8th - October 7th) 辛酉

Those among you who own a business should ensure that all your deals are on the straight and narrow. If not, the chances of you encountering losses as a result of dodgy deals are very high, and it's too steep a price for you to pay simply to cut a few corners. Additionally, in order to make successful speculative investments in the property field, you'll need to have some valuable knowledge on the subject. In other words, doing your homework will pay off handsomely. And to make romantic relationships work, and thrive – this will require that both partners give each other the requisite amount of space.

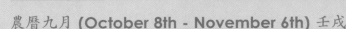

農曆九月 (October 8th - November 6th) 壬戌

Where health is concerned, you'll have to watch out for potential bronchitis. Those of you who are asthmatic will find your symptoms flaring up and it's possible that some of you might develop it at this point in time, especially if using this room. If you're an artist, consider putting your works up for exhibit at this point in time, because this will greatly increase your reputation and credibility. The media is an ideal vehicle for those of you in the mining or agriculture industries to promote yourself and advertise your services – as an increasing amount of customers will lead to greater profits.

農曆十月 (November 7th - December 6th) 癸亥

If you're travelling this month, you should expect some sudden changes or last-minute problems that necessitate the buying of travel insurance. Being prepared for these spontaneous changes could make the situation a lot easier to bear with! Those in the artistic, marketing and consulting fields will do well this month, particularly if they have to travel to conclude deals. In terms of health, be careful of your spine and potentially risky injuries.

農曆十一月 (December 7th 2018 - January 4th 2019) 甲子

This is a stressful month for those sleeping in this bedroom, resulting in stomach upsets and ulcers. However, if you're keen in broadening your knowledge in religion, spirituality, or metaphysical studies – this is the room for you! There is a good opportunity this month as well, to make favourable financial gains from property deals abroad – so travelling to close business deals will only bode well for you.

農曆十二月 (January 5th - February 3rd 2019) 乙丑

Scrutinise all legal documents very carefully before you commit yourself to them, in order to pre-empt any potential complications later on. In terms of relations and communication with others, you may be involved in aggressive disputes this month. To mitigate the risk of finding yourself in such a scenario, avoid using this room, if you can. In terms of physical safety, handle all sharp instruments with care to prevent yourself from being injured.

| Main Door | Northeast | Bedroom Sector | Southeast |

	SE	S	SW	
E	8	4	6	W
	7	**9**	2	
	3	5	1	
	NE	N	NW	

農曆正月 (February 4th - March 4th) 甲寅

This is not a good month to engage in strategic negotiations, as you will only find yourself plagued by losses in the long-term. Err on the side of caution, especially if you're uncertain. What's more, couples and newly weds should avoid using this bedroom this month. The energies abiding in this sector will bring about disharmony, miscommunication and tension to their relationship.

農曆二月 (March 5th - April 4th) 乙卯

If you're a salaried employee, you will stand a chance to gain authority and recognition, but this will be at the expense of your personal life. More hours will need to be logged at the office along with more responsibilities. If you are in the share and equity markets, this month should show a good profit, this is provided if you actually cash in your shares. However, you will need to be sure to bank in this money rather than let it slip through your fingers.

農曆三月 (April 5th - May 4th) 丙辰

If you are involved in extreme sports, you will need to be careful of injuries this month. Property deals abound, but you should be circumspect and shrewd, especially when entering into new deals. Make sure that you are completely happy with all the details before you sign on the dotted line, and even then, be sure that you are well-versed with the fine print. If you're a lawyer or in legal service, you will find that your services are in demand this month – so good luck!

農曆四月 (May 5th - June 5th) 丁巳

Your bosses may demand quite a bit from you this month and make advancements at your expense. Stress is inevitable. However, if you use this sector's room, there is a possibility of moving homes, as property investments are good and a significant change is needed. The change is likely to do you good as well.

農曆五月 (June 6th - July 6th) 戊午

If you have children, particularly those who use this bedroom – be on alert. Rebellious children will get into fights at school, and end up getting hurt by sharp metal objects and metal implements. If you have business deals planned, try to postpone it as there will be sudden changes in negotiations that could result in possible losses. This is a stressful month for relationships in general, so do not make any important decisions about the future at this point. Otherwise you are likely to make the wrong one.

農曆六月 (July 7th - August 6th) 己未

Be on the watch for malicious parties at work. These people are only out to see you stumble and fall, so watch what you do and say – especially around colleagues you don't trust. Relationships will be off to a bad start at the beginning of the month, but things will eventually smooth themselves out as the month draws to a close. On the bright side, you may well find plenty of opportunities to invest in real estate or property this month.

農曆七月 (August 7th - September 7th) 庚申

You should make the most of this month and take advantage of the support from your superiors this month by launching new ideas and projects. They will be useful as a valuable sounding board and mentors. Speculative investments will provide short-term gains, but you need to be careful of greed, as it could cost you quite dearly. If you're married, this month brings quite a few disputes into focus.

農曆八月 (September 8th - October 7th) 辛酉

This is a month of new beginnings and start-up ventures. If you are thinking of embarking on a new project, then this is the time to have a go. In general, you can expect recognition, rewards and advancements in your career if you're using this bedroom. Generally, good news and celebrations await those using this bedroom, especially if they're married or in a relationship and keen to start a family.

農曆九月 (October 8th - November 6th) 壬戌

This is a good month to consolidate both professional and personal relationships, although the start may be a little rocky. Investments in property or real estate may bring in good profits, but it is easy to get stuck in this field and make losses rather than profits. You will need to plan your path carefully. In general, you can expect your Wealth Luck to be strong but you will need to work through involved and prolonged deals before you can benefit from the resultant profits.

農曆十月 (November 7th - December 6th) 癸亥

This will be a favorable month for business owners, especially young and up-and-coming entrepreneurs who will find this to be an ideal time for launching their businesses into the market. This is because favorable receptions are to be expected. For individual investors, capital gains in their portfolio are possible but they may choose to hold on to them for even higher gains in the long run. Additionally, the positive energies of this bedroom enables business negotiators to close important financial deals from an advantageous position.

農曆十一月 (December 7th 2018 - January 4th 2019) 甲子

Speculative investments and business deals will have the potential for financial gains this month, especially if there is a natural Water feature in this sector of the property. Similarly, occupants of this bedroom who are in a family business will find smooth progress and perhaps even new business opportunities coming their way. Hence, it would be best to take advantage of the positive energies of this sector's room for their career and business. Enhancement of their reputation and credibility in terms of their personal branding, is also in the cards, especially if they strategically make use of the positive energies here.

農曆十二月 (January 5th - February 3rd 2019) 乙丑

The unperturbed progress of last month comes to a screeching halt. It would be best to leave investments and business deals alone for the time being, with a note to revisit it next month. Your personal and working relationships will also be impacted and are likely to be strained by factors beyond your control. All important decisions should be postponed to the following month. The energies of this sector can go on to negatively impact your health, so watch your diet and do not place unnecessary strain on your back, because digestive ailments and back pain are likely to arise for those using this bedroom.

SE	S	SW
8	4	6
7	**9**	2
3	5	1
NE	N	NW

E (left side), W (right side)

農曆正月 (February 4th - March 4th) 甲寅

Rumour-mongering and politics will be on the increase this month and it would be advisable to distance yourself from this problem because there is a likelihood that it could end in legal issues. Rivalries and competition intensifies, with unpleasantness as the usual outcomes. If you're already ill and in poor health, be careful of lung problems this month, as it could develop into more serious problems, especially if there are negative structures outside this room.

農曆二月 (March 5th - April 4th) 乙卯

It is possible to say the wrong thing, or even have things twisted out of context, especially when it comes to people in the communications and media industry, this month. You will need to think things through before articulating them out loud. Those in the engineering and construction industry should take care of new deals, as these could result in a breakdown with certain negative outcomes. Again, this will be a problem with negative publicity due to misunderstandings and miscommunications.

農曆三月 (April 5th - May 4th) 丙辰

If you're in property development, you could make instant money from investments deals this month but you will need to know when to get out of the market. Otherwise you could end up losing more than you gain. In a sense, this requires some crafty yet careful planning on your part. This is not a good room to use when preparing for important examinations, as it is not favourable for studies and academic preparation. In general, particularly if you use this room, sudden problems will arise this month, and these should be handled carefully as it could get out of hand and end up being a legal mess.

農曆四月 (May 5th - June 5th) 丁巳

This is a good month for those who love to travel, as the energies of the month are on your side. Budding entrepreneurs will also find this time of the year to be perfectly ideal in airing their ideas or inspirations, and pursuing their dreams accordingly. However, you will need to be careful of unstable emotions on your part; these emotions might threaten to taint or tarnish your reputation and public image. It's always wise to keep a tight rein on your emotions, instead of letting them get the better of you.

Northeast Sector Main Door

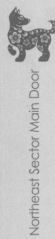

| Main Door | Northeast | Bedroom Sector | East |

農曆五月 (June 6th - July 6th) 戊午

Good news for real estate or property developers or investors: You'll stand to realise substantial gains from your investments. And if you're feeling lucky, perhaps this is the best time to take on your competitors, especially if you wish to widen your customer base. If you're a scholar or a student, you'll find that using the East room will be a boost for studying, particularly if you have to sit for examinations.

農曆六月 (July 7th - August 6th) 己未

Avoid new ventures this month, as these are likely to hit snags and obstacles that could end up with legal problems. Excessive competition at work depletes your energy and weakens your immune system. Try to avoid the emotional turmoil of a dog-eat-dog competitive work environment by attempting to lay low and opting not to play the game. If you're a man, you may suffer from an increased sense of depression this month.

農曆七月 (August 7th - September 7th) 庚申

Good publicity brings you into the limelight this month, and this is likely to result in career advancement. You will need to be enthusiastic enough to make the most of the networking opportunities that will come your way in order to increase your visibility. If you're a woman with investments or a business abroad, you will find that this is a good month for you, especially if you have travel to conduct deals abroad.

農曆八月 (September 8th - October 7th) 辛酉

This is a good month to attract new customers and clients to your business, and this will in turn provide you with good financial returns. This is also a month to expand your property investment portfolio, as good financial profits are likely to be made as well. Where your personal life is concerned, it will be a good month to focus on your relationships and work on building intimacy and trust as you will feel close to your partner or spouse, and communication is smooth.

農曆九月 (October 8th - November 6th) 壬戌

Retail cash deposits should be made with care this month, as this is a weak area for business in general. It is unwise to make any important business or personal decisions this month, as the outcomes will be unfavourable and you may come to regret these choices later. To the best of your ability, you should err on the side of caution as much as possible. This is a good month for the communications industry and generally a month of enhanced reputation.

農曆十月 (November 7th - December 6th) 癸亥

Do not be involved in office politics and rumour-mongering at the workplace this month. Be warned that there will be competition and rivalries coming your way and it will only intensify. Focus on your work and on being productive instead. Cut out the noise. When it gets too much, try to distract yourself in areas of your personal interest. Health-wise, those who have pre-existing medical conditions should be mindful of its reoccurrence, especially if is a respiratory problem and there is a presence of Negative Sha in this sector.

農曆十一月 (December 7th 2018 - January 4th 2019) 甲子

Fire hazards are very likely this month, so check the electrical circuits and wiring in your home, as well as all your gas outlets. Don't be negligent or careless with your safety. People sitting for important examinations should avoid using this room, and pregnant women should also refrain from using this bedroom – or possible complications could arise.

農曆十二月 (January 5th - February 3rd 2019) 乙丑

It's a good month for female entrepreneurs to venture into markets abroad, because there will be substantial profits to be gained from deals and agreements concluded in another country. But in general, people using this room should refrain from beginning new commercial ventures this month. You're likely to face some serious obstacles from the start, which will delay your progress and waste your time. It will be best for you to wait for another time. Be prepared for heartbreak this month, as possible romantic flings you're involved in could turn out to be short-term.

West Sector
Main Door

This section contains the monthly outlook for all 12 months of the year for different bedroom sectors, in a property with a West Sector Main Door.

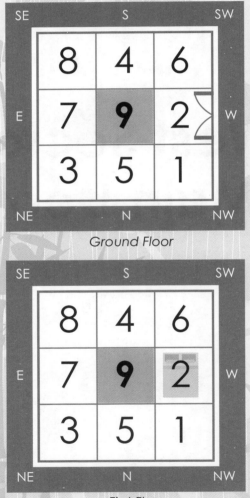

Ground Floor

First Floor

農曆正月 (February 4th - March 4th) 甲寅

Be careful in your business dealings this month, as things are not what they seem and rivals are out to deceive you into deals which will not be financially sound. Be alert so that you're not easily trapped or cheated. If you are involved in competitive sports, you will do better in competitions away from home this month. If you're married, you need to be prepared for arguments and tension this month. There is a risk that the domestic realm may be wreaked by disharmony.

農曆二月 (March 5th - April 4th) 乙卯

Health problems are a risk this month. Mouth ulcers and throat problems will plague those using this bedroom, so you need to take extra care. Older people in politics will find that they make good headway in the political field and become recognised for the work they do within the community. Those who wish to invest in goldmines should do so this month, as it is a good time to do so and receive good outcomes.

農曆三月 (April 5th - May 4th) 丙辰

Real estate ventures will be successful and bring great financial success but you should make sure that all the legal issues are covered, as there could be problems later on. Run through all contracts with a fine-toothed comb! There is a chance for romance to prosper this month but be careful of gossip, as others are out to get you into a trap. Health-wise, there is also a risk of some form of recurring illness.

農曆四月 (May 5th - June 5th) 丁巳

This sector is a good sector for those writing important exams soon, and for scholarly work. It will also be a good month for dabbling in real estate and property, or if you work in these fields. Daughters-in-law and mothers-in-law will have a hard time getting along this month, and the best solution would be having room to breathe and less interference in one another's affairs.

Main Door	West	Bedroom Sector	West

農曆五月 (June 6th - July 6th) 戊午

Make sure that any deals concluded this month does not rely on capital, as this may end in losses that could be potentially serious. If you're a salaried employee, you will have a difficult month as you will find that no matter how hard you work and how much extra effort and time you put in, commensurate financial remuneration is not forthcoming. There is a possibility of mental and emotional strain which may cause stress this month. Try not to let stress get to you too much or your mental health will suffer.

農曆六月 (July 7th - August 6th) 己未

There is a chance of superior property deals this month if you do your homework well, but don't neglect to tie up all loose ends as these may result in legal issues later. If there is a need to sign legal documents, be particularly careful this month, exercising extreme caution and double-checking all that you sign. Those using this bedroom this month may suffer from serious illnesses this month, so see a doctor if something seems amiss.

農曆七月 (August 7th - September 7th) 庚申

If you work in the literary field or if you're an author, this month sees you enjoying the fruits of your labour and experiencing a boost to your reputation. Money can be made from real estate-related fields this month, so long as the deals have been thoroughly worked out. There will be strife and disharmony between in-laws this month, so extra patience will be required to make the relationship work. Exercise tolerance as well, as it can go a long way!

農曆八月 (September 8th - October 7th) 辛酉

This month, make sure that all your fines and taxes are up to date or you may just find yourself in trouble with the law! But generally, this is a good sector for those who are involved with religious and spiritual endeavours. Couples should avoid using this room, as it is not conducive to good relationships and intimate ties. You might find yourself distant with each other or constantly at odds.

農曆九月 (October 8th - November 6th) 壬戌

If you happen to be suffering from a chronic illness of any sort, be sure to mind your health this month. The risk of your ailment rearing its ugly head again is very likely, so adopt a healthy lifestyle and consult your doctor at the first sign of trouble. In terms of finances, however, you're likely to do well this month – particularly if you're in the property business or dealings.

農曆十月 (November 7th - December 6th) 癸亥

Do bear in mind that confusion may come into the decision-making process if you are using the bedroom this month, so it is preferable to refrain from making any key decisions at this point. If this can't be avoided, seek the help of trusted confidants who can be objective about your situation. Pregnant women should be careful if they are using this room this month, as there is a risk of miscarriage or untimely delivery. Ensure that you take the proper precautions. If you're a student, you should avoid this sector for studying or revision purposes - especially if you are facing important examinations this month.

農曆十一月 (December 7th 2018 - January 4th 2019) 甲子

Those of you who run a company and need to employ more staff members this month, it will be best to postpone this to a more favourable time. Otherwise, you risk selecting people who are the skim of the cream, as opposed to the cream of the crop! If there are negative formations outside this sector this month, it could cause deteriorating vision or even blindness for the people using this room. However, don't worry unnecessarily but just take the proper preventive measures.

農曆十二月 (January 5th - February 3rd 2019) 乙丑

Reign in any temptations you might have to engage in speculative investments or high-risk ventures. You will probably end up with a lot less than you expected. This is not the right time for you to commit to major deals. Otherwise, you will only be incurring losses. Elderly women using this room should consult their doctor at the first sign of abdominal troubles. Otherwise, this could risk becoming something very serious, with long-term consequences.

West Sector Main Door

Main Door	West	Bedroom Sector	Southwest

農曆正月 (February 4th - March 4th) 甲寅

For those of you using this room, this is the month when your efforts and capabilities are recognised by your superiors, and things start looking up as far as your job is concerned. You've been doing something right all this while, so keep up the good work. Real estate or property specialists will be pleased to welcome repeat-customers, and new ones as well, as they find their client base expanding. Additionally, couples looking to conceive and start a family should use this bedroom this month.

農曆二月 (March 5th - April 4th) 乙卯

Those of you involved in consulting businesses, think tanks, strategic decision-making processes, and others whose work requires wisdom and intelligence and critical thinking, will attract fame and good fortune this month. In other words, your talents and capabilities will finally get its due reward. Generally, for most of you, your wisdom and intelligence at work will be recognised and superiors will entrust important projects and deals to you that could result in advancement and promotion. In other words, it may be your month to shine at work, so don't shrink from the limelight! For those wanting to start a family, this will still be a suitable month to do so.

農曆三月 (April 5th - May 4th) 丙辰

This is generally not a good month for those in the entertainment industry, as well as the electrical and electronic industries. Demand for your services and products will be somewhat diminished, resulting in a loss of profits. Defer any important decision-making as far as personal and professional relationships are concerned to a more suitable time, because it will be hard for you to be rational and logical this month when emotions are running high. Elderly people using this room this month will be more susceptible to heart attacks and strokes, so they might want to consider moving to another room.

農曆四月 (May 5th - June 5th) 丁巳

You will receive the accolades, recognition, advancement and financial rewards that you've worked so hard to achieve in your professional life. So it's time to kick back, put your legs up and let the accolades pile up! Investment and merchant bankers who specialise in stocks, equities and corporate deals and mergers also stand to make substantial monetary gains on-the-job, so double your efforts if you want to gain more out of it. Couples using this room will enjoy a heightened relationship with closer ties and a better sense of fulfillment.

| Main Door | West | Bedroom Sector | Southwest |

農曆五月 (June 6th - July 6th) 戊午

Lawyers and professionals dabbling in the legal field will find their services much sought-after this month, as others become familiar with your name and expertise. Salaried employees should be on the lookout for disputes and office politics at the workplace this month, as power struggles are taking place in full force. But stay out of them, to avoid running into any legal entanglements later on. Where matters of the heart are concerned, don't give your heart away too easily this month. Any romantic flings that crop up this month are likely to be just that – flings, and nothing more.

農曆六月 (July 7th - August 6th) 己未

Couples will have a happier month this month and they will do well in your chosen careers as well. Both your professional and personal lives will complement the other nicely, leading to contentment. Children using this bedroom this month will be rebellious and difficult to control and parents may have to exercise greater authority than necessary. If your job involves strategic thinking or analysis, you will find that you have the chance to advance your career and make a name for yourself this month. Don't hesitate to grab the opportunities to promote yourself.

農曆七月 (August 7th - September 7th) 庚申

Investment and merchant bankers concluding deals in the share and equity markets this month will benefit from good profits in the months to come. Therefore, if something appears promising, do your best and go for it! You will receive the recognition, career advancement and financial reward you deserve this month, propelling your career to new heights and bringing a new level of job satisfaction. Newly-married couples will find this to be a very good month for harmonious relationships and you will enjoy better communication and improved ties.

農曆八月 (September 8th - October 7th) 辛酉

For those of you trying to make an honest living from a regular job, don't bother with trivial disputes or arguments at the workplace this month, which could fester into legal complications if blown out of proportion. Ignore your rivals and the proliferation of backstabbers at work and concentrate on your job. The rewards are a lot more fulfilling than being caught up in office politics. Those who are actively involved in the trading of stocks and shares will be pleased to know that there will be gains to be made from their transactions. Garner the input and help from more seasoned investors, if you're unsure on how to proceed.

農曆九月 (October 8th - November 6th) 壬戌

Engineers, technicians and individuals involved in the technical and engineering professions, will find their career prospects looking more promising this month. Keep up your good work, as it can lead to possibilities that have never occurred to you before. The sweet taste of success will come to you in time. Investment deals, especially risky ones, are a big no-no this month, unless you're particularly looking forward to ending up with legal problems on your hands! Athletes and sportspersons should also guard against any sports-inflicted injuries; particularly those affecting their legs and feet.

農曆十月 (November 7th - December 6th) 癸亥

Your elder family members who have been sleeping in this room may develop lung diseases and as such, if symptoms start to emerge, it is imperative to consult the physician. Besides that, tension may also arise from family relations. However, it is recommended to keep the peace, because lashing out in public may be an ineffective way to resolve the conflict. In terms of work, there is a high likelihood that you will suffer from fraudulence by a senior colleague.

農曆十一月 (December 7th 2018 - January 4th 2019) 甲子

If you sleep in the bedroom in this sector, you will tend to enjoy optimal health conditions and fulfilling relationships. So take advantage of a good thing, and see if you can extend your run of good luck! What's more, long–term investments will finally yield considerable profits for you, especially if you are using this bedroom. In addition, your prowess and capabilities at work will also gain the respect and recognition of your superiors, who might just be tempted enough to reward you for your exertions!

農曆十二月 (January 5th - February 3rd 2019) 乙丑

This month may not be the optimal timing to make important decisions in personal and professional areas, since it will be harder for you to remain rational and logical this month and your emotions may run high. Move any elderly family members out of this bedroom this month, lest they become susceptible to heart disease or even a stroke. This is generally not a good month for those in the entertainment and electrical industries as well, because demand will not be very encouraging, particularly if they happen to be a market player.

| Main Door | West | Bedroom Sector | South |

SE	S	SW
8	4	6
E 7	**9**	2 **W**
3	5	1
NE	N	NW

農曆正月 (February 4th - March 4th) 甲寅

People with an artistic and creative bent will find the energies of this room benefiting them this month, especially if you pursue commercial opportunities abroad. You'll be able to garner both mass attention and critical acclaim. At the workplace, you'll need to tread carefully, as office politics are at an all-time high. It could become unhealthy and out of control, so try not to get involved. Parents of children using this room may need to be more patient than necessary, as their children are liable to be influenced by peer pressure and be more rebellious than usual.

農曆二月 (March 5th - April 4th) 乙卯

For those of you in relationships, you should give your partner some breathing space this month, especially if you find that both of you are more quarrelsome than ever lately. It would also be advisable for you to keep an eye open for health issues, particularly breast cancer or liver ailments – if you happen to be using this bedroom. It will also prove to be a volatile, unstable month to indulge in the stock market. Therefore, it would be better for you to hold on to your money just a little longer.

農曆三月 (April 5th - May 4th) 丙辰

It's a good time to go on a vacation that you've dreamed for a long time, as you've earned this time off and should rightfully claim it! Chances are, you might also be able to embark on a little fling while you're abroad. Bear in mind that these are likely to be short-term ones, rather than anything lasting. Professionals in the marketing and consultation businesses should consider going ahead and publishing a research paper that they've been working on long enough.

農曆四月 (May 5th - June 5th) 丁巳

This month, keep a strong watch on your back and what you say. Malicious individuals are out to get you in any way possible, so don't give them ammunition to launch any attacks. Where your health is concerned, pay close attention to head or brain-related injuries. In any case, seek professional medical treatment instead of letting it slide. Those among you involved in the artistic and creative fields will enjoy success this month, although you might have to travel to earn your income. But this can be a positive thing, as being in a new place with fresh sights and sounds can serve as fodder for your hungry muse!

Main Door	West	Bedroom Sector	South

農曆五月 (June 6th - July 6th) 戊午

If you're actively involved in the real estate and property field, and wish to realise your returns on investment, then this is the month to do so. Professionals and enthusiasts dabbling in the metaphysical and esoteric fields will also benefit from the energies of this room. However, if you happen to be a married woman sleeping in this room, don't be surprised to find your relationship with your mother-in-law to be slightly tense this month, especially if you both live under the same roof. Don't give in to your emotions and where possible, avoid contact with your in-law to avoid potentially explosive conflicts.

農曆六月 (July 7th - August 6th) 己未

Couples who want to find that loving feeling again should consider using this room, as it will keep the home fires burning! However, be careful of any significant water features located outside this sector, as that could lead to one of the partners straying or becoming involved in an affair. Specialists in the media and consultation industries will be able to enjoy much fame and publicity this month, so let your talents and capabilities shine! This room will also benefit academics, scholars, and researchers, as well as students.

農曆七月 (August 7th - September 7th) 庚申

This is not a month for female employees, as they will not find the support or encouragement from their superiors to be forthcoming or readily available this month. If you're female, don't let this get you down too much, as you should plan your goals and workload accordingly, to reduce the effects of any sudden hiccups – and doing so will allow you to be in control. This is not a month to use this bedroom for students and scholars sitting for important examinations, as your results will be worse than you expected. But there are good outcomes from any joint-venture projects you undertake in the financial world.

農曆八月 (September 8th - October 7th) 辛酉

Romantic relationships come under strain this month and couples using this bedroom will find that their relationships are a little more tense than usual and plagued with petty quarrels. Consider going off on a trip together to strengthen ties, or doing some activity or hobby together that can remove you from your daily cares, at least for a little while. If you're involved in management and consulting, this will be a good month to expand your business. Professionals in the literary and media fields will also do quite well this month, as inspiration just seems to flood you!

農曆九月 (October 8th - November 6th) 壬戌

This month, you'll have to be careful of the legal documents that you sign. Ensure that you read the fine print and if you're not sure what's going on, enlist the help of a legal professional to ensure that everything is above board. It's also a month to be careful of your words and how you say your words or otherwise that something you said in jest or anger will come back to haunt you! Those of you who have been feeling upset and unappreciated by your bosses and superiors this month need to continue to lay low and avoid drawing attention to your concerns, as this is not the time for it. It might only backfire on you.

農曆十月 (November 7th - December 6th) 癸亥

Marital relations will be strained this month so tolerance will need to be exercised by everyone involved. Domestic disputes and family issues are likely this month, but this will affect females using this bedroom more than men. However, you do need to watch out for backstabbers. Be alert and stay focused or otherwise you will act out of confusion.

農曆十一月 (December 7th 2018 - January 4th 2019) 甲子

In terms of finances, this is not a good month to invest in the stock market, as the risk factor works against you. Give your partner some breathing space this month, especially if both of you are at loggerheads more frequently than expected. It would also be advisable for you to keep an eye open for health issues, particularly breast cancer or liver ailments, if you happen to be using this bedroom.

農曆十二月 (January 5th - February 3rd 2019) 乙丑

Students using this bedroom to study will find that they have good results in the upcoming important examinations. You will be able to focus more extensively on your academic work. This is a good month to engage in business expansion or to build alliances with overseas partners. In terms of relationships, if you're single, you will find this to be a relatively good month but without long-term prospects.

SE	S	SW
8	4	6
7 (E)	9	2 (W)
3	5	1
NE	N	NW

農曆正月 (February 4th - March 4th) 甲寅

Windfall gains are possible this month, so look to realise these profits in your portfolio. You just never know how much you might cash in! This is a good month for networking and developing new client and business relationships, so you'll need to put yourself out there and work hard at forming new contacts. Children using this bedroom will tend to be very independent this month, but if you're a parent, you'll have to be prepared for some rebellious behaviour.

農曆二月 (March 5th - April 4th) 乙卯

Postpone or avoid engaging in important business negotiations this month, unless you wish to risk getting entangled in a legal dispute. Your luck with the law is not good this month. Generally speaking, this is a stressful time of the year for both professional and personal relationships, so resist the temptation to commit to any major decision about the future. And you might also want to consider temporarily relocating young boys or your infant sons to another bedroom this month, as they may suffer from leg injuries or cuts from a mishap by remaining in the West.

農曆三月 (April 5th - May 4th) 丙辰

If you're a business owner, you will spend a lot of time over declining profits that, in turn, will demotivate your employees. You will need to work harder to keep employees' morale up. Find more creative ways to make them feel like they belong and have something to work toward. Accidents during travels are possible, so you will need to keep your travels to a minimum. Your health may be affected this month, with muscle, joint and nerve problems arising to give you some trouble.

農曆四月 (May 5th - June 5th) 丁巳

There is good news this month. You will be blessed with good health and relationships. As such, make the most of this good run in luck to engage more aggressively in deals that will bring you rich financial rewards, particularly if you happen to be dabbling in the travel or construction industry. Similarly, fund and investment managers will find their stratagems coming into fruition this month. Well done, and remember; it pays to plan carefully and think wisely ahead.

Main Door	West	Bedroom Sector	Southeast

農曆五月 (June 6th - July 6th) 戊午

Big changes will help revive stagnant careers and businesses this month. Try to approach things with a fresh perspective and relegate old ways out the window, especially if they don't give you good results. If would be best for you to keep young children out of this room this month, as they may be prone to injury by sharp metal objects and any metal implements. Do not let your arguments with anyone get out of hand, as these could end in lawsuits.

農曆六月 (July 7th - August 6th) 己未

If you're single and keen to embark on a relationship, this month will prove to be good to you! However, in general, remember that success breeds contempt and jealousy among others. So watch out for those who try to undermine you, but don't fixate on their actions or words. By giving them your time of the day, you give them victory as well. On the property and real estate front, go ahead and invest prudently. Your investments, however, should be made with a view to generate long-term income.

農曆七月 (August 7th - September 7th) 庚申

Those in the construction and engineering business will find that business picks up this month and there will be a chance to make good investments abroad. If you're required to travel for business, you should jump at the chance! This is a good month for those who have taken investment positions in the preceding months or who work as fund managers in the futures markets to realise their financial gains. Marital relations prove to be harmonious and rewarding for those using this bedroom this month as well.

農曆八月 (September 8th - October 7th) 辛酉

Good news and celebrations await those using this bedroom this month. You will receive recognition for something you have succeeded in and promotion is likely as a result. You will finally feel rewarded for all the hard work you've put in. If you're in a long-term relationship and have long thought about marriage, this will be a good month to pop the question.

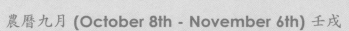

農曆九月 (October 8th - November 6th) 壬戌

There are real estate and property investment opportunities this month but concluding the deal will be more laborious than usual, so you'll need to be ready to put in some effort. Your personal relationships will be strained this month and it will require a concentrated effort to keep them stable and out of rocky ground. Jealousy will cause people to plot against you and try to cause your demise but do not let this bother you too much, as it will turn out well in the end.

農曆十月 (November 7th - December 6th) 癸亥

Investment and opportunities are likely to be in abundance this month, especially for those in the business of communications. However, your relationships will be troubled by passionate and possessive emotions which are likely to develop into jealousy and trust issues, if you're using this bedroom. Both you and your partner will need to keep your emotions at bay. Take extra care where your health is concerned, especially if you have pre-existing respiratory conditions. This is also applicable if you have negative features outside this bedroom in this month.

農曆十一月 (December 7th 2018 - January 4th 2019) 甲子

For business owners, your business ventures will benefit the most compared to other areas of your life, if you are occupying this bedroom. If you are involved in a family business, you will do well this month and travelling abroad will bring in new business prospects and expand your clientele. Those in the banking, finance and share market, will have investment opportunities that have the potential for future earning – be it for work or on personal basis. You will also benefit from the energies of this room if you are in the field of competitive sports. You should do well this month as far as recognition and performance is concerned.

農曆十二月 (January 5th - February 3rd 2019) 乙丑

If you are a business owner, your business is likely to give rise to potential problems – be it operational, financial or issues caused by your employees. The likelihood of having to "firefight" these problems is high and it would be wise to have contingency plans that will be able to resolve or mitigate its effects. Your health may be effected this month, with muscle, joint and nerve problems arising to disrupt your schedule. Your physical well-being is also at risk, so it would be wise to keep your travels to a minimum this month.

Main Door	West	Bedroom Sector	East

農曆正月 (February 4th - March 4th) 甲寅

Lawyers, advocates and solicitors, and those dabbling in the legal profession will find this month to be a fairly favourable one. For this month, it pays to be prudent and discreet with the amount of information you share with the world. The risk of robberies and theft is high, so don't share information with others if you've recently come into some wealth. Those involved in a serious relationship might find things to be a little strained or tense this month. It might be better off giving each other room to breathe instead of trying to find a quick fix.

農曆二月 (March 5th - April 4th) 乙卯

Property deals could go sour owing to a breakdown in negotiations, which is a direct result of a miscommunication, especially if you are in the mining, minerals and semi-precious stones industries. Avoid new romantic relationships this month, as these could end up in scandals and cause more misery than joy for you. It will be best for you to focus on another aspect of your life. Do not make any major personal or business decisions this month, as discussions over these matters may have been clouded with miscommunication. You will end up making some bad choices if pressed into it.

農曆三月 (April 5th - May 4th) 丙辰

This is a good time to watch your health, especially if you've been feeling rather poorly of late. Otherwise, you risk falling ill and acquiring some form of blood disease or suffering from food poisoning. Males, in particular, have to avoid over-indulging in alcohol for both physical and mental reasons. If you happen to work in the civil service or you are a politician, this is the time to keep a low profile and avoid attracting unnecessary attention to yourself, as it will likely backfire and set your cause back a few steps.

農曆四月 (May 5th - June 5th) 丁巳

Seek the limelight at work if possible, and let people know what you're doing. Your ascent up the career ladder should thereby proceed in a smoother manner. Students and anyone who's due to sit for important examinations soon will also do well to tap into the positive energies of this room. Stay away from nightclubs and places of unsavoury reputation this month, or you could attract more trouble than you know what to do with!

Main Door	West	Bedroom Sector	East

農曆五月 (June 6th - July 6th) 戊午

Practice tolerance in both your professional and personal relationships this month – at all times. Romance will be somewhat tricky to negotiate this month, but don't just think with your heart – use your head too and common sense will tell you what to do. Those of you who are involved in the real estate business, though, should keep abreast of the latest market trends in order to benefit from it. Being highly observant and vigilant should pay off handsomely for you in the future.

農曆六月 (July 7th - August 6th) 己未

This looks set to be a favorable month for people working in the communications industry, so seize the opportunity to enhance your reputation and expand your clientele. However, avoid making any significant investments this month, as Wealth Luck will not be on your side. You may be greeting losses instead of gains! You might also face some intense business rivalry or competition at work, with the situation being further compounded by the risk of theft or burglary this month. Stay calm and keep your wits about you, it will be more than needed at this point.

農曆七月 (August 7th - September 7th) 庚申

Those of you working as salaried employees, stay out of office politics and gossip, as you could well find your words being used against you by your rivals or enemies. You might also find your relationships with others plagued by conflicts and disagreements, no thanks to jealousy rearing its ugly head at the wrong time. Seek first to understand others, before you make yourself understood. And needless to say, think before you say or do anything that will cause you regret later on.

農曆八月 (September 8th - October 7th) 辛酉

Certain niggling health problems come to the fore this month, so drink lots of water, get plenty of rest and be on guard for any possible throat ailments. This is also the time of the year when communication is at an all-time low, and misunderstandings abound. As such, couples need to be more patient and understanding of each other's emotions and wants. At work, be sure to communicate coherently, otherwise you risk having your words being misunderstood or misrepresented, thereby leading to stickier problems.

農曆九月 (October 8th - November 6th) 壬戌

Expectant mothers need to seriously consider changing bedrooms, at least until the month's over. This is done to negate the risk of pregnancy complications. Married females living in close quarters have to be careful of getting into a tiff with their mothers-in-law, as these could have long-term consequences. However, on the bright side of things, your personal and professional relationships are looking good this month, so take advantage of them to expand your network of contacts.

農曆十月 (November 7th - December 6th) 癸亥

If you're in sales, you will have a bumper month this month, but you should be aware that misunderstandings could take place. Therefore, you should make sure that all your clients understand and acknowledge the small print before any documents are signed or deals are closed. Those in the cell phone industry will see an upsurge in sales this month. Rumour-mongering and general bad vibes between people will increase this month. It will be advisable to distance yourself from indulging in gossip and idle chatter as misunderstandings could arise.

農曆十一月 (December 7th 2018 - January 4th 2019) 甲子

Property deals could go sour owing to a breakdown in negotiations as a result of a miscommunication, especially if you are in the mining, minerals and semi-precious stones industries. Do not make any major personal or business decisions, as the discussions over these matters may have twisted things out of context, or even deliberately misconstrued certain aspects. In your personal life, avoid beginning new romantic relationships this month, as these could end badly or invite scandal and cause more misery than joy for you.

農曆十二月 (January 5th - February 3rd 2019) 乙丑

It's a good month to take a holiday, so if you've long wanted to pack your bags and go for a well-deserved break, this month would be the month to do it. Those with respiratory problems should be careful when using this sector this month, as ailments may flare up and cause some complications. You should keep the signing of documents to a minimum, or it should preferably be left to a more suitable time. This is because there will be a rise in misunderstandings occurring this month.

農曆正月 (February 4th - March 4th) 甲寅

Those among you who are involved in the real estate and property market should aggressively market yourselves, as this is a good chance to make money. This is not the month to be overly humble or self-effacing when it comes to your talents and capabilities! Those in the service industry will have opportunities to make money this month, but you will need to pay all taxes earned as the tax officials will be on your tail otherwise! On the home front, do note that there is a potential for disharmony between mother and son relationships this month. Anticipate arguments that could result in family feuds.

農曆二月 (March 5th - April 4th) 乙卯

If you've been feeling poorly of late, you will need to be extra vigilant this month because the risk of physical injuries is quite high. Seek the advice and treatment of a physician at the first sign of trouble; otherwise the situation could well become serious. The risk of fraud and theft is also high this month. Nothing's absolutely certain, but you can always play your part in averting such risks, by ensuring that good security controls are in place. There will be windfall gains for those involved in business ventures with overseas or offshore partners.

農曆三月 (April 5th - May 4th) 丙辰

If possible, avoid traveling for business-related purposes, as the outcomes from such trips will not be favourable to you. It would just be an added expense that won't really lead to anything solid. If you've been toiling at your job and sense that a promotion is just waiting for you, you just might be right! And if it comes, you will be elevated to a position with more power, status and authority, which as you probably know is more than well-deserved. Male adolescents using this room will be slightly more temperamental and rebellious than usual, so parents will need to be prepared!

農曆四月 (May 5th - June 5th) 丁巳

Resist the temptation to gamble and indulge in any form of speculative investments this month, unless you wish to risk accumulating huge financial losses – which, let's face it – no one does! If you have by chance come into extra money lately, it would be advisable for you to remain discreet and prudent on your financial status. There are people out there keen to stretch out their itchy fingers and take what's not theirs. Also, be careful of health problems that will appear in the form of ulcers, gallstones or liver-related ailments; have these treated at the first sign of trouble.

| Main Door | West | Bedroom Sector | Northeast |

農曆五月 (June 6th - July 6th) 戊午

Monitor your employees or staff closely this month, as there's a chance that there might be certain individuals who might be up to no good at work. Fraud or theft is likely, as is betrayal of any kind. But don't automatically start suspecting everyone on your staff – just be more discreet and observant. Those among you who make a living from the literary, creative or artistic fields will be pleased to know that good tidings await you this month, in the forms of fame, reputation and money. Those suffering from depression or any mental problems might want to consider moving out of this bedroom for the duration of the month to prevent aggravating your condition.

農曆六月 (July 7th - August 6th) 己未

There's a likelihood of disputes brewing within your family members, so try to prevent it from escalating into something serious. Also, pay attention to personal safety this month as the risk of robberies and muggings is high. Bear in mind this month that by failing to keep abreast of current trends and staying on top of your game in your industry - you will only risk losing your share of the market or even niche market. This month, additionally, pay particular attention to communication. Lack of it could potentially undermine your endeavours and set you back.

農曆七月 (August 7th - September 7th) 庚申

Couples using this room might run into a spot of trouble, so both partners must be patient and tolerant. Avoid listening to others but actually listen to each other instead. Refrain from playing the blame game and pointing fingers, as this will only make the situation worse. Additionally, stay away from gambling this month, as the result will be a significant loss of wealth. Those in poor health should avoid using this bedroom this month as all forms of illnesses could take a turn for the worse.

農曆八月 (September 8th - October 7th) 辛酉

This promises to be a profitable month for most people using this room, but especially for those in the construction industry. Seize every opportunity to embark on business trips, as these will yield positive outcomes for you. Couples using this bedroom should be more sensitive to each other's emotions this month. Be more tactful and sensitive in your daily interactions and avoid taking each other for granted. Keep a look out as well for liver-related problems, or any feeling of light-headedness, especially if you notice the presence of a negative form outside of this sector. Always seek immediate treatment at the first sign of trouble.

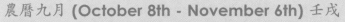

農曆九月 (October 8th - November 6th) 壬戌

You will do well to hold your tongue, rather than offer unsolicited advice to those who are incapable of appreciating your good intentions. Instead, focus on building yourself up. Where business is concerned, review and go over your strategies. This is a good month for strategising and decision-making in general, but not for business expansion and growth. Be prepared for unexpected surprises as well, if using this bedroom. Nothing is quite what it seems.

農曆十月 (November 7th - December 6th) 癸亥

Business deals and contracts need to be well-scrutinised as even a small oversight may end up being a costly mistake. Make sure that all decisions are discussed with your spouse, or otherwise this could lead to stressful relations with your partner. Health problems could surface in the form of stomach-related issues; and this is especially true for the older women in the house, and for those using this bedroom, specifically.

農曆十一月 (December 7th 2018 - January 4th 2019) 甲子

Do not be tempted to become embroiled in fights this month, as you will come off second best. It will be best to maintain dignity by maintaining your silence! If you are in the legal profession you will do very well this month, as your persuasive powers will come to the fore. Marital discord will be a problem for couples who use this bedroom this month.

農曆十二月 (January 5th - February 3rd 2019) 乙丑

Hostile and aggressive takeovers are possible and if you sleep in this sector's bedroom, you should be aware of competitors who will take you on as well. This is a favourable bedroom for children, as it will be beneficial for their studies and academic work. Health problems may come in the form of liver trouble this month and if there are negative structures outside this sector, then the impact will be worse.

Main Door	West	Bedroom Sector	North

農曆正月 (February 4th - March 4th) 甲寅

Expectant mothers should avoid using this bedroom this month, as the risk of miscarriage is quite high. If you're a business owner or manager involved in the tourism, travel or media businesses, you should be prepared for your sales targets to fall slightly below the mark this month. On the other hand, scholars and academics will find the energies of the month auguring well for their reputations. Go forth and publish that paper you've being toiling away at, or present your findings at a conference. This will be a good way for your star to shine brighter.

農曆二月 (March 5th - April 4th) 乙卯

This month, you should steer clear of any high-risk investment deals, as they could well burn a hole in your bank account at the end of the day. Those working in the entertainment industry will find it tough (and very lonely) this month, with your superiors and co-workers apparently being unable or unwilling to back you up – when you need it the most. Remember that you can still make a difference by working smart, instead of just working hard! Health issues to watch out for are eye or heart-related problems.

農曆三月 (April 5th - May 4th) 丙辰

Prepare for some backstabbing and betrayal from within the company. If you own or manage one, be sure that you keep your eyes on all of your employees. Gastrointestinal problems will plague the elderly using this bedroom, so they will need to take extra care where stomach issues and troubles are concerned. There is a possibility of concluding property deals this month but as soon as there is any indication of volatile, argumentative bargaining to secure the investment, you should immediately withdraw from the deal as the outcome will not be worth the effort.

農曆四月 (May 5th - June 5th) 丁巳

Get a qualified electrician or technician to check the wiring of your property because the risk of fire hazards is high. Those among you who are advocates and solicitors, might find it hard to put your points across this month in presenting your case in court. Don't be unduly frustrated, though. If you keep your wits about you, and remain calm and patient as you go about executing your duties. Married couples or those of you in committed relationships will also be put to the test this month. But don't allow a bad patch to ruin your entire relationship. Instead, find ways to overcome the bad patch.

| Main Door | West | Bedroom Sector | North |

農曆五月 (June 6th - July 6th) 戊午

If you are due to sit for an important examination soon and do not wish to be distracted, then it would be wise to avoid using this bedroom, this month. Head injuries or lung ailments are the significant health problems that you need to look out for. Those of you in the communications and public relations industries will also find miscommunication to be rife. In general, Wealth Luck is poor for those using this bedroom, so refrain from making any investments for the time being.

農曆六月 (July 7th - August 6th) 己未

Good profits can be made from conservative property deals but to benefit from these opportunities, you will need to watch the markets carefully. Carefully avoid taking any untoward financial risks. Younger children in the home may have health problems this month in the form of ligament, muscles and tendon injuries. In general, relationships don't fare well this month and those using these rooms should be patient with their loved ones. Avoid getting impatient and losing your temper, because it will only make things worse. As much as possible, avoid falling into petty arguments.

農曆七月 (August 7th - September 7th) 庚申

Unless you're prepared to face up to the consequences or repercussions of a casual fling, no thanks to a night of binging – do not overindulge in alcohol, or spend too many evenings at the pubs and nightclubs. You might find that you're taking away one type of stress and bringing on another! Also, those suffering from poor health should seriously consider moving out of this bedroom, to mitigate the risk of having their health worsened by a skin or liver ailment. This month promises to be a challenging one at work as well, where rivals and competitors will heat up the competition and challenge you considerably.

農曆八月 (September 8th - October 7th) 辛酉

Those involved in the legal or arbitration businesses will be pleased to know that with the proper amount of effort, you will be able to enjoy the fruits of your labour sooner than you expected. However, for this month, you should refrain from giving personal loans, especially to relatives and family members, as you can't afford to be impudent and you might not see the money again. Children using this bedroom are likely to be more rebellious and difficult to control or discipline this month.

農曆九月 (October 8th - November 6th) 壬戌

Ambitious or optimistic as you may be, this is simply not the right time to embark on a new enterprise or venture, as the probability of tasting early success is very low. Instead, it might be more prudent for you to wait for a more suitable time to make your move. The end results could be a lot sweeter! Resist the temptation to gamble and engage in any form of speculative investment, as you may end up poorer than when you first started. Elderly ladies suffer from the risk of appendicitis or oral disease if they use this room this month, consider putting them in another room.

農曆十月 (November 7th - December 6th) 癸亥

Couples might find their relationship undergoing a rough patch this month. Bear in mind though, that this is not the time for confrontation or bickering. Instead, be patient with each other, and see if you can temporarily use another bedroom for the duration of the month, in order to mitigate the possibility of arguments or misunderstandings. And if you're trying to conceive, this bedroom is definitely not the one to use.

農曆十一月 (December 7th 2018 - January 4th 2019) 甲子

Females using this room must be careful of injuries or legal matters arising from car accidents. Personal safety is important this month, as there is a risk of robbery and theft. Take extra precautions with your personal belongings and valuables. Children will be more rebellious, so it will be best to use common sense when dealing with them. Getting impatient will only prompt them to react.

農曆十二月 (January 5th - February 3rd 2019) 乙丑

Invest carefully in conservative, long-term property deals and you stand to reap the benefits of your investments, in time. If you run a business or a family venture in particular, it's time to pay more attention to your staff this month, as some could be backstabbers or betrayers. You should also watch out for nerve and tendon injuries if you use this bedroom.

Main Door	West	Bedroom Sector	Northwest

農曆正月 (February 4th - March 4th) 甲寅

Those aspiring to achieve literary successes should showcase their talents this month. You'll find that people are receptive to what you offer and you have a greater chance of meeting publishers, agents and editors. If you're in professional or competitive sports, you will do well this month and you should maximise efforts while the going is good. However, do bear in mind that mental instability and emotional stress are significant problems this month for those using this bedroom.

農曆二月 (March 5th - April 4th) 乙卯

Water-related industries such as tourism, travel, logistics and spa, will have some positive publicity and should return favourable profits as a result. Those of you who work in those fields are likely to see a bigger bonus this year! Spouses may feel a bit neglected this month, as one partner is busy making money while the other is being sidelined. Ensure that you devote enough time and energy to your relationship and don't sacrifice it for the sake of your career. Look into property investments this month, as there are good deals to be had with good financial rewards that could keep you comfortable for some time.

農曆三月 (April 5th - May 4th) 丙辰

Short-term passionate flings rather than long-term affairs will be the result this month for people using this bedroom. If you have any romantic feelings about someone and want them fulfilled, it's best to keep this in mind. It's a month to mind your own business, because if you meddle in other people's affairs, you are likely to get into arguments rather than be on the receiving end of a wave of gratitude. Resentment and anger are the likely results. Office politics are simmering to boiling point this month and this will therefore, be a period of sharp competition and intense rivalries.

農曆四月 (May 5th - June 5th) 丁巳

Make a name for yourself in your chosen field of industry this month, as you stand to make greater acquaintances and thus establish and cement your position. Try to go after joint-venture deals and partnerships that you began awhile back, as the outcomes are likely to bring strong profits in your favour. This is the month to go for broke, rather than sit back and wait for the opportunities to fall into your lap!

| Main Door | West | Bedroom Sector | Northwest |

農曆五月 (June 6th - July 6th) 戊午

Try to put off all important decision-making to another point in time, as any decisions you do make right now will likely have the opposite effect of what was intended. If possible, request the input of clear-minded and objective confidants or people you trust. Expectant mothers are advised to use a different room this month, as there is a risk of complications. Likewise, individuals using this room should be prepared for possible accidents while on one of their travelling trips.

農曆六月 (July 7th - August 6th) 己未

Those of you involved in the world of academia will find that you receive recognition for your work this month if you use this room. People will finally start to know you for the work you do. Be careful if you are involved in any joint ventures and partnerships this month, because these may just have hidden legal entanglements that will take you by surprise. Romantic relationships will be on the upswing this month for those using this bedroom, but you need to be careful if there are water features outside this sector.

農曆七月 (August 7th - September 7th) 庚申

Overseas and offshore business opportunities will enhance the bottom line for your business this month, so grab these opportunities as they crop up. Those in the furniture business will find that financial gains will be made this month. However, a loss of wealth and legal problems are possible this month, as a result of betrayals and rumours spreading about your business. You may need to watch your back and safeguard your interests as much as possible, and employ some form of damage control if the backbiting becomes too rampant.

農曆八月 (September 8th - October 7th) 辛酉

If you're married, you should be careful of third-party gossip causing you some amount of tension in your relationship. Guard against unwarranted and unreasonable jealousy, as this will cause a certain amount of problems. There is a chance of miscarriage for pregnant women using this sector this month, so if it's possible to move to another room, do it! Those in the real estate business will find that property deals return good profits this month and you are likely to enjoy some good financial gains.

農曆九月 (October 8th - November 6th) 壬戌

Use your inner talents of wisdom and knowledge to gain the promotion you deserve. If this requires you having to speak up about your talents and abilities and making it known, so be it! You've been humble and self-effacing for far too long. If you're involved in professional and competitive sports, you will do well in international competitions this month, if you use this bedroom. Elderly individuals should be careful of head injuries, especially if there are negative features and structures outside this sector.

農曆十月 (November 7th - December 6th) 癸亥

This is still a month to show off your true talents and abilities, as superiors will finally notice you and give you the promotion you have always wanted. Personal relationships will be tense and difficult for those using this bedroom this month, and you will have to work harder on your communication. You can maximise the benefits of being in the limelight and avoid working with people who do not know you very well.

農曆十一月 (December 7th 2018 - January 4th 2019) 甲子

Those in the travel and logistics business should make use of the opportunities to make new deals or build alliances with overseas partners this month. It will be best for you to make an effort to cultivate these opportunities instead of waiting for it to come your way. This is an excellent bedroom to use if you are in the literary, mining, metals and engineering industries, as financial gains are plentiful.

農曆十二月 (January 5th - February 3rd 2019) 乙丑

This is generally a month to mind your own business, because if you meddle in other people's affairs, you are likely to get into arguments rather than be on the receiving end of a wave of gratitude. Office politics are at their height and this will be a month of sharp competition and intense rivalries. Short-term passionate flings rather than long-term affairs will be the result this month if you use this room, so keep your expectations modest.

Southwest Sector
Main Door

This section contains the monthly outlook for all 12 months of the year for different bedroom sectors, in a property with a Southwest Sector Main Door.

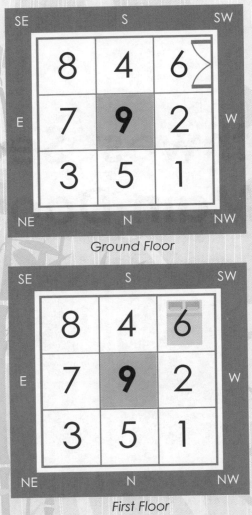

Ground Floor

First Floor

農曆正月 (February 4th - March 4th) 甲寅

If you're keen on increasing your profits, this will be the month to do it. However, try not to be too hasty or careless when it comes to signing any legal contracts or documents, as you may succumb to the fraudulent manipulations of some unscrupulous people. Or, you might also end up getting much less than what you expected. This is not a good room for couples that are looking to start a family. Where health is concerned, occupants could suffer from kidney or head-related ailments and injuries.

農曆二月 (March 5th - April 4th) 乙卯

Couples using this room will have a better month, as there are improved communication ties. They will be able to enjoy a smoother, more intimate relationship that will leave them both feeling fulfilled. For those of you working in the marketing and consulting fields, or in research and development, you will find that business starts to pick up this month. There is also a very good chance of promotion among the senior female employees. Travel bodes well for you this month, as you'll be able to close lucrative property deals while you're abroad.

農曆三月 (April 5th - May 4th) 丙辰

Elderly males using this room should be careful of certain health problems, particularly if you are susceptible to diseases or ailments affecting your lungs and blood circulation system. Those of you who hold a position of authority and power at work will have to be prepared for possible defiance from your subordinates. Parents will face a similar situation at home, with your children. People who dabble in the share market will stand to make some good financial gains this month.

農曆四月 (May 5th - June 5th) 丁巳

You will find that your success at work will increase for reasons that you are not exactly clear about. However, there is no reason to be worried – just enjoy it! Those among you in the real estate and property businesses will find profit from a lot of your dealings this month. Salaried employees who are looking for ways to increase their pay and gain greater benefits will stand a chance of fulfilling their ambitions this month.

| Main Door | Southwest | Bedroom Sector | Southwest |

農曆五月 (June 6th - July 6th) 戊午

Be prepared for intense business rivalry at work, which could lead to intense backstabbing and jealousy. You will need to watch your back, and avoid getting involved in an argument or confrontation. Otherwise, it would get blown-out of proportion. Therefore, make an effort to keep your emotions under control and strive to stay in control of the situation, instead of being overly-reactive. Politicians will find their reputation improving among the masses this month, so enjoy your burst of popularity and make the most of it. In general, people using this room should guard against kidney troubles and must closely monitor their health.

農曆六月 (July 7th - August 6th) 己未

Some of you who use this room will be more susceptible to flus and colds, or illnesses that attack your respiratory systems. Therefore, you should maintain a healthy lifestyle and change your daily habits so that you boost your immune system. If a particular illness, even though minor, takes a long time to cure – be sure to get professional medical treatment. It's a good time to make an appointment with your boss to discuss possible salary increments or promotions. Beware that there are jealous, resentful individuals keen to bring you down, though.

農曆七月 (August 7th - September 7th) 庚申

Couples who are newly-married will find this to be a good month, as their relationship will be harmonious and intimate, with many happy moments enjoyed together. Salaried employees who have been patiently waiting for a promotion and further recognition, will find their wishes being granted this month. In general, it's a favourable month for property and gilt investments. So, don't be afraid to make a bold move, as the gains are likely to be very good.

農曆八月 (September 8th - October 7th) 辛酉

A favourable month is in store for you, especially if you're in the field of academics, or sitting for a major examination. You're likely to pass all tests with flying colours! For those of you required to travel for work and business purposes, you will find that your trip yields immensely successful outcomes. People who are in steady, committed relationships will find that ties are more harmonious than ever and that your partner is as equally sincere and committed as you are.

農曆九月 (October 8th - November 6th) 壬戌

Those among you who are involved in professional and competitive sports will find this a good month, as you'll be able to obtain good results in all your tournaments and competitions. Faithful employees will find that all their efforts will be rewarded this month with more than just a pat on the back, so they can expect some financial gains to come their way! Elderly members of the household should be treated with care and understanding, as they might become somewhat stubborn when it comes to health issues this month. Bear in mind that they might be more afraid than anything else.

農曆十月 (November 7th - December 6th) 癸亥

For those of you using this sector's bedroom this month, you will be under a lot of stress. In the workplace, your superiors will expect a lot from you and will start pressuring you to produce better results than before. Keep your head in the game and focus on your career goals, especially since now it is not a good time for partnership. Avoid investing in the financial sector because certain deals will not be what they seem – resulting in either poor investment choices or scams.

農曆十一月 (December 7th 2018 - January 4th 2019) 甲子

For those of you in the marketing, consulting or research and development industries, you will do very well this month. If you're an elderly female, you will be in for a promotion this month. It might also be extremely beneficial for you to travel for work or pursue property deals that will bring you great returns. In terms of love, couples using this room will be able to cultivate a harmonious relationship, where communication will be smooth among the two of you.

農曆十二月 (January 5th - February 3rd 2019) 乙丑

For parents, your kids can be quite a rebel this month. Move them to a different room, if you can, to curb their negative behavior. Financial-wise, you are encouraged to not partake in speculative investments. But bear in mind that this would be an opportune time to seek out new clients for your business, especially if you're in engineering. As for males who are in this room, they're prone to health issues related to stomach ailments, especially if they do not practice healthy eating habits.

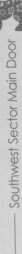

農曆正月 (February 4th - March 4th) 甲寅

Your fine negotiation skills will be able to net you substantial financial gains from your investments, so go ahead and seize every opportunity that presents itself. This is also an ideal month to establish a joint-venture or partnership with another party, more so if you're looking to expand your business or capitalise on a larger portion of equity ownership. Mergers and expansions will bode well for you at this point. Those among you in a steady, committed relationship and wish to take your relationship to the next level, this will be the ideal month to do it, preferably over the course of a romantic dinner or weekend getaway.

農曆二月 (March 5th - April 4th) 乙卯

On the domestic front, problems with the in-laws may plague those who share a home. Therefore, it is best to avoid contact or even move away for the month to prevent any major disagreements and quarrels. Those of you working in metaphysics and alternate therapies industries should use the media to promote and market your business, as you will find it very fruitful and beneficial. However, most of you in general, have to be careful of female subordinates or superiors causing problems at work by making sudden unexpected changes this month.

農曆三月 (April 5th - May 4th) 丙辰

Couples and newlyweds will want to avoid using this room to sidestep any unnecessary tension and conflicts that could arise. If this isn't possible, be tactful and tolerant when dealing with your loved one, especially when arguments occur. Furniture manufacturers and shop-owners will find this to be a favorable month. However, it is always advisable to carefully go over all legal documents before signing. Otherwise, you risk inviting unnecessary future complications. You'll want to use this bedroom for all meditative, religious or spiritual pursuits, if you're so inclined. The energies present here will allow your mind to be at peace and allow you to reach a greater sense of spiritual fulfillment.

農曆四月 (May 5th - June 5th) 丁巳

Those of you in the financial and banking industries might need to travel abroad to conclude deals. Grab the opportunities, because these overseas deals will yield many profits. This is also a good month for people involved in professional and competitive sports, as your reputation enjoys a good boost. However, you'll need to be prepared that the financial benefits won't be as quick to arrive. Where health is concerned, lung or kidney problems are likely for people who use this bedroom, particularly if there are negative features located outside. It would be safer to avoid using this sector for the duration of the month.

農曆五月 (June 6th - July 6th) 戊午

Unfortunately, this will not be a very good month for most endeavours. Marital bliss won't be there to be enjoyed for those among you who are married, so give each other some breathing space this month and be patient. Things will get better once this month is out. Keep a sharp eye out for any negative features outside this sector, as these indicate the risk of a possible infection, or worse, liver or breast cancer. Where finances are concerned, hold on to your money and do not invest in real estate or property at this point in time. If you do, you'll only recoup losses.

農曆六月 (July 7th - August 6th) 己未

Expectant mothers should avoid using this bedroom this month, as they risk having pregnancy complications or a possible miscarriage. Females who are ready to enter the world of romance and dating again should be careful of the people they choose. There is a strong risk that they may fall for someone with a shady personality, or one who is not who he seems. Those of you who make a living from your artistic or creative talents, you may need to travel this month to earn your keep. It will, however, be ultimately worth your while and prove to be immensely beneficial.

農曆七月 (August 7th - September 7th) 庚申

People who are seeking new romantic involvements will find yourself struck by cupid's arrow this month and will have favourable luck meeting new partners. Artistic and creative people will also benefit from using this sector, particularly if they are seeking to market their skills abroad. Those of you who are parents may find that your children seem to be more prone to picking fights with others. You might want to consider relocating them to another bedroom. You certainly don't need them to be continuously engaged in some form of unfriendly or unhealthy rivalry!

農曆八月 (September 8th - October 7th) 辛酉

This month, you will need to tread carefully, as hidden agendas and ulterior motives may affect your business affairs. Make sure that you fully understand what you're in for, before you finalise any important deals. Pay attention to the small details so that you don't miss out on anything. On the domestic front, you could well experience some trouble arising from a misunderstanding between the ladies in your household; particularly between mothers and daughters-in-law. Be fair and tactful in handling any such situation or you risk making it worse. Health-wise, keep a look-out for ailments affecting your abdominal region, or even possible stomach and pancreatic troubles.

農曆九月 (October 8th - November 6th) 壬戌

You'll want to use this bedroom if you're sitting for a major examination soon, or happen to dabble in the academic, literary or media fields. The energies here are conducive for just such endeavours. Newly-weds and couples in a committed relationship will also find this room to be an ideal bedroom for romance and cultivating solid, loving ties. However, you will need to be careful of any significant Water forms or features outside this sector, as these indicate the possibility of scandals or infidelity, with the possibility of betrayal.

農曆十月 (November 7th - December 6th) 癸亥

If you're thinking about expanding your business, this would be the ideal month to do so. As a business owner, it will be good for you to establish a joint-venture or a partnership. Always keep an eye on opportunities that will benefit you in the long run. Good news! Your investments will only bring you financial profits and if you manage to get your hands on those sweet deals by using your negotiation skills – you're set to go. If you're in a committed relationship, you're advised to take it to the next level and put a ring on it!

農曆十一月 (December 7th 2018 - January 4th 2019) 甲子

You will be plagued with health complications this month. This is largely due to your high stress levels. Always be prepared to face tough competition at work, which is caused by your productivity and effectiveness in the workplace. This is also a good month to invest your money in the property market, especially if you need to travel to one place or another to conclude a particular deal.

農曆十二月 (January 5th - February 3rd 2019) 乙丑

For couples, you will have a harmonious relationship with your partner due to the positive energies found in this sector. And as for those of you in the literary field, your new written work will bring about favourable outcomes. This will earn you the fame and fortune that you've long desired. For those on scholarly pursuits this month, it's good to know that you can sleep in this room or to study in it, thus benefiting from its good energies for the best results.

| Main Door | Southwest | Bedroom Sector | Southeast |

農曆正月 (February 4th - March 4th) 甲寅

Excellent commercial opportunities beckon to those involved in the marketing and consultation industries with corresponding financial gains to be made by the shrewd, prudent businessperson. And if you also happen to own a portfolio of properties, this would be a suitable month to sell or divest a part of your portfolio, to cash in on the profits from your investments. Academic Luck features strongly for those using this bedroom, so go ahead and enroll for that self-improvement course or any other course that will add to your existing repertoire of skills!

農曆二月 (March 5th - April 4th) 乙卯

Those in banking and the finance industries using this sector's room will be rewarded and recognised by their superiors this month. Individuals in competitive sports will find success in their international activities or competitions, resulting in possible fame and recognition this month, as well. You will need to be careful of illness, especially with kidney problems being the most likely health issue plaguing you.

農曆三月 (April 5th - May 4th) 丙辰

Athletes and long-distance runners should take care of their joints this month, as injury is possible, especially through over-exertion. Employees will find that they are stressed at this point in time, as superiors step up the pressure for them to perform and increase their expectations. This is a difficult month to make profits, so a more conservative approach to wealth management and investment should be adopted.

農曆四月 (May 5th - June 5th) 丁巳

This promises to be a pleasant and productive month for those using this bedroom. There will be substantial profits to be made from the travel or construction business. Also, this is a good time of the year to engage in speculative investments, especially if you wish to make a quick buck. You need to know, however, when to stop engaging in such investments, and of course, when to gain from them. Couples using this bedroom this month, will find their relationship harmonious and thriving.

| Main Door | Southwest | Bedroom Sector | Southeast |

農曆五月 (June 6th - July 6th) 戊午

Young boys using this sector should stay away from any sort of machinery, as there could be injuries to their legs. This is a stressful month for relationships, so do not make any important decisions about the future. If possible, hold off all important relationship talks and decisions to the next month. Big changes and bold new steps will be needed to revive stagnant careers and floundering investments.

農曆六月 (July 7th - August 6th) 己未

You may be disappointed to find that your efforts are not bearing the results expected. This is the time to consider whether you've been doing things right and the right things well! Similarly, this is an ideal month to engage in property deals, but ensure that proper planning has been undertaken, if you wish to profit from your investments. You may also find your personal relationships to be more strained and tense than usual this month. Be tactful, sensitive and patient to preserve harmony in your relationships.

農曆七月 (August 7th - September 7th) 庚申

Take advantage of speculative investments this month, as these will provide short-term gains. However, you will need to be careful of being too greedy or it will end up costing you dearly. Marital relations prove to be harmonious and rewarding this month for those in this room. This is a good month for those who have taken investment positions in the preceding months or who work as fund managers in the futures markets to realise their financial gains and make some profit out of it.

農曆八月 (September 8th - October 7th) 辛酉

Couples looking to start a family should make use of the good energies of this bedroom, this month. This is the month that you will receive recognition for something you have done, for example, publishing a paper in the field of psychology. Short-term flings and passionate romances await those who use this bedroom, this month.

農曆九月 (October 8th - November 6th) 壬戌

Business-owners should not overemphasize targets and profit margins, because you'd only be stressing out and demotivating your employees unnecessarily. Instead, sit down with them and come out with a realistic business plan to improve the fortunes of your company. Likewise, Romance Luck won't exactly be on your side this month, so spend your energy on other more rewarding endeavours.

農曆十月 (November 7th - December 6th) 癸亥

For those of you who invest in property, this would be a good month for you. This would also be the month to sell and divest your existing portfolio. Thereafter, you'll be able to gain substantial profit from your investments by improving your skills. Take advantage of the strong Academic Luck this month to pursue more knowledge or additional skills. There will also be great commercial opportunities, especially for those in the marketing and consulting fields – where financial profits await.

農曆十一月 (December 7th 2018 - January 4th 2019) 甲子

If you're in the banking and financial sectors, you will find your efforts being recognised by your supervisors this month – only if this bedroom is used for this month, of course. And if you're a professional athlete, you will deliver outstanding performances in competitions. Your name will be in lights and your new status will only bring about international accolades, this month. In terms of health, you should pay attention to possible kidney problems as it is the likeliest health issue bugging you.

農曆十二月 (January 5th - February 3rd 2019) 乙丑

For those of you using this bedroom, this month, you should be careful with the possibility of developing abnormal ulcers and lower back pain. Career-wise, you might fight with your partner a lot. You're both advised to focus on your careers now because romance will not be good this month.

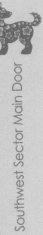

Southwest Sector Main Door

農曆正月 (February 4th - March 4th) 甲寅

It's a volatile month for relationships, as disagreements caused by jealousy and suspicion are likely to cause some gloom in love ties. You'll have to make more of an effort to keep the relationship on an even keel. People working in the legal and judicial fields will do well this month, because they're bound to be inundated by requests for their services. Elderly women using this room and prone to stomach ailments might want to consider temporarily moving into another room for the month.

農曆二月 (March 5th - April 4th) 乙卯

Communication in general will suffer from a temporary collapse this month, so don't rely on word-of-mouth deals and agreements. Get everything down in black and white. Likewise, don't count on people delivering the right message to others this month, as the threat of lawsuits is high. Where possible, have a written message prepared instead. Romance also takes a backseat to bickering this month, as miscommunication is rife, driving a wedge between partners. In that same vein, be prepared for arguments and conflicts at the workplace. Understand that this is a temporary glitch and avoid overreacting to explosive situations.

農曆三月 (April 5th - May 4th) 丙辰

Those of you who have steadily been working hard and putting in extra labour will find your efforts being recognised, and perhaps even rewarded, this month. Continue to do the good work – even when it seems that you're plugging away alone, someone is always observing! If you work as a politician or civil servant, you need to keep a low profile this month in order to avoid unnecessary scandals and gossip. If you invest in properties, you're likely to see good profits this month – but you'll need to travel to meet with quality buyers and close your deals.

農曆四月 (May 5th - June 5th) 丁巳

Elderly ladies using this room should be aware of potential health troubles in store. There will be signs of illnesses, and even if these seem minor, you need to get them checked out to ensure that it isn't anything serious. Students who will be sitting for examinations soon should avoid using this room, this month, because it will not be conducive for your learning and studies. There is some female trouble to be expected at work and at home, so if there are messy fights or conflicts involving females, whether in the domestic or professional sense, steer clear out of it!

| Main Door | Southwest | Bedroom Sector | East |

農曆五月 (June 6th - July 6th) 戊午

This month might leave you smiling in satisfaction, as it will generally be very smooth and productive. This will be true both in professional or personal sense. In addition, newly-married couples who have just embarked on an exciting new life should use this bedroom for its positive energies. Property investors should be bold this month and invest in the properties of their choice, as it will likely lead to good results. However, ensure that you read the fine print of all documents before committing to anything.

農曆六月 (July 7th - August 6th) 己未

Fire hazards are a serious threat this month. Protect yourself by double-checking all your electrical wiring and systems, preferably by an experienced professional. Don't just limit this to your home – if you own a business, get your office and work space checked out too, especially if you sleep in this room. Decisions are best left to another time; both for professional and personal ones. Injuries are also a risk this month, and it's possible that you might suffer from a broken limb if you engage in risky contact sports, or extreme physical activities.

農曆七月 (August 7th - September 7th) 庚申

In matters of the heart, single people should avoid expecting a serious relationship out of anything new. The outlook for long-term relationships is dim, but that doesn't mean that you can't enjoy a few casual relationships and gain some valuable dating experience! If you've been huddled away in your lab or workspace, busily crafting something new and ingenious – this is the time to share your inventions with the world! There will be good publicity and word-of-mouth that can help propel your career forward. Negative structures located outside this sector can lead to an increased risk of fire hazards.

農曆八月 (September 8th - October 7th) 辛酉

There will be unending minor health troubles coming your way, especially if you're using this room, this month. Although they're not really serious, it can still cause you uneasiness. Always pay attention to throat ailments, or to toothaches and gum infections. Get the help of a professional immediately – instead of avoiding it and hoping that it goes away. You will also be plagued with miscommunication issues with the people who are close to you. This will not be a good month for love pursuits either, as your new crush or romance will lead to something scandalous, instead of happiness.

農曆九月 (October 8th - November 6th) 壬戌

Sweet young female with the silver tongue and the face of an angel – you'll be the bane of red-blooded men everywhere. This month, men have to be careful of this sort of temptation, as otherwise you'll only find yourself entangled in a compromising and embarrassing situation! Guard against frivolous temptation. Be very careful with your personal safety this month, as there is a risk of robbery and theft. If you run a business, avoid embarking on any new ventures, and instead, seek to eliminate internal fraud committed by dishonest employees.

農曆十月 (November 7th - December 6th) 癸亥

Do not let yourself be cheated by smooth-talking individuals who present seemingly irresistible offers to you. Chances are, they are only out to relieve you of your money. This warning goes out especially to those in the courier, logistics, freight and transportation industries. If you're a Gua 2 person, be forewarned that the risk of a robbery or burglary looms over your head this month. Singles will, however, find their personal life 'taking-off', with a newfound romantic interest from within their circle of friends or acquaintances.

農曆十一月 (December 7th 2018 - January 4th 2019) 甲子

When it comes to matters related to property – this will not be the time to invest. Avoid getting involved in property deals, as they could end up in legal disputes. Additionally, you might not want to take that plane ride to close that business deal this month, because business dealings this month, in particular, could lead to losses. As for relationships, you and your partner might feel strained but you're advised to face the issue straight on and resolve them. By avoiding and not talking about it at all, you will only turn small issues into huge, never-ending problems.

農曆十二月 (January 5th - February 3rd 2019) 乙丑

For those of you working in the communications industry, do consider investing in new capitals this month. It will be the most opportune month to do so. As for those who are on scholarly pursuits (be it academicians, researchers and scholars), their hard work will be recognised, if this bedroom is used this month. Women who are pregnant will need to be careful if they chose to sleep in this room. You're advised to make different arrangements for a different room instead.

SE		S		SW
8		4		6
E	7	**9**	2	W
	3	5	1	
NE		N		NW

農曆正月 (February 4th - March 4th) 甲寅

It will be a rewarding month for people involved in the academic, creative, and literary fields. You will find your career moving ahead by leaps and bounds. But do keep in mind that what's success to you is reason for envy to someone else, so be prepared for jealous, petty people keen to speak ill of you when your back is turned. But don't let them get you down; you will do well to simply ignore their shallow actions. Young children using this room might be at risk of being injured by sharp objects and metal implements.

農曆二月 (March 5th - April 4th) 乙卯

Those among you who make a living as counsellors, life coaches and trainers will find this month to be a bumper month – as you will literally be inundated with new clients seeking your help and assistance. If you work as senior personnel in your corporation, you should be vigilant against third parties who are out to extort large sums of money from you. Keep your friends close, but keep your enemies closer! If you've long been involved in a tumultuous and unsettled personal or professional relationship, you'll find this to be the month that puts it all to an end.

農曆三月 (April 5th - May 4th) 丙辰

Accidents and mishaps may plague you this month, so be careful when you're out travelling, even if this means venturing out your front door! However, this particularly applies to road-related mishaps – so be careful when you're on the road or when you're driving. If you have children, you will find that your teenage daughters are apt to be more rebellious than usual this month. Open the channels of communication to find out exactly what's wrong, instead of reacting with emotional anger.

農曆四月 (May 5th - June 5th) 丁巳

Avoid investing in high-risk portfolios this month, because you'll only stand to lose – not gain! In general, it's a good month to keep an eagle eye on all your financial expenditures. It's easy for your money to trickle out of your fingers at this point, and you don't want to see that happen after all the effort you've put in. Be especially vigilant, as there is a heightened risk of armed robberies and thefts. In terms of health, do consider relocating to another bedroom if that's possible; otherwise, you're at risk of suffering from ulcers, gallstones and gastrointestinal issues.

| Main Door | **Southwest** | Bedroom Sector | Northeast |

農曆五月 **(June 6th - July 6th)** 戊午

If you want to make money at this point in time, it's time to ask for help! Others with accumulated expertise and wisdom in financial matters will able to offer you advice that is worth gold – so listen up. But do be careful whom you approach, as there is a proliferation of fraudsters lurking about, just waiting to pull the wool over your eyes. You'll be feeling mentally and emotionally down this month, and just feeling out of spirits in general. Don't beat yourself over it, as everyone feels this way in varying degrees at different points in their lives. However, if it feels like unmanageable depression or simply something you can't cope with – then do not hesitate to seek professional help or simply see a counsellor or therapist.

農曆六月 **(July 7th - August 6th)** 己未

Be careful when you're travelling and out and about, as there is an increased risk of accidents. This could be caused by your own negligence, so don't let yourself get distracted when you're travelling on the road. But in general, your professional life is set to receive a boost, because there are great opportunities for career advancement, which will lead to more power and authority at the workplace. Parents may find that their male teenage children using this room will be more rebellious than usual, so they should consider using another room, if it becomes too problematic.

農曆七月 **(August 7th - September 7th)** 庚申

There are some health problems that will come to the fore this month. This will manifest itself primarily in the form of liver troubles. Profits might come your way in the form of smart property investments, so strike a deal if it feels particularly right! There is a continued threat of robbery and theft for people using this room, this month, so for those of you who have just come into some money – ensure that you share this information with only the people you trust the most, as others might use it in a devious way.

農曆八月 **(September 8th - October 7th)** 辛酉

For students and scholars sitting for important examinations this month, this would be the room to use. It bodes well for your studies and revision. People involved in the media and marketing industries will find this month bringing with it achievements and honour, so get ready to enjoy your moment in the spotlight! Your past efforts and labours will finally get its due. In general, however, people using this room might have to battle some emotional volatility and psychological problems, so take extra care if you're already prone to depression and mental instability.

農曆九月 (October 8th - November 6th) 壬戌

This month, put on your strategic thinking hat and plan ahead carefully. Having a solid arrangement will allow you to grab the opportunity that comes your way, and with proper timing and calculated efforts, significant financial rewards will simply fall into your lap! In general, this month bodes well for all thinking and intellectual activities, so be sure that you carefully and deliberately think through what will benefit you tremendously. Students will benefit from the energies of this room for their academic and educational activities. The results are likely to be seen in their examinations!

農曆十月 (November 7th - December 6th) 癸亥

Speculative investments, especially in the property market, will return with good investments this month. Relationships should improve so take advantage of this good month to take your spouse away for a treat or a vacation together. People involved in professional sports should be careful of injuries to the legs and feet.

農曆十一月 (December 7th 2018 - January 4th 2019) 甲子

Those in the oil and gas business should take advantage of good business deals offered to them this month. Printing and publishing houses will do well this month with profits coming mostly from overseas sales. This is a tough month for relationships.

農曆十二月 (January 5th - February 3rd 2019) 乙丑

A financially challenging month awaits you with the possibility of betrayals and loss of wealth. However, those using this room should expect the unexpected, as changes are likely to bring good fortune for those using this bedroom. Good news will come to those who use this bedroom, this month, so long as they are involved in travel and travel-related activities.

Southwest Sector Main Door

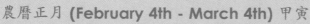

農曆正月 (February 4th - March 4th) 甲寅

This is not a month to get involved in any major decisions or business deals, as these will not end up as good investments and may even result in some losses. There is a possibility of concluding property deals this month, but as soon as there are any hints of volatile, argumentative bargaining involved in securing the investment, you will need to withdraw from the deal. It will definitely not be worth the fight. Gastrointestinal problems will plague elderly females using this room, so they will need to take greater care of their health.

農曆二月 (March 5th - April 4th) 乙卯

Business partners should be aware of possible fallout from tension and stress this month, as this will result in loss of wealth. You will also need to take some time out and relax, or risk having to lose your finances. In general, this will be a difficult month for business owners and managers, as sales targets will be difficult to meet. This is especially true for those in the tourism, travel and media business industries. Academics and scholars will find an increase in reputation this month, especially if they decide publish their research and papers in their fields of expertise.

農曆三月 (April 5th - May 4th) 丙辰

Things are not looking so bright for people using this room this month. You find yourself unable to communicate and see eye-to-eye with both your co-workers at work, and loved ones at home. Tempers are easily frayed and seemingly minor disputes escalate into major quarrels. You will have to exercise greater effort in being patient and forgiving. Avoid any long-distance travel this month, as there is a high risk of accidents and obstacles.

農曆四月 (May 5th - June 5th) 丁巳

You should try to avoid using this room as much as possible, for the duration of this month. Otherwise, emotional problems may affect your peace of mind, and your relationship with others. Things get even worse when you have difficulty finding the underlying sources of the problem. It might be necessary for you to talk to people or seek help, in order to get the load off of your chest. Psychological problems are nothing to be ashamed of and sometimes we are unable to overcome them on our own, no matter how hard we try.

Main Door	Southwest	Bedroom Sector	North

農曆五月 (June 6th - July 6th) 戊午

Where matters of the heart are concerned, you can expect your relationships to be stormy and troubled. In other words, you can be prepared for a certain amount of drama to take place! Health-wise, you'll find yourself prone to leg injuries, liver ailments and/or other forms of illnesses. Seek medical treatment if you notice something highly irregular. For those of you in the entertainment business, or if you run a nightclub, bar or pub, you might want to keep a closer eye on your finances this month, especially when it comes to your dealings with external third parties.

農曆六月 (July 7th - August 6th) 己未

Where health is concerned this month, you would be better off taking care of your own health and seeking immediate treatment from your doctor at the first sign of an illness. Don't neglect or put off attending to obvious warning signs. Do not engage in any high-risk ventures this month, especially where property and real estate are concerned. The chances of incurring huge amounts of losses are very high! And by 'high-risk' ventures, we are also talking about gambling, games of chance and speculative investments. Leave the lottery and numbers game to another time, when the chances of winning are higher!

農曆七月 (August 7th - September 7th) 庚申

For those of you who are involved in the tourism, travel and/or media business, this might be a challenging month for you. As such, refrain from making any major decisions this month. Chances are, you would already be in a confused and irritable state of mind, and this doesn't augur well for your sense of reasoning and judgment. Expectant mothers should not use this bedroom, as this will only result in pregnancy complications. Where possible, move into another bedroom for the time being.

農曆八月 (September 8th - October 7th) 辛酉

Health problems affect the people using this bedroom this month and you might run into complications with your kidneys or blood circulatory system. Where relationships are concerned, your relationship with your partner will also be affected, due to a possible interference by a third party. This could also lead to some pretty tense arguments. If you're working in the tourism, courier and logistics industries, you'll find yourself having to double your efforts this month. Help or support from friends, superiors and mentors will not be forthcoming, but don't give up easily as perseverance will pay off.

農曆九月 (October 8th - November 6th) 壬戌

Those of you involved in professional and competitive sports should watch how you go about in practice and competition, to prevent against injuring your tendons, ligaments or bones. Keep an eagle eye on the property market this month and seize any good deals that come your way! Should you, however, encounter any hostile competition that threatens to derail your investment plans in the property concerned, pull out of the deal immediately. You might also want to be on the lookout for malicious, petty-minded people who will be out to backstab you and spread rumours and gossip.

農曆十月 (November 7th - December 6th) 癸亥

Miscommunication seems to be the order of the day, and indeed, it can spell trouble for both personal and professional relationships. Hence, those whose jobs require them to utilise their communication skills on a daily basis will be most affected. Lawyers and legal counselors, especially those born in the Year of the Snake, might want to consider delaying or postponing any litigation cases, as their argumentative and persuasive powers are weak this month.

農曆十一月 (December 7th 2018 - January 4th 2019) 甲子

If you happen to be sleeping in this bedroom, then be sure to look out for office politics this month. No one seems to be talking to each other and everyone is out to 'get' someone else. And if you're an employer or business owner, there is a chance that you might be betrayed by your own employees or subordinates. Look out as well for health issues, particularly lung problems and joint pains. Consult your physician at once should you find yourself feeling poorly.

農曆十二月 (January 5th - February 3rd 2019) 乙丑

Those in the political arena will find that friends and acquaintances will be around this month to help them with their political aspirations. Tensions will mount between colleagues, and between staff members and superiors, as a result of stress in the workplace. Speculative investments, positions on the stock exchange or even gambling, will return potential heavy losses this month.

農曆正月 (February 4th - March 4th) 甲寅

Relationships should be good this month, so if you wish to take it to a new level, you should do so and don't let your fear or inhibitions hold you back. Remember, fortune – and Romantic Luck – favour the brave! Let your intelligence and innate wisdom flower, as it will lead to opportunities that bring about a promotion, or a greater sense of authority at the workplace. This is the month to show the boss what you are made of, so don't hold back! It is time to gain the rewards for your hard work. Health-wise, be careful of eye and heart problems, especially if there are negative formations outside this sector.

農曆二月 (March 5th - April 4th) 乙卯

It will prove to be a favourable month for employees who are hoping for a career promotion, as the results are likely to be quite spectacular this year. Evidently, all your hard work and initiative have impressed all the right people! Business owners will make money this month, particularly if you are in the oil, gas, or mining industries. Travelling can bring about positive benefits at this time and this includes possible new investors with new venture opportunities and partnership deals.

農曆三月 (April 5th - May 4th) 丙辰

A fairly competitive month is in store for you at work, with office politics at their height. You need to avoid getting involved with your rivals, as you are sure to end up on the losing side. Avoid also taking sides in any feuds that seem to be taking place, especially the subtle ones! This month, romance is best left alone. Not only are things likely to end badly, but it might also tarnish your reputation. In terms of personal safety, avoid driving while under the influence of alcohol this month, as there is a good chance that you will get caught and have to pay a heavy fine or sustain a few injuries.

農曆四月 (May 5th - June 5th) 丁巳

Politicians and public servants will have a good month enjoying excellent public support and may even find themselves rising up the ranks in government or in their parties. You will be able to receive plenty of help from other individuals this month, and they will help you break past some of the more persistent barriers and overcome those pesky obstacles. Still, be wise and discerning about whom you choose to trust, as there are plenty of wolves dressed in sheep's clothing, out to take you for a little spin. If there was ever a time you need to put on your skeptic's cloak, this month will be it.

Main Door	Southwest	Bedroom Sector	Northwest

農曆五月 (June 6th - July 6th) 戊午

Romantic relationships are plagued by the shadow of the green-eyed monster this month. As much as possible, couples should avoid using this bedroom to avoid inviting undue trouble. In addition, pregnant women should move out this room and into another where possible. There is a likelihood of serious complications, or even a miscarriage, if they continue to use this room.

農曆六月 (July 7th - August 6th) 己未

This is a good room for children and scholars to use as a study, especially if they are facing important examinations this month. It generally bodes well for academics and exam preparations, thus resulting in favourable results in tests. Those involved in ports and transportation will do well financially this month, as deals increase and profits also start to multiply accordingly! Couples are likely to benefit from the good energies of this room for the month, particularly if there is a well-situated mountain outside.

農曆七月 (August 7th - September 7th) 庚申

Business booms for those in the furniture or publishing industry this month, so do your best to try to attract more customers – because it will result in greater profits. Look for overseas and offshore business opportunities in particular, as those will enhance the bottom line even more. Couples using this room may experience some marital discord this month. Patience and tolerance will be needed in liberal amounts so as to not further aggravate the tension in the relationship.

農曆八月 (September 8th - October 7th) 辛酉

This is precisely the month for you to offload property from your portfolio, as this strategy will result in good financial gains. Always think about what you need to do and then proceed to make it happen – perceptively! For pregnant ladies, it would be best for you to avoid this room, this month. If not, you might risk some complications or there could be even be a possible miscarriage. Do not accept information and opinions from others at face value this month. This is because you are bound to be surrounded by individuals who are only looking out for their own interests this month. Be cautious and careful – so that you're not charmed by sweet talkers!

農曆九月 (October 8th - November 6th) 壬戌

For those of you in the creative industry, this will be a positive month for you. There are chances for you to make a name for yourself in the industry and bask in the limelight. There will also be good financial profits that are set to follow – so what are you waiting for? Seize the moment. As for couples, they should be careful of temptation this month – giving in will only lead to tension with their partners. Always avoid turning into a jealous monster or being ruled by paranoia due to your suspicions. Finally, you will be able to get help from mentors and helpful individuals around you, this month. So, do whatever you need to do to make your dreams come true and you will be getting the support and assistance you need!

農曆十月 (November 7th - December 6th) 癸亥

For those of you who are in the entertainment industry or those who are running or are employed by health clubs, you will do well to sleep in this sector this month. Be proactive and ask for an increase in salary and for a new position with more authority and status. This month should prove to be a boon for restaurant owners, as there is a chance of profits.

農曆十一月 (December 7th 2018 - January 4th 2019) 甲子

This is a good month for relationships, so investing time in this partnership will bring its own rewards. It's also a good time to sell some favourable property investments, as these will turn into exceptional financial gains. Bankers and financial institution employees will see positive career development this month and this will most likely come in the form of a pay raise.

農曆十二月 (January 5th - February 3rd 2019) 乙丑

Romance is on the cards this month, but you should expect short-term passionate flings rather than anything long-lasting. There should be an improvement in interpersonal relationships amongst family members and friends, so use this time to strengthen your ties. This is a month to mind your own business because if you meddle in other people's affairs, arguments and ill will rather than gratitude, is likely.

| Main Door | Southwest | Bedroom Sector | West |

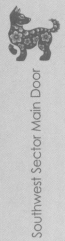

農曆正月 (February 4th - March 4th) 甲寅

Couples, either those married or in long-term relationships, will face arguments and disharmony this month. Both parties need to remain calm and tolerant, as otherwise the situation is likely to deteriorate into a tense one. If you're close to cutting a deal this month, you should not be deceived by appearances. Probe deeply into each one and evaluate them objectively, otherwise, you risk spending quite a bit of money. In general, you need to be careful of all business deals this month – as rivals and competitors are out to deceive you.

農曆二月 (March 5th - April 4th) 乙卯

If you are interested in spiritual or metaphysical knowledge and practices, you may want to use this bedroom. But do ensure that you check outside this sector to ensure that there are no negative features or structures outside, as otherwise the opposite effects are likely, and you will run into obstacles and problems. Real estate agents, as well as those looking to sell their houses, should make their best offer to prospective buyers. This enables you to reap good financial benefits.

農曆三月 (April 5th - May 4th) 丙辰

This is a very good month to make large investments in property and real estate, as the returns will be extremely good. Therefore, if you've long had an eye on one, don't hesitate to acquire it at this point in time. Those among you in the upper-social circles of society will find that this month brings with it plenty of opportunities to rub shoulders with the rich and famous, and you will be able to be introduced to the crème-de-la-crème of society. However, those of you who are married should be careful that your spouse is not seduced by a rich and powerful person who is only out to have a good time.

農曆四月 (May 5th - June 5th) 丁巳

Those of you who are married should minimise the amount of contact you have with your in-laws. If you do so, you'll be able to eliminate quite a bit of troubles and conflicts that will serve to increase your stress. In general, however, this is a good room to use. Ensure that you manage all your work-related stress well, otherwise it could start to affect your health. This could appear in the form of stomach ulcers and digestive-tract issues. Take it easy and give yourself plenty of rest.

| Main Door | Southwest | Bedroom Sector | West |

農曆五月 (June 6th - July 6th) 戊午

Be careful when you drive and are on the road this month, as you might risk getting into an accident. Don't be reckless and negligent when you're in the driver's seat. Real estate and property deals that are struck this month are likely to bring about profitable gains. However, personal relationships will be rather strained and tense this month, so do exercise plenty of tact and sensitivity when dealing with your partner.

農曆六月 (July 7th - August 6th) 己未

Pregnant women should avoid using this room, this month, as it could lead to complications – or in the worst-case scenario, a miscarriage. Likewise, students and scholars should also avoid this room, if they're sitting for important examinations. Try to use another room if possible, as this room will likely bring about poor results. It's a good month for you to invest in property and real estate, so make an effort to select the best type of property that gives you maximum returns.

農曆七月 (August 7th - September 7th) 庚申

This month, you'll have to be a lot more skeptical than usual as certain people will make an effort to come off like butter wouldn't melt in their mouths! Remember, if something or someone seems too good to be true, it probably is. Be careful of the papers and documents you are required to sign and check it through several times to ensure that you don't misinterpret the fine print. Students and scholars should avoid using this bedroom for their studies and revision. The energies here are not conducive for such work. Avoid making any major decisions this month, as well.

農曆八月 (September 8th - October 7th) 辛酉

This is a good bedroom to use, especially if you're looking to become involved in spiritual issues, or if you wish to develop your spiritual cultivation. Those of you who work as salaried employees should be careful of falling into arguments and disputes at the workplace this month, because if it gets particularly nasty or serious, it could end with a legal dispute. Those among you who are involved in romantic relationships will find themselves embroiled in constant quarrels and arguments.

農曆九月 (October 8th - November 6th) 壬戌

There are plenty of good opportunities and openings this month that enable you to make more money. However, don't be too excited or greedy and become carried away, as the constant pursuit for more will only lead to more stress and discontent. If you're single, you'll be happy to know that love seems to be on your side this month! There will be opportunities to meet your ideal partner. At the same time, keep an eye out for your business operations, if you're a business owner.

農曆十月 (November 7th - December 6th) 癸亥

Be careful of business dealings this month, as things are not what they seem and rivals are out to deceive you into deals which will not be financially sound. Couples need to watch for potential discords in marriage, arguments and family disharmony. Do not be deceived by appearances this month and evaluate all new deals conclusively; otherwise, these could end up costing you quite a bit of money.

農曆十一月 (December 7th 2018 - January 4th 2019) 甲子

Eye problems will cause health issues for those using this bedroom, this month. Avoid partnerships and joint ventures, as things are not good this month and will not have favourable outcomes. Stubbornness and a lack of logical thinking will cause employees to make some bad decisions that are likely to result in financial losses.

農曆十二月 (January 5th - February 3rd 2019) 乙丑

This is a month to make large investments in property and real estate, as the returns will be extremely good. Those in the upper-social circles of society will find that this month brings with it plenty of opportunities to rub shoulders with the rich and famous. And for those of you who are married, you should be careful that your spouse is not seduced by wealthy individuals who are out to only have a good time.

South Sector Main Door

Main Door	South	Bedroom Sector	South

This section contains the monthly outlook for all 12 months of the year for different bedroom sectors, in a property with a South Sector Main Door.

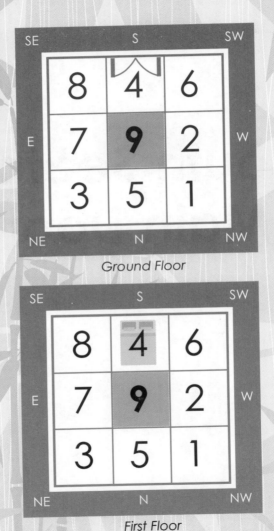

Ground Floor

First Floor

農曆正月 (February 4th - March 4th) 甲寅

The home will be far from a safe haven and refuge from the troubles of the world this month, as most squabbles and tension are likely to arise on the domestic front. There will be a lot of family disputes and issues arising that are likely to trouble you and cause some upheaval in your ties with others. In particular, these disagreements are likely to affect the female occupants more than the others. Relations between married couples are also likely to be strained this month, so you will do well to remember to exercise lots of forbearance and patience.

農曆二月 (March 5th - April 4th) 乙卯

This will be a good month to focus on self-cultivation, as this room bodes well for these pursuits. If you intend on embarking on a course in self-improvement and development, such as physical fitness regimes or motivational seminars and talks, then this would be the ideal room to use in order to enjoy favourable results. If you're likely to be travelling quite a bit this month, then it would be best for you to consider investing in some travel insurance. You might run into a few problems while on the move, and you'll be better able to deal with these issues with some form of protection in place.

農曆三月 (April 5th - May 4th) 丙辰

This will be a good month to get studious! All things related to academics and scholarly activities will enjoy favourable luck, so if you're sitting for important examinations or writing theses, and other such activities along those lines, then you would do well to use this room. Writers and literary types who want to put out new work and receive a favourable response will find this the ideal month to look around for publishers and agents. Travel activities will also allow you to reap benefits, as it will be a good time to expand your business or forge new alliances and partnerships.

農曆四月 (May 5th - June 5th) 丁巳

Couples who use this room will find that the air is heavy with tension and discord this month. Strained relations could lead to frequent disagreements or quarrels. One way to deal with it would be to travel together to another place, as travelling will help to dissipate some of the tension. Those of you in the financial and literary fields will find that you're able to bring to fruition many of your deals that are based abroad. The benefits of these deals are two-fold, as you'll also be able to cement your reputation and status through these negotiations in addition to reaping the financial benefits.

Main Door	South	Bedroom Sector	South

農曆五月 (June 6th - July 6th) 戊午

To prevent yourself from sustaining huge financial losses that could severely set you back, avoid getting into gambling, or any speculative financial activities. In line with that, you should also avoid getting into any property deals or investment, either, as the results could be far from good. Females using this room should consult their gynecologists this month to ensure that there are no unexpected complications or troubles. Married couples are likely to face quite a bit of tension and disagreements this month, so be patient with each other.

農曆六月 (July 7th - August 6th) 己未

Married couples using this room might find themselves walking on eggshells this month, as the likelihood of the female partner being argumentative is high. As a result, she is also most likely to bear the burden of the constant disagreements and may suffer as a result. Those of you who need to embark on any travel trips should take the necessary precautions and invest in a good insurance policy, as the chances for negligence or accidents while travelling are rather high.

農曆七月 (August 7th - September 7th) 庚申

It's a good month for relationship ties in general, and those using this room will find it especially beneficial to consolidate both personal and professional relationships. If it's the latter, don't hesitate to strike up deals or negotiate pacts that will merge both parties closer together, as this will only work in your favour. Where personal relationships are concerned, it will be a good time to make romantic relationships official, or even take the next step and put marriage plans in place. You'll also find that opportunities to travel might actually boost your reputation and stature this month, putting your name in bright lights in whatever industry or field that you're in!

農曆八月 (September 8th - October 7th) 辛酉

More room to breathe – literally and figuratively! – is what is needed among couples using this room this month, and you'll find your relationship improving by leaps and bounds. You'll be inclined to be more tolerant of each other, and accepting of each other's quirks and flaws, when there is more breathing room between the partners. However, where finances are concerned, there will be huge financial losses, especially if you decide to dabble in gambling and speculative investments. This might be a time to keep your wallets firmly in your bags and pockets! Individuals who own businesses, or entrepreneurs in general, will want to ensure that they keep to the straight and narrow at this point in time. Don't try to take shortcuts by involving yourself in illegal deals, as otherwise this could backfire in a bad way and result in some serious legal implications for you.

農曆九月 (October 8th - November 6th) 壬戌

This is a good month to pack your bags and take off on a jet-setting trip around the world – or even to at least one other destination! It also bodes well for your travel activities, so if you've been itching to go on a holiday or on a trip, this is the right time to do so. Your travel trips are likely to go well, and you're bound to gain quite a bit from your travels as well. It's a month of growth and happiness for couples who use this room, and those of you in long-term relationships will find your ties growing warmer, closer, and more intimate. If you're a part of a serious relationship and would like to take things further, then make the most of this month and use this room to derive its positive benefits. However, for women who are pregnant, you would be better off not using this room for the duration of this month.

農曆十月 (November 7th - December 6th) 癸亥

It will be good to tap into the energies of this bedroom this month, especially if you wish to consolidate both your personal and professional relationships. However, be mindful of the fact that any negative structures present outside this sector may bring about problems in your relationships, particularly romantic relationships. Academic endeavours will not go over very well this month, either. Don't use this room if you are due to write your exams anytime soon.

農曆十一月 (December 7th 2018 - January 4th 2019) 甲子

This is a month to be more patient with your partner or spouse. Giving each other breathing space will be necessary, as there is a risk that this will prove to be a trying month for your relationship. Management consultants and real estate and property professionals should, however, find the energies of the South conducive enough to net them substantial financial gains. Those of you who are writers and want to get your work published will also find this sector useful for the month.

農曆十二月 (January 5th - February 3rd 2019) 乙丑

Ailing folk, especially ladies, should be more mindful of their health this month, as health problems come to the fore, especially respiratory ones. Spine injuries are also likely. Consult your physician at the first sign of trouble and don't let illness accumulate. You also need to prioritise safety at work, especially if your job entails handling knives, sharp instruments or heavy machinery on a regular basis. Married men may have some trouble with their spouses this month, so lay low and don't fan the flames of discord!

| Main Door | South | Bedroom Sector | Southeast |

SE | S | SW

8	4	6
7	**9**	2
3	5	1

E | | W

NE | N | NW

農曆正月 (February 4th - March 4th) 甲寅

Couples who work hard at their relationship will be rewarded with a harmonious month, even though there may be a few arguments to occasionally disrupt the peace. The best advice would be to exercise forbearance and refuse to give in to emotional mood swings. Windfall gains are possible this month so look to realise these profits in your portfolio but it is important that you put the money in the bank, rather than let it slip through your fingers. On the health front, lung infections could be a possible risk if you use this bedroom.

農曆二月 (March 5th - April 4th) 乙卯

If you are in the banking industry, you can look forward to an increase in your salary package this month due to the hard work that you put in that is finally noticed by your superiors. However, this may be a lonely month for females using this bedroom. If you're a professional sportsperson, this will be the ideal month to display your talents and skills to the world as others will sit up and take notice.

農曆三月 (April 5th - May 4th) 丙辰

Speculative property investments will give high returns this month, especially if you are in the entertainment business. Therefore, pay attention to the ways you can make this work. In terms of health, stomach-related ulcers and back pain will be a problem for you, especially if you use this room this month. Relationships will be strained this month and no important decisions about the future should be taken at this point.

農曆四月 (May 5th - June 5th) 丁巳

Do not let superiors take advantage of you and end up making gains at your expense. You will need to watch your back and safeguard your own interests. Be more cautious with what you share and with whom. If you're in management and consulting, you will do well to expand your businesses this month, as both profits and clients abound. Improved health is in the cards so if you are in need of recovery or recuperation from a health ailment, then try to use this bedroom this month.

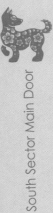

| Main Door | South | Bedroom Sector | Southeast |

農曆五月 (June 6th - July 6th) 戊午

Don't be too easily swayed by any romantic interludes you encounter this month. Chances are, these will only turn out to be short-term flings – no matter how passionate things may appear at the start! Be realistic about your expectations. Look forward instead to being rewarded for your diligent efforts at work, in the form of a promotion and salary increment. Indeed, this promises to be a month of good tidings, celebrations and happy events for those using this bedroom.

農曆六月 (July 7th - August 6th) 己未

Wealth Luck smiles upon you this month, although you'll need to be both diligent and persevering to enjoy the fruits of your labour at the end of the day. In fact, there will be substantial profits to be made by investing in long-term real estate or property deals. Just ensure that these are viable and proceed carefully. Watch out for disputes with your partner or spouse as well, and deal with any tacky situation swiftly and tactfully to prevent it from getting out of hand.

農曆七月 (August 7th - September 7th) 庚申

If you're in the logistics or the travel industry, you will find that you have improved profits this month! Couples using this bedroom will have a happy month together. If you're keen to start a new family, then this will be a good month to begin trying. Bladder-related ailments will be a problem to those using this bedroom this month, so see your doctor if you suspect an infection.

農曆八月 (September 8th - October 7th) 辛酉

Competitive athletes will find their performance during tournaments surpassing even their own expectations this month. What's more, salaried workers will be able to rise to positions of power and authority in their respective careers. You only need to be careful of jealous rivals who are out to undermine you. The energies of the Southeast spell success, achievements and financial gains, although if you're using this sector you may experience a feeling of loneliness or isolation.

農曆九月 (October 8th - November 6th) 壬戌

You are advised to adopt a more conservative approach to your investments and wealth management techniques to preserve your wealth. This appears to be a relatively 'lethargic' month, when progress will be slow. Hence, if you're a manager or boss you should instead focus on motivating your staff in order to boost their morale for the months ahead. In addition, those using this bedroom will be susceptible to bone and joint pains this month. See your doctor if you feel something's amiss.

農曆十月 (November 7th - December 6th) 癸亥

For couples, you will need to pay extra effort in maintaining your relationship. Generally it will be a positive month despite some occasional arguments. Additionally, there will also be the prospect of making a big difference in your pockets this month as there is a prediction of you making a huge profit. This should be the time for you to embark on some market research and craft new strategies to enhance your portfolio. Always remember that it's important for you to re-invest. In terms of health, there will be possible lung infection.

農曆十一月 (December 7th 2018 - January 4th 2019) 甲子

Individuals using this bedroom should be careful of sprains, bone injuries or arthritis. It is extremely important for you to prevent it from happening by taking the necessary medication or prevention methods. If you find something amiss, immediately consult your doctor, especially when you're caught in physical trauma of sorts. You should also be careful with sharp metal objects as those items could lead to you getting hurt or injured. While business may seem slow to pick up this month, do not be afraid to take on risky changes for the greater good of the company.

農曆十二月 (January 5th - February 3rd 2019) 乙丑

Individuals in the entertainment industry will enjoy high profit this month, from speculative property investments. In terms of health, you might find yourself suffering from abdominal ulcers or lower back pains – so be sure to see the doctor regularly – prevention is better than cure! As for relationships, tension will be high this month. Couples are warned from making any big decisions at this month.

Main Door	South	Bedroom Sector	East

農曆正月 (February 4th - March 4th) 甲寅

Individuals in the legal and judicial fields will do well this month, and they will also see some recognition and advancement at the workplace. For others, they will find that this is a somewhat challenging month, as rivalries intensify and competition becomes strong. This will affect both employers and employees, and put a damper on the morale. It will be important to keep an eye on the future and see the bigger picture. The green-eyed monster rules the roost in the domestic sphere this month, and as a result, you're likely to be knee-deep in fights and quarrels as a result. Keep your relationship free of suspicion and finger-pointing as much as possible.

農曆二月 (March 5th - April 4th) 乙卯

Words said and words misunderstood will be the general theme this month, as misunderstandings are rife and relationships are likely to be a little tense as a result. This applies to both personal and professional ties, so you might want to be a little careful with what you say and how you convey your message. Negative forms or features located outside this particular sector and room will negatively affect any of your business dealings, as legal tussles are likely to be the result of it. But, in general, you will need to be sensitive and attuned to all the legal details in all of your business deals this month, because otherwise you're liable to face some problematic issues in the future.

農曆三月 (April 5th - May 4th) 丙辰

You'll have to guard against jealousy creeping into your relationships this month, or it could result in a lot of painful arguments. If you're able to put things into perspective and exercise a lot more patience, things will go smoothly for you. You should avoid using this room as a study, as there could be sudden disruptions that might cause your examination results to go in an entirely different direction than you had hoped. Possible gossip or rumours might plague the people using this room, resulting in a loss of reputation or credibility. Endeavour to keep your head above water and avoid doing anything that will cause further speculation.

農曆四月 (May 5th - June 5th) 丁巳

Stress and turbulent emotions might be the hallmarks of this month, but travelling about this month will help you enhance your reputation. Your public image will receive a much-welcomed boost. If you're working in a legal capacity, or in a legal advisory of any sort, your services will be much needed this month – all signs point to business booming for you!

農曆五月 (June 6th - July 6th) 戊午

You might find it difficult to keep the true fires of love burning brightly if you're using this room this month. Short-lived romance may be one of the things you have to deal with. However, if you're a salaried employee and on a secure payroll, don't just wait for the cheque to come in at the end of the month. This is a good time to go scouring about for some opportunities to make extra side income. Finances are looking good in general, and if you've made property investments earlier, you're likely to see the gains.

農曆六月 (July 7th - August 6th) 己未

Health issues are of primary importance this month, so try to make your own well-being a priority. The possibility of limb injuries is high, and you may also experience some food poisoning issues. Also, get your blood checked to make sure nothing is amiss. Where work is concerned, those of you in the travel and communication industries will find this a bumper month in terms of increased status. You'll enjoy enhanced status and recognition in your field, and will likely also see promotions and advancements in your career.

農曆七月 (August 7th - September 7th) 庚申

As much as possible, you need to reign in the party animal in you this month and spend some quiet time at home. Too much time spent at bars and nightclubs will only invite unwanted trouble into your life at this point. However, you do require the center stage spot at this point in time – where your career is concerned. Any publicity you get as a result of the work you do will result in strong career advancement, so don't shy away from the limelight where your job's concerned! Females using this room, in particular those who invest in enterprises and businesses located abroad will profit well from it – enough to make some sustainable financial gains!

農曆八月 (September 8th - October 7th) 辛酉

Money is coming in this month – specifically through opportunities made and realised through real estate. However, it doesn't come easy, as misunderstandings and quarrels are likely to plague you before you're able to see the gains. Where your work or business is concerned, you're able to make some financial profits by attracting new clientele and customers to your enterprise. But you need to be ambitious and strong, as the only way to attract new people is to take on your competitors headfirst. Children and young people using this room will do well in their studies, as the sudden changes brought upon them in their work will benefit and help them to obtain the results they want in their examinations.

農曆九月 (October 8th - November 6th) 壬戌

They say if you've got it, flaunt it, but you're better off keeping your extra wealth under wraps this month! There is a risk of robbery and theft for those using this room, so it's best to keep a low profile where money matters are concerned. Your relationships are rife with emotional undertones this month, so you'll be better off having a clear head about matters at hand. Separate reason from emotion and don't confuse your feelings with the issues you're facing.

農曆十月 (November 7th - December 6th) 癸亥

Rumour-mongering and politics will be on the increase this month and it would be advisable for you to distance yourself from this problem. It is likely to end in legal issues for those involved. Those who are ill should be careful of lung problems this month, as it could develop into cancer if there is a negative structure outside of this sector. Power struggles for authority at work will intensify, usually with unpleasant outcomes, so you will do well to play it cool and lay low.

農曆十一月 (December 7th 2018 - January 4th 2019) 甲子

Arguments and disputes within the workplace abound, and those involved should try to keep away from these issues especially if they are in the construction business. There will be a vast amount of negative publicity involving those in the professional sporting arena resulting from misunderstandings and miscommunication. If you're a business owner, robbery and theft will plague your business this month, so you will need to establish better audit checks to curb this tendency.

農曆十二月 (January 5th - February 3rd 2019) 乙丑

Those in the media and publishing industries will find that investments made this month will be profitable from the start but make sure that all legal issues are in place. Misunderstandings will drive a rift between couples this month, so if you're the other half, ensure you do your bit by communicating honestly instead of stifling grievances and letting it erupt later. Sudden problems will arise this month but these problems should be handled carefully as it could get out of hand and may eventually need the involvement of lawyers.

| Main Door | South | Bedroom Sector | Northeast |

農曆正月 (February 4th - March 4th) 甲寅

Speculative investments, especially in the futures market, will lead to profits. This is a month where you can afford to play around with your money! If you're in merchant banking or equity dealing, you'll be able to negotiate some favourable deals and strike a good profit. Couples using this bedroom will need to be discreet and tolerant of each other, as disputes and arguments will be prominent this month. If there's nothing nice to say, then you're better off not saying anything! You may suffer a loss of income through legal issues caused by financial problems this month – so be on guard and be careful!

農曆二月 (March 5th - April 4th) 乙卯

If you're in the legal field, you will do well financially this month, but bear in mind that you won't be seeing the money and rewards for your efforts immediately. These can only be claimed at a later date. There is a heightened increase in risk of robberies and theft this month. Those who want to change careers or who want to start new businesses should do so this month, because the opportunities will be there and the results are likely to be good.

農曆三月 (April 5th - May 4th) 丙辰

Clarity of thought will favour those who need to make important decisions this month, so those of you facing big decisions needn't be overly worried! Just be calm and consider your options without too much of an emotional to-do, and you're likely to reach a conclusion easily. If you're involved in business, hostile takeovers from rivals and enemies are possible; so you need to be prepared with some retaliatory plans. Be ready for some fierce competition and be ready to fight back! Romantic interludes should be avoided this month, as it will only bring about trouble and heartache.

農曆四月 (May 5th - June 5th) 丁巳

Bite your tongue, and you may just save yourself a world of potential trouble by doing so. This is not the month to fly off the rails and give in to your emotional outbursts! Also, see if you can delay or postpone any major business decisions to a more favourable period, because otherwise they're all likely to go wrong. If you're feeling sick and unwell, then using this room will only make your condition worse – so see if there's a chance for you to move into another room temporarily.

South Sector Main Door

農曆五月 (June 6th - July 6th) 戊午

Professionals in the engineering and technical fields will find their skills and talents recognised by their bosses and superiors, resulting in a possible promotion and salary increment for them. This is definitely good news for you! But for those of you in the position of an employer and a boss, don't be too surprised or overwhelmed if you find your employees seemingly working against each other. They could just lack a clear sense of direction and a sense of purpose! This is when you need to step in and set some clear guidelines. Those of you using this room will also find your emotions a little too close to the surface this month. If you slip into depression and find yourself overwhelmed, don't hesitate to seek help from another – or even to consider professional help and therapy to get you back on your feet.

農曆六月 (July 7th - August 6th) 己未

Recognition and praise could come your way at work, with bouquets instead of brickbats thrown at you! With this recognition there exists a chance to get promoted, and to have your status and authority at the workplace also strengthened. Don't be too modest – you've done your work and you deserve your time to shine, so step forward accordingly. Parents might have to deal with difficult, rebellious sons if their sons are using this room. A change of rooms might restore peace to the household and calm their rebellious natures.

農曆七月 (August 7th - September 7th) 庚申

It would be best to avoid making important business decisions this month if you sleep in this room, because disputes are possible – particularly those born in the Year of the Goat. Along with this comes the possibility of slander, as well. Those in business should toe a conservative line this month, because if you risk stepping out of line, a possible demotion is what will greet your efforts! It will be best for you to play by the rules and consider attempting any risks only in the future. Couples using this bedroom this month must be patient and tolerant with each other, especially since both of them will be listening to others instead of each other.

農曆八月 (September 8th - October 7th) 辛酉

If you own or run a business, be super vigilant of rivals posing as allies, because this will result in losses for their enterprise. Sketchy individuals will be heading your way this month, so exercise skepticism and always be on guard. Couples should make an effort in their relationships this month, as well. Neglecting your other half could result in poachers honing in on your territory! In other words, don't neglect to pay attention to your partner, or you might find others are more than willing to step into your shoes. Newfound fame and enhanced reputation will bring an increase in wealth for those in the literary and creative arts fields.

農曆九月 (October 8th - November 6th) 壬戌

Those in the analytical, research, statistical, or scientific fields will benefit from the good energies of this sector and find breakthroughs in their line of work. What seemed mired in uncertainty before, will now seem crystal clear! If you're in the mining and construction industries, then you will find this to be a good month to make inroads into your competitors' markets. If you're reluctant to implement the changes that are required in your line of work, you'll find this an immensely challenging month indeed. It's best to adapt to the new requirements and exercise your creative-thinking muscles.

農曆十月 (November 7th - December 6th) 癸亥

Be forewarned that the presence of any negative features outside this bedroom will cause the individuals of this sector to be particularly prone to head injuries this month. If you're using this room, be extremely cautious when using sharp, metal implements as well. However, if you're a merchant banker or equity dealer you will find this month fairly profitable, during which you will be able to generate more income thanks to favourable and profitable deals.

農曆十一月 (December 7th 2018 - January 4th 2019) 甲子

Elder men using this bedroom may find their health failing, with a possible emergency surgery required to solve matters. Vigilance and a close monitoring of the health will be needed to put into action. Similarly, if you work with heavy or dangerous machinery on a regular basis, you should prioritise your safety to minimise the risk of meeting with an accident at the workplace. Employers should also monitor their staff closely, as there's a possibility of dishonest employees attempting to defraud them.

農曆十二月 (January 5th - February 3rd 2019) 乙丑

If you're an employer or manager, there is a risk of employees are out to short-change or defraud you this month, so ensure that the necessary security procedures are in place and conduct regular audits. What's more, rivals and competitors will also do their best to prevent you from getting that promotion you deserve and thus using this bedroom means that you'll be setting yourself up for a fall this month. Domestic problems will be also be a likelihood. This is in part due to financial disputes and issues amongst family members.

South Sector Main Door

農曆正月 (February 4th - March 4th) 甲寅

Couples using this room for this month will find their relationship ties somewhat strained, and testy at points. Even seemingly normal and ordinary arguments could get blown out of proportion. If using another room is unlikely, then bear this mind and avoid getting into any serious discussions this month. Those of you who are business owners and managers in the tourism, travel, and media industries will also find it to be tough. You'll have some trouble meeting your sales targets. Health-wise, bladder and kidney problems should be anticipated.

農曆二月 (March 5th - April 4th) 乙卯

Be on guard for fire hazards this month and check out all the electrical wiring in your home. If you run a company, try not to focus so much on creating profits and boosting your financial standing. You have more important things to look into and that includes ensuring that your employees are satisfied. Focus on building team morale, because if that is flagging, no amount of planning can take your company further.

農曆三月 (April 5th - May 4th) 丙辰

High-risk investment deals are a no-no for this month as well. The results could be bad, and this is especially true where property deals are concerned. It would be best to stake your bets on this another time. If you own a business, don't think about expansion at this point. Instead, seek to consolidate your position and use it to leverage new connections. There will be a time in the future to make things bigger than they are.

農曆四月 (May 5th - June 5th) 丁巳

Couples will continue to have problems in their relationship. Your best bet is to prevent these from becoming serious full-fledged arguments. Be objective in evaluating each problem, and don't let your emotions take the reign. If it seems like solving certain issues in your life feels like you're beating your head against the wall, then take a step back and relax. Not every problem needs to be solved immediately. Some solutions will come to you with patience, in time.

| Main Door | South | Bedroom Sector | North |

農曆五月 (June 6th - July 6th) 戊午

You might find your kidneys, or your eyes, acting up this month. Get the problem checked out immediately. Don't prolong it or the repercussions could be bad. Those of you in relationships should be prepared for an inevitable chill in your ties as a result of using this room. Try to find ways to infuse some warmth and closeness in your interactions with each other. If you're a CEO or a director of your company, the lack of motivation among your employees should be the key problem that you try to solve this month. This should take priority over other strategic and business implementations you might have planned.

農曆六月 (July 7th - August 6th) 己未

Any health issues this month, even seemingly minor ones, should be thoroughly checked out. Don't put off going to the doctor if you have, or you'll have to pay for your oversights later on – and the consequences could be serious. Better to be safe than sorry. Pregnant women should avoid using this room for the month, or complications could arise. You will also stand to lose some in property dealings, so if something seems too risky then it's better to avoid it altogether.

農曆七月 (August 7th - September 7th) 庚申

Financial losses are still quite possible for this month, so it's best to toe the line and avoid risking anything. That means speculative financial investments are a big no-no! Gambling is another high-risk activity that you'll do best to avoid. You'll find yourself having to beat down tough competition this month, which will leave you feeling drained of energy. Try not to drown your sorrows in alcohol, if you can help it. Drinking too much this month could result in casual relationships with less than casual outcomes! So be on guard, and try to be on your best behaviour to ride out the stress of this month.

農曆八月 (September 8th - October 7th) 辛酉

There is trouble in paradise this month for those of you who are in relationships and marriages. Be careful that small arguments and disputes don't turn into something nasty and serious. Lay low if you have to. You'll find that your employees, if you run a business or corporation, to be less than helpful this month. So if need be, avoid scheduling major projects and tasks that require their serious collaboration and input. This would be a better time to go at it alone.

農曆九月 (October 8th - November 6th) 壬戌

Again, this is another month to avoid risky transactions. This is especially true where property deals are concerned. You'll stand a chance to lose money, rather than gain it. You might also want to avoid diving into anything new this month, as the chances of it enjoying success are slim to none. It would also be a good idea to avoid this room if you're feeling generally listless and poor of health, as the energies present here could exacerbate the issue. This is particularly true if you're having gastrointestinal issues.

農曆十月 (November 7th - December 6th) 癸亥

Scholars and academics will find their reputation greatly enhanced this month. If you're in this field, it will be a good month to publish your papers and research, and make a mark in the world! Business partners, however, need to look out for any tension or cracks in their partnership, which could lead to both parties suffering from financial losses. And if you've been feeling sickly of late, then this sector is definitely not the best sector to use this month, as you could end up aggravating your condition.

農曆十一月 (December 7th 2018 - January 4th 2019) 甲子

Investments should be avoided, as these could bring about huge amounts of losses if it goes awry, and there's plenty of chance for that happening this month. This promises to be a rollercoaster sort of month, where stress may eventually take its toll on your health and emotions, if left unchecked. Those in the explosives or any other industry involving fire or inflammable chemicals, need to guard against business losses, as well. In general, take things easy and try to play it safe.

農曆十二月 (January 5th - February 3rd 2019) 乙丑

This month, expectant mothers need to watch out for pregnancy complications, and where possible, refrain from using this bedroom this month. It would also be advisable to avoid all real estate investments, as they may well burn a huge hole in your finances, if things go wrong. If you own or run a business, it's time to concentrate on core affairs instead of embarking on ambitious expansion schemes.

| Main Door | South | Bedroom Sector | Northwest |

農曆正月 (February 4th - March 4th) 甲寅

There will be career advancements for those in the transportation industry. They will receive the promotion that they have been hoping for. Those in the entertainment industry should seek opportunities for career advancement this month, as their passion and excitement will get them ready for something new. Those who work in the 'hands-on' industry will find this is a good month for them, as there are many benefits to be had.

農曆二月 (March 5th - April 4th) 乙卯

If you're involved in the real estate industry, then this would be a good month for you to consider some sound investment opportunities. If you're single and looking for some romance this month, then this would indeed be the room to use! If you're into professional sports and athletics or work with machinery, it will be good for you to take advantage of the opportunities at your disposal.

農曆三月 (April 5th - May 4th) 丙辰

Be careful not to drink and drive this month or you could get into an accident while on the road. This room doesn't bode well for relationships this month, either, as the likelihood of these ties ending badly and causing a dent to your reputation is quite strong. At work, you'll have some personal battles as well – colleagues who are jealous of your success and envious of you will not hide their need to compete. Don't play into their hand, or else you'll get sucked into a vicious game that will leave no winners.

農曆四月 (May 5th - June 5th) 丁巳

Go all out in striking foreign deals this month, because the outcome will be profitable. Don't stick to your usual network of connections this month; consider expanding to include people from abroad, as well, in order to incur some benefits. Go all out there and be visible – this is not the time to be a wallflower! Politicians will find that they enjoy a favourable month, leading to good support from the grassroots that can propel their careers forward.

Main Door	South	Bedroom Sector	Northwest

農曆五月 (June 6th - July 6th) 戊午

If you're a business owner, progress is likely to be slow or even stagnant this month. Don't beat your head against the wall trying to move past the obstacles; instead, just use this month as a cushion and lie low, while finding ways to consolidate your position. It will be of no use to you to consider ploughing ahead when the time is not right. You may be a little fragile where health is concerned; watch out especially for your lungs. Head injuries are also possible.

農曆六月 (July 7th - August 6th) 己未

For this month, this room bodes well for Academic Luck. If you're a student using this room for studies, you'll find that it will benefit you when you sit for any examinations this month. Any deals located abroad or in other countries will need to be concluded and closed this month, especially if it involves some form of asset acquisition. This room also bodes well to further your romantic ties, and it is appropriate for furthering relationship ties – however, this will only work if there is no natural water in this sector.

農曆七月 (August 7th - September 7th) 庚申

Couples who use this room might run into a spot of romantic trouble this month. If your relationship is strained and tense, don't give in to your temptation to be short with your words and hurtful with your actions. Instead, it would be better for you to be more tolerant and understanding of each other. If you're involved in the furniture business, you will find that profits will pour in! Generally, those using this room should be circumspect in behaviour and speech, as there is a good chance that lawsuits might haunt you, and people will talk about you behind your back. Don't give them fodder for gossip; keep a low profile.

農曆八月 (September 8th - October 7th) 辛酉

Expectant women should avoid using this room for the month, as miscarriages could result. In general, if you're in poor health or feeling unwell and frail, avoid this room altogether, otherwise you will be prone to illnesses. Marital tension is rife for couples using this room. Be more tolerant of each other, as no one is perfect and every person comes bundled with a package of flaws. The more you strive to understand each other, the stronger your relationship will be – and the chances of being bothered by trivial differences will lessen.

農曆九月 (October 8th - November 6th) 壬戌

Generally, this will be a favourable month for most. Relationships will go well, and you will do well where your career is concerned. All that you need to succeed and make inroads at work is already in you; so use your knowledge, wisdom, and unique talents to get ahead. Be proactive in doing this, and take the initiative, and the results will be in your favour! This is an especially good month for Gua 6 individuals to highlight and showcase their own talents.

農曆十月 (November 7th - December 6th) 癸亥

Couples using this bedroom will see an improvement in marital relationships this month. Show off your true talents and abilities at work, as superiors will finally notice you and give you the promotion you deserve. Those negotiating or planning to conclude new deals should do so now, as these are likely to come out in your favour.

農曆十一月 (December 7th 2018 - January 4th 2019) 甲子

If you're trying to climb the corporate ladder, you should make use of the good energies in this bedroom. This is because it's a good month for you to achieve favourable results. For couples, it will be positive for those using this bedroom this month – they can expect closer ties and a harmonious environment. Business expansion is also rather auspicious this month as your staff will prove to be most supportive of your endeavours.

農曆十二月 (January 5th - February 3rd 2019) 乙丑

Amateurs who are considering entering the professional arena should launch their careers now but should be careful of being cheated or manipulated. Be wary of anyone who seems to be taking you for a ride! This is a competitive month at work, with office politics at their height. Avoid getting involved in any of it, as you are certain to end up losing if you take on your rivals at this point in time. Health is weak this month for older men using this bedroom, particularly for those with weak lungs.

Main Door	South	Bedroom Sector	West

農曆正月 (February 4th - March 4th) 甲寅

Domestic disharmony might be the theme for the month, as you'll find yourself mired in arguments with your family members more frequently. You'll need to exercise greater patience and tolerance. Try not to dwell only on the negative side of things and see the good side of everyone even when in the midst of an argument. If you're a student using this room and you're taking examinations this month, your results might not be favourable – you might want to consider temporarily using another room. In general, confusion reigns for this period of time and you'll find it difficult to make important decisions.

農曆二月 (March 5th - April 4th) 乙卯

Those of you embarking in new relationships this month should not take things seriously, as you may be putting in more hope than is necessary. Things may not be what they seem, and after awhile the real situation will shine through. The females in this house might tend to be stubborn and foolish, which means that you shouldn't make important decisions this month. Otherwise, you risk looking back on these decisions later and wondering why on earth you made them!

農曆三月 (April 5th - May 4th) 丙辰

If you're in real estate and property development, you're likely to find this a good month to make beneficial property investments. The gains will be profitable. If you've been gunning for a promotion or seeking to be elevated to a higher position in society, then this could be a very fulfilling month for you. You'll be able to attain and realise your expectations and goals. Those of you with heart and eye problems will find that these problems will aggravate you this month.

農曆四月 (May 5th - June 5th) 丁巳

If there are elderly ladies using this room in your house this month, they will have to pay close attention to their health. This is particularly so because they are susceptible to gastrointestinal ailments and illnesses that can lead to more serious and major problems if left untreated. If you're living with your in-laws, this is a month for you to maintain your distance. Even if you don't live in the same household, try to minimise your contact with them, as your interactions will be frosty.

South Sector Main Door

農曆五月 (June 6th - July 6th) 戊午

You'll find disagreements and arguments rife this month, and if you get too carried away and become trapped in these quarrels – legal problems are what you're likely to face! You may also find yourself entangled in arguments with your spouse or partner. Bearing this in mind, it will be best to bite your tongue more often than not, than to give in to the temptation of saying exactly what you feel! For those of you who have outstanding fines and summonses, especially traffic-related ones, clear them up this month or the law could catch up with you sooner than you think! This applies to your tax returns as well.

農曆六月 (July 7th - August 6th) 己未

This is a difficult month for those of you in merchant banking, shares, and stock trading, as your deals will sometimes fall flat. Your profits will start to dwindle, as a result, and cause some serious losses. In general, this is not a good month for you to get involved in financial markets at all, as sustaining heavy losses might be the only result that arises out of this. Women who use this room should be careful of illnesses and accidents, which could lead to some grave consequences.

農曆七月 (August 7th - September 7th) 庚申

If you're working in the media, consulting and marketing industries, you'll find that investing in property will actually lead to profits. Make the most of this favourable time to do so. If by chance, you find yourself having to spend more time with your in-laws this month, you will face an increased risk of arguments and tension. To prevent unwanted conflicts, it might be better to just take a holiday or use alternative accommodation. Where health is concerned, women are more likely to suffer from gastrointestinal problems. Don't ignore these problems and hope that it will go away, as it will only become worse with time.

農曆八月 (September 8th - October 7th) 辛酉

If your work involves logistics or strategy and deduction in any way, you will find this month to be quite challenging. As such, if you're looking to hire fresh minds, it might be best to defer this to a more favourable time in the future. Hiring new people now could result in getting the stubborn and less-intelligent (even idle) employees who could only cause you more losses than gains. If you're single and on the lookout, then this is the month when romance could strike from Cupid's bow! Make an effort to expand your social circle and meet new people.

農曆九月 (October 8th - November 6th) 壬戌

If you find yourself of weak and in poor health of late, don't just hope for the symptoms to go away. It would be better for you in the long run to get it checked out sooner rather than later. If you're thinking of making some additional income through investment ventures, you can do no better than going into real estate this month. You're likely to see some good profits as a result. If you're a married woman, however, it will behoove you to have your guard up! There are sweet-talking wealthy men about who would only want to use you for their own gains, so don't be easily swayed or smitten.

農曆十月 (November 7th - December 6th) 癸亥

This is not an ideal bedroom to use, especially if you're trying to conceive. In fact, it will only bring about more complications for you and your spouse. In terms of personal space, if your house is fairly old in years in terms of building structure, then you might want to have a qualified electrician check the wiring to negate the risk of a fire hazard this month. At the workplace, matters will be somewhat tense with jealousy and unhealthy rivalry, especially amongst certain female colleagues, causing chaos and problems.

農曆十一月 (December 7th 2018 - January 4th 2019) 甲子

If you're in real estate and property development, you could find yourself gaining recognition and being promoted this month. However, in your personal life, this is potentially a month of mental instability, so if you suffer from depression, then the situation could be exacerbated if you use this bedroom this month. If there are negative structures outside this sector, then there is as strong possibility of car accidents occurring this month so be extra careful when you're on the road.

農曆十二月 (January 5th - February 3rd 2019) 乙丑

As a reminder of the previous month, rivals, subordinates and colleagues are looking to undermine you this month. You may want to be careful about how much you divulge to certain people about your new ideas and projects. Tread carefully at the workplace and try to keep a low profile. Personal and professional relationships are positive and smooth this month. If you need to change your home, this will be a good month to do so, as you will make some financial gains.

| Main Door | South | Bedroom Sector | Southwest |

農曆正月 (February 4th - March 4th) 甲寅

If you're in the real estate industry, then make the most of the positive energies of this month! Consider investing in some worthy property deals, as you're likely to receive good profits in return. If you're working in the insurance field, you are also likely to expand your business. Business will be good and you'll benefit tremendously from it all. You'll also find yourself battling bouts of depression and dealing with tumultuous emotions and feelings.

農曆二月 (March 5th - April 4th) 乙卯

If you're in the literary and academic fields, this is a good month for you to receive recognition and rewards that can lead to both fame and advancement! This is most definitely a beneficial month in store. Analysts will find this to be an exciting month, as your career will take off as a result of your smart and strategic positioning in the equities market. Partnerships and alliances do well this month, especially for those who invest in their future together.

農曆三月 (April 5th - May 4th) 丙辰

There will be a heightened risk of family discords and tension for this month. Try not to let your emotions be blown about by every wind or you'll risk saying the wrong thing and offending people. Negative structures outside this room during the month indicate a high possibility of the son in the family turning against the father or having some intense disagreements. Where work is concerned, you will find that there is a lot of internal fighting going on, leading to heightened office politics. It would be best to keep your head down and stay out of it. Health-wise, older men using this room should pay attention to any health problems that arise out of blood and lung disease or complications.

農曆四月 (May 5th - June 5th) 丁巳

There are some good news for investment and merchant bankers, as you'll be able to conclude certain deals in the share and equity markets that will bring you good profits. Those of you work a salaried job will finally gain long-awaited respect and accolades from your superiors – which could happily lead to a pay raise or even a promotion. If you're using this room this month, you will be plagued with anxiety. You may be feeling somewhat fragile emotionally and prone to suffering from excessive loneliness. It would be the best time not to retreat from friends and loved ones, but to try to spend more time with them to appease the isolation you feel.

| Main Door | South | Bedroom Sector | Southwest |

農曆五月 (June 6th - July 6th) 戊午

Where health is concerned, elderly people should be on guard against possible kidney ailments. Get yourself checked out early if things seem amiss. Couples who are using this room will also find that they are more prone to arguments and fights. If you're bickering with each other non-stop, then you should take some time away and consider going on a vacation. If you run a business with a partner, you will also find yourself arguing over the slightest thing. It will be a matter of each of you attempting to assert control over the other.

農曆六月 (July 7th - August 6th) 己未

If you've been a hardworking, faithful employee in your company thus far, you'll get your just rewards and benefits this month! Your efforts will not go unrecognised. Those of you who run or manage a company should take it easy on your staff and employees this month, especially if you need to achieve your goals urgently. They will respond better and produce better work, if you take the pressure off of them. If you're a professional sports player, you will find yourself outshining your competitors this month.

農曆七月 (August 7th - September 7th) 庚申

If you're using this room this month, your efforts will go unnoticed by your boss or superiors, in the workplace. A certain feeling of invisibility might creep in, as well. You will have to work harder to obtain the simplest form of acknowledgement. Don't bend over backwards to receive recognition – just roll with it and bear in mind that this time will pass soon. You might want to make an effort to invest in property transactions this month, as there is a chance of making good financial gains. People who use this bedroom this month will find that anxiety, stress and mental pressure, start taking its toll. Make an effort to learn how to distress and relax, otherwise the repercussions will only affect you.

農曆八月 (September 8th - October 7th) 辛酉

If you dabble in speculative investments in equities and stocks, you'll find that this a good month to make some profits from it and enjoy some financial gains. But remember to always resist the urge to shout about your profits to all, as it will be better for you to maintain a low profile. If you're an academic, or involved in the literary field, this will be a great month for bouts of new inspiration and ideas – and better still, these are likely to lead to good financial gains as well. Newly-weds who are using this bedroom will find this month to be conducive for enhancing growth and development.

農曆九月 (October 8th - November 6th) 壬戌

Be extra careful when you're driving and on the road this month. The risk of accidents is particularly high. Don't cut corners and be cautious. Adolescents using this room this month will be particularly fractious and rebellious, and will continue to test the boundaries set by their parents. Parents will have to be particularly patient and unyielding, at the same time! If you work in the engineering industry, you'll find yourself on the good side of your bosses and superiors and a pay raise is entirely possible this month!

農曆十月 (November 7th - December 6th) 癸亥

Those in the manufacturing industry will find this to be a good month with minimal labour disruptions and a generally improved output. Couples wishing to start a family should use the good energies of this sector this month in order to get a positive start. If there are negative forms outside this sector this month, then the older women of the house should be careful of possible mental instability and being emotionally depressed.

農曆十一月 (December 7th 2018 - January 4th 2019) 甲子

Your health and relationship prospects will be good this month, and those involved in the logistics, courier and tourism industries will prosper accordingly as well. What's more, if your job entails strategic decision-making or sound analytical skills, then go ahead and show them what you're made of! That will allow you to carve a reputation for yourself, which in turn, should further brighten your career prospects.

農曆十二月 (January 5th - February 3rd 2019) 乙丑

Couples will have a happier month this month and are likely also do well in their chosen careers. Avoid putting children in this bedroom this month, as they are likely to become rebellious and difficult to control. Employers should be careful with labour relations this month, as workers are likely to be somewhat defiant. As a result, they might be difficult to manage and will be prone to challenging authority.

Southeast Sector
Main Door

This section contains the monthly outlook for all 12 months of the year for different bedroom sectors, in a property with a Southeast Sector Main Door.

Ground Floor

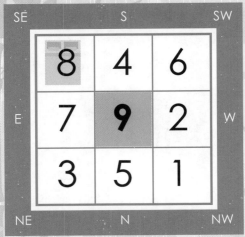

First Floor

農曆正月 (February 4th - March 4th) 甲寅

In terms of relationships, if you are single and looking for a connection you should use this bedroom. If you work in the agricultural industry, you will find your profits much improved, with the presence of new suppliers further boosting business prospects. Bear in mind, though, that health problems in the form of gall bladder and nerve problems threaten to plague those using the West bedroom this month. Seek medical treatment at the first sign of trouble.

農曆二月 (March 5th - April 4th) 乙卯

This month brings lots of success, achievements and financial gains with employees being able to rise to positions of power and authority. This is especially true if you're in the travel industry. Individuals involved in competitive sports will do well in the internal arena this month, especially if travel is involved. If you have investments in property, you should cash in your investments this month to realise the investment profits.

農曆三月 (April 5th - May 4th) 丙辰

If you're a business owner, you'll notice a slowdown this month. As such, employers will be concerned with declining profits and employees will be under greater pressure. Accidents are likely this month so it will be best to be careful when you're up and about and on the move. Property deals abound but not all of these will be profitable so you will need to be astute in your dealings.

農曆四月 (May 5th - June 5th) 丁巳

Do not let your superiors take advantage of you and make gains at your expense. Be circumspect and don't be overly -accommodating or you may find yourself drained of energy and time. Consulting and management businesses should seriously consider expanding their businesses, as it will bring in new clients this month. This is a good month to unbundle your property portfolios (if you have them) because there are generous profits to be made.

Main Door	Southeast	Bedroom Sector	Southeast

農曆五月 (June 6th - July 6th) 戊午

This month, you should focus on academic activities or self-cultivation that is likely to result in personal growth. Think about developing new skills and capabilities; the energies of this sector in this month augur well for such pursuits. Do not make any important business decisions this month, as at best, these will not be in your favour and at worst, these will end in losses. Children should be careful of injuries to the limbs caused by sharp metal objects and implements, particularly if they use this room.

農曆六月 (July 7th - August 6th) 己未

If you're in the real estate and property industries, there is a chance to enjoy some outstanding profits this month. This is especially the case if there is the presence of water in this sector. If you wish to take your relationship to the next level, you should do so this month and make use of the favourable energies of the sector. Older women who use this sector this month should not dismiss minor stomach ailments because these could develop into something more serious.

農曆七月 (August 7th - September 7th) 庚申

This is a good month for those who have taken investment positions in the preceding months or those who work as fund managers in the futures markets to realise their financial gains. If you're in the oil and gas industry, you will make good money this month as financial gains are on the upswing. If you're married and interested in starting a family, the favourable energies of this sector bodes well for you.

農曆八月 (September 8th - October 7th) 辛酉

This is a month of celebration, good news, and happy activities, particularly if you use the Southeast room. You will receive recognition for something you have succeeded in and a promotion is likely as a result. The good vibes for your relationship continue this month and it will be a great time for you to work on improving your communication with each other.

農曆九月 (October 8th - November 6th) 壬戌

If you're in the property and real estate industries, you should be able to benefit from long-term deals this month. This is because many financial opportunities are likely come your way but you will find that you are unable to make use of most of them. So, grab the opportunities when you can. Your relationship may be off to a rocky start this month, but take comfort that the end results will be positive for you and your partner.

農曆十月 (November 7th - December 6th) 癸亥

Have you been eyeing that dream home that recently caught your attention? Then this could be a good month to invest in property so that you could make that dream home a reality. Don't be impatient in concluding other types of deals, as you need all the facts and information at your disposal before you can make the final decision. Salaried employees should be mindful of superiors, who are out to profit at their productivity and expense by exploiting them.

農曆十一月 (December 7th 2018 - January 4th 2019) 甲子

Where possible, postpone all deals to a more suitable period in time as chances are your dealings this month will be less than profitable. In fact, chaos and unexpected changes may plague your business this month, thus resulting in unbudgeted losses. However, stagnant careers and flailing enterprises may still be revived if you're prepared to make drastic changes to your business where necessary.

農曆十二月 (January 5th - February 3rd 2019) 乙丑

Elderly women using this bedroom should guard against acquiring any potentially chronic stomach ailments this month. Seek the advice of your doctor at the first sign of trouble. On the other hand, the energies of the Southeast bode well for those who desire to take their relationship to the next level; so tap into them accordingly, if that's what you seek. Be vigilant for any lucrative property deals headed your way. When opportunity comes a-knocking, seize them at once!

Southeast Sector Main Door

農曆正月 (February 4th - March 4th) 甲寅

In terms of industries, those in the fashion, apparels and cosmetics industries will find this to be a fairly profitable month, as long as they plan their business strategies carefully. This is a good month to embark on your travels, whether for business or pleasure, as you'll find them smooth-sailing and beneficial. In any case, be mindful of any potentially unpleasant situation that could well lead to disagreements amongst the ladies in your household.

農曆二月 (March 5th - April 4th) 乙卯

If you're a full-time salaried worker, you should explore means of making some side income this month, as you stand to benefit from some Indirect Wealth Luck. In other aspects, however, using this room may not be a good idea. If you're looking to enhance your Romance Luck, then try not to use this bedroom this month. Avoid using this sector as well, if you happen to be pregnant and do not wish to encounter any complications during this period.

農曆三月 (April 5th - May 4th) 丙辰

There will be animosity amongst the women of the house this month and it could lead to arguments and disagreements if allowed to get out of hand. If you're a woman, then, you should strive to exercise patience and forbearance in your interpersonal dealings with family. Those of you who work in the media and publishing industries will find that investments made are likely to be profitable from the start.

農曆四月 (May 5th - June 5th) 丁巳

If you're single, do not expect any romantic flings to develop into anything long-term or serious. Instead, just enjoy the moment while it lasts! Career-wise, it's a good month for businesswomen. You will find this to be a favourable month when it comes to concluding deals abroad. You may need to travel, though, to secure your source of revenue. Scrutinise all documents carefully or have your lawyer vet through them. This is so you can prevent running into any legal complications in the future.

| Main Door | Southeast | Bedroom Sector | East |

農曆五月 (June 6th - July 6th) 戊午

If you're studying or sitting for your examinations soon, you will want to use this room. If you're one half of a couple, you will need to be patient with your partner as frayed tempers are likely. That aside, this is a suitable time of the year to widen your customer base and source of revenue, by planning how to attract new customers to your business.

農曆六月 (July 7th - August 6th) 己未

Be selective with your business dealings this month, and only invest in those in which you're fairly certain will bring you the returns expected. Above all, be careful of people out to trick you and watch out for scams. Bear in mind this month that while your reputation, status and public image take a boost, your mental condition is in jeopardy of deteriorating, particularly with the additional stress brought about by overwork and too much travelling.

農曆七月 (August 7th - September 7th) 庚申

If you're a woman and you have investments or businesses abroad, you will find that this is a good month, particularly if you travel to get some deals and negotiations done. In general, any documents that need to be signed this month should be scrutinised carefully or possibly even given to lawyers, as hidden obligations may be involved. Fire hazards will plague your business this month and increased vigilance should be maintained throughout the month to prevent any danger.

農曆八月 (September 8th - October 7th) 辛酉

If you're a scholar or a student, this bedroom will be good to use this month for preparation and helping you focus in your studies or scholarly pursuits. For business owners or entrepreneurs, this is a good month to attract new customers and clients to your business that will in turn give you good financial returns. If you're married and have long wanted to start a family, this room will be a good one to use this month.

農曆九月 (October 8th - November 6th) 壬戌

Retail cash deposits should be made with care, as this is a weak area for the business this month. This is generally a good month for the communications industry and also a good month of enhanced reputation and standing. You should also work hard to improve your reputation if you need to network to get noticed. Men should be careful of women with the gift of the gab who might entice them into uncompromising situations.

農曆十月 (November 7th - December 6th) 癸亥

You'll need to be extra safe on the road this month, as chances of injuries are high. This goes the same for those who work with heavy machineries. Take extra care, especially when you're the running risk of mechanical injuries this month! As for those in sales, you might be tested this month due to miscommunication issues. Try and see things from your client's point of view and also ensure that all messages delivered are clear. Health-wise, those with lung disease should avoid this sector at all costs due to the Negative Sha – if not, this could lead to cancer.

農曆十一月 (December 7th 2018 - January 4th 2019) 甲子

If you're in a relationship, trust issues will develop among you and your partner, if this room is used this month. This could lead to a strained relationship. There will be a lot of miscommunication problems in your daily dealings with work or when it comes to matters related to your business – especially when handling terms of agreements and contracts. Therefore, be cautious and ensure that you spell everything out to prevent any problems later on. You will need get your lawyers to look through the documents or contracts before concluding any business deals this month.

農曆十二月 (January 5th - February 3rd 2019) 乙丑

Females who use this bedroom will find themselves quarreling and arguing with others easily. These unwanted situations mostly involve their in-laws and as such, it is important for them to choose their words carefully. In terms of business, your employee might commit fraud – watch everything they do like a hawk and do not let any shady activities pass you by. For those who are pregnant, you're advised to avoid using this bedroom as there is a strong chance of a miscarriage.

| Main Door | Southeast | Bedroom Sector | Northeast |

農曆正月 (February 4th - March 4th) 甲寅

This is a good month for those in real estate, and this will be your chance to increase property portfolios. There are many money-making opportunities and the achievement of fame and recognition for those who are constantly on their toes this month. So, if you've been working hard, you're likely to get your reward! If you're in marketing, event planning and advertising, you're also in for a bumper month.

農曆二月 (March 5th - April 4th) 乙卯

If you are interested in changing careers or starting a new business, then this is the month to do so, as the changes will bring about good outcomes. Those in the public relations sector will find this to be a difficult month, with a lot of problems coming your way. If you're in the legal field, you will find that your skills are in high demand this month, if you use this bedroom, thus resulting in increased profits.

農曆三月 (April 5th - May 4th) 丙辰

Arguments and disputes, especially regarding finances, may affect the relationship between you and your partner or spouse, this month. You should ensure that emotions don't overpower reason. And if you happen to work with machinery on a regular or daily basis, be sure to prioritise your personal safety. Injuries on the road or while travelling are also a possibility, so ensure that you've all the necessary insurance policies in place and don't be careless with your travel documents.

農曆四月 (May 5th - June 5th) 丁巳

You are strongly advised to stay clear of any speculative investments or gambling activities this month, as the outcome could result in financial loss. If you have been shrewd enough to make substantial financial gains, you should remain discreet and humble about your newfound wealth. Flaunting it could result in some unwanted results. Using this bedroom this month might also make you particularly susceptible to respiratory or auto-immune diseases this month. See a doctor at the first sign of trouble.

Southeast Sector Main Door

農曆五月 (June 6th - July 6th) 戊午

Try not to travel if possible this month, as your journeys will tend to be problematic. Those using this bedroom will also be prone to emotional and psychological disturbances, and this could lead to depression if left unchecked. Nevertheless, there will be good financial prospects for professionals in the literary, arts and other creative fields – with your newfound fame and enhanced reputation contributing to your Wealth Luck.

農曆六月 (July 7th - August 6th) 己未

This is not a favourable month to travel for business, as the journey will be plagued by problems throughout. Therefore, try to take things easy and don't move about so much. If you're a parent, this will be a difficult month particularly if you have a son. If he uses this bedroom, he is liable to be rebellious.

農曆七月 (August 7th - September 7th) 庚申

Avoid all investment opportunities this month as these are likely to turn sour. If this is unavoidable, then all contracts should be carefully scrutinised by a legal team. In terms of health, women using this room should be careful of potential breast lumps and should check with their doctor as soon as possible. If you're in a relationship, you will have to be willing to listen to your partner instead of what others are saying.

農曆八月 (September 8th - October 7th) 辛酉

Newfound fame and an enhanced reputation will bring an increase in wealth, if you're in the literary and creative arts fields. Individuals in the engineering field will have the opportunity to gain prominence this month and this is likely to result in a pay raise. Underhanded tactics are on the increase this month and you would be well advised to be on the lookout for possible fraud and deceit.

農曆九月 (October 8th - November 6th) 壬戌

Personal safety should be made a priority this month, as there is a possibility of being robbed and mugged. A lack of communication will cause problems in relationships, so endeavour to try and be more open with your partner. If you work in the analytical and research fields of technology and science, it's a good month – particularly if you use this room to make headway in your work and professional achievement.

農曆十月 (November 7th - December 6th) 癸亥

Those who trade at markets or manage restaurants will find this to be a financially rewarding month. If you have outstanding fines or taxes owing, you may be in trouble with the law and should pay all outstanding penalties as soon as possible. Illnesses affecting the stomach and intestines will be a significant problem this month.

農曆十一月 (December 7th 2018 - January 4th 2019) 甲子

Mentors and counsellors will find that they are inundated by new clients looking for help and support. Those artistically inclined, especially sculptors and carvers, will find that they attract increased commissions for their work. This is a favourable month for those in the construction industry, especially if they are required to travel to conclude deals.

農曆十二月 (January 5th - February 3rd 2019) 乙丑

A financially challenging month awaits you with betrayals and loss of wealth being very likely. Profits being realised this month should be invested wisely by those who cash in their gains. Good news will come to those who use this bedroom so long as they are involved in travels.

Southeast Sector Main Door

農曆正月 (February 4th - March 4th) 甲寅

This month, try to settle any lawsuits out of court if possible, as a prolonged legal entanglement will only be detrimental to you in the grander scheme of things. Professional relationships won't exactly be favourable for you this month, so tackle every potential issue with your business partners carefully. Expectant mothers are also advised to go for a full medical checkup or consult their gynecologist, if they're using this bedroom, as complications are likely.

農曆二月 (March 5th - April 4th) 乙卯

You may be dismayed to find the stress and pressures of life taking its toll on your relationships this month. Manage your lifestyle carefully, and seek a work-life balance in everything you do. In terms of physical health, look out for eye ailments and the possible risk of a stroke for elderly people if using this bedroom. There is also the risk of a fire hazard this month, particularly with older properties and electrical wiring – so get that checked out.

農曆三月 (April 5th - May 4th) 丙辰

There is a possibility of concluding property deals this month, but as soon as common sense and wisdom is applied, the deals will tend to dry up. In other words, you may need to be quick on the ball and be willing to take a risk this month if you want to see a significant profit. You will also have to be careful of people working against you, as there are rumbles of disloyalty. Students preparing for important examinations should not use this bedroom this month, as it does not bode well for academic pursuits.

農曆四月 (May 5th - June 5th) 丁巳

Watch out for any miscommunication, especially if you specialise in the cell phone or IT industries. This is the time to mitigate the risk of losses due to disputes and misunderstandings. Lawyers and legal professionals will also find it hard to put their cases across, as will those who rely on their vocal abilities/prowess for a livelihood, such as motivational speakers. Don't worry unduly, as this is only a momentary glitch that will right itself soon.

| Main Door | Southeast | Bedroom Sector | North |

農曆五月 (June 6th - July 6th) 戊午

Avoid all investment deals this month, as a significant financial loss is likely. If you're a business owner or manager, you should monitor your employees closely this month as disloyal subordinates could try to undermine your efforts quite frequently. Health-wise, the elderly are particularly prone to head injuries and bone problems this month. Hence, it may be wise to have them undergo a full medical check-up if they happen to be using this bedroom.

農曆六月 (July 7th - August 6th) 己未

Where possible, refrain from embarking on long-distance travel this month. This is indeed an unfavourable time of the year where there will be potential for calamities and mishaps. Therefore, take it easy and just go with the flow. Be resilient and things should sort themselves out, eventually. Maintain a low profile, avoid undertaking anything ambitious or adventurous this month, and you will do just fine.

農曆七月 (August 7th - September 7th) 庚申

Problems will be difficult to rectify this month, as the cause is not easily identifiable. Lawyers will find it tough-going in terms of your career trajectory, as you will find it difficult putting your case across and making a name for yourself. Those in the communications industry should take a back seat with regards to financial investments and business expansion, as this is a very difficult month to gain profits and new prospects.

農曆八月 (September 8th - October 7th) 辛酉

If you're in competitive sports, you'll find competitions an uphill battle this month. Bear in mind also that stress and anxiety might cause some amount of depression and emotional turbulence this month, particularly if you're using this bedroom and there are negative structures outside it. If you're in a new relationship, you should ease off a little this month and give the fires some 'space' to really flare up!

農曆九月 (October 8th - November 6th) 壬戌

This month, any joint ventures or partnerships should be delayed until a more auspicious time. Real estate and property transactions will be unprofitable this month, so it is better to take a low profile until things start to improve. Health problems may include liver and kidney problems, if you're using this bedroom.

農曆十月 (November 7th - December 6th) 癸亥

Avoid gambling this month, as there is a strong possibility of losing property or even your entire fortune! Those in ill health should watch out for kidney problems, especially if they're cancer-related. If you have made profits from investments, it would be wise to cash in on these gains at this point in time.

農曆十一月 (December 7th 2018 - January 4th 2019) 甲子

You may be dismayed to find the stress and pressures of life taking their toll on your relationships this month. Manage your lifestyle carefully and seek a work-life balance in everything you do. Look out as well for eye ailments and the possibility of suffering from a stroke, if you happen to be using this bedroom. Get a qualified electrician to check the wiring and electrical appliances in this sector of your property as well, especially if your premises have been around for quite a while.

農曆十二月 (January 5th - February 3rd 2019) 乙丑

This is not the time to start new ventures or businesses, as the possibility of success is limited. Those of you who are in the property and real estate fields, and are in the know should be able to make quick, beneficial financial gains this month. Mothers and older women will find that their relationships are under strain this month.

Southeast Sector Main Door

SE	S	SW
8	4	6
7	**9**	2
3	5	1
NE	N	NW

農曆正月 (February 4th - March 4th) 甲寅

This is a month to ask for the promotion you wanted especially if you are in the food and beverage or media industries. Be assertive and don't shy away from receiving the recognition and rewards from your work. Business owners in the restaurant business or entertainment industry will see a boom this month. In addition, there might also be a risk of heart- or eye-related problems this month.

農曆二月 (March 5th - April 4th) 乙卯

Business owners will make money and employees will experience career advancement, especially if they are in the oil and gas industry or the mining industry. If you're in the metals, precious stones, and jewellery business, you will also enjoy handsome profits this month. Travelling brings positive benefits, including new investors into the business or even new venture possibilities – so cultivate the opportunity to move around quite a bit.

農曆三月 (April 5th - May 4th) 丙辰

Avoid getting involved in office politics, as you are certain to end up losing if you take on your rivals. It will be best to stay out of the sniping and underhand disloyalty. Health-wise, you will need to watch out for drinking problems this month and it will be best to limit your intake of alcohol overall. If you're married and using this bedroom, jealousy might be a problem you have to deal with.

農曆四月 (May 5th - June 5th) 丁巳

Politicians and those in public service will have a good month enjoying public support this month, and you may even find yourself rising the ranks in the government or within your parties. You will need to network more this month, as it is a good time to make new contacts and connections, and spread your influence. There will be plenty of mentors and people ready to help you out, but you should still watch out for those who might want to undermine your work.

Southeast Sector Main Door

農曆五月 (June 6th - July 6th) 戊午

It will be difficult to make progress in anything this month, so it would be best to take a back seat and consolidate your position. It might be wise for you to sit down and hatch a plan for the future instead of taking action at this point. Turnover will be affected for those in the travel, courier and logistics business, so lie low and work through the tough month and you are likely to emerge shining.

農曆六月 (July 7th - August 6th) 己未

Asset acquisition will be successful this month, especially if it involves overseas travel. Make the effort to explore new opportunities while abroad. Romance will bloom for those using this sector as a bedroom. Take advantage of this good time to seek out prospective partners, if you are single. Engineering-related businesses will have a good month, as the media attention will bring in new customers.

農曆七月 (August 7th - September 7th) 庚申

The good luck with businesses overseas, continues this month, therefore, business owners should continue to find more possibilities in this similar vein. Ensure that you take advantage of your network of contacts, because you never know what might come up. There will be some arguments that will come to the fore this month and you must try to deflate the tension before legal troubles arise.

農曆八月 (September 8th - October 7th) 辛酉

If you're married, you and your partner need to talk to each other instead of listening to others. This is because third party gossip will cause tension in the relationship. Keeping the lines of communication open and frank will help to dispel a lot of the strain. Your decision-making power will be somewhat weak this month, so consider the wisdom of others for important decisions that cannot be postponed to a later time.

農曆九月 (October 8th - November 6th) 壬戌

This is a good month for those in the creative industries, as they will be in the limelight and there is a chance for them to make a name for themselves. But, remember, you'll have to make an effort to get out there and present yourself, as others will definitely respond to you in kind. Remaining in the shadows and being overly modest will not get your foot in through the door!

農曆十月 (November 7th - December 6th) 癸亥

Married couples should consider going on a holiday together this month. Pharmacists and those employed in the entertainment industry are likely to do well this month. Children will also benefit using this room, as their examination results will be positive and they will achieve much academic success.

農曆十一月 (December 7th 2018 - January 4th 2019) 甲子

For business owners, they will be able to make profit and returns from their ventures. As for those who are employed, they will be able to climb the corporate ladder successfully – this is especially true if they happen to be from the oil and gas or mining industries. If the Northwest bedroom is used, those who are in the jewelry or jade businesses will be able to enjoy good returns. Additionally, the choice to travel for work will be fruitful as there will be new investors and new projects on the horizon.

農曆十二月 (January 5th - February 3rd 2019) 乙丑

This is a month to avoid making important personal or financial decisions, as you will find that you're not able to make clear decisions. Couples using this bedroom should be tolerant of each other this month, as there is a risk of communication leading to conflicts and arguments.

| Main Door | Southeast | Bedroom Sector | West |

	SE	S	SW
E	8	4	6
	7	**9**	2
NE	3	5	1
	N		NW

農曆正月 (February 4th - March 4th) 甲寅

Jealous parties threaten to undermine or sabotage whatever good efforts you've put in at work. Do your best to resist any attempts by such malicious people to provoke you into an argument or dispute, which will only take away all the good work you've done, so far. There is, however, some extra cash to be made from side investments. If you're a doctor or in the medical field you will find that others are keen to utilise your services this month.

農曆二月 (March 5th - April 4th) 乙卯

Promotion is likely this month, although your workload is likely to increase. Use your networking capabilities to explore previously unchartered territories for new business. Lung infections and problems are likely if you're using this room. Older women who use this room this month may also be prone to health problems. If you live at home with any elderly females, pay more attention to their health and well-being this month.

農曆三月 (April 5th - May 4th) 丙辰

Personal and professional relationships are positive and smooth this month, so make the most of it by having discussions and negotiations or meetings that are necessary. This is a good month to invest in property developments, as returns will give you favourable income. If you need to change your home, this is also a good time to sell, as you will gain favourable profits.

農曆四月 (May 5th - June 5th) 丁巳

If you work as a judge or a doctor, you'll find this month bringing you an increased workload that improves your reputation. In general, you need to pace yourself this month. Try not to be everything to everybody, as you will only spread yourself thin and this will not work in the long run. There is increased competition at work and colleagues are apt to be acrimonious and argumentative.

| Main Door | Southeast | Bedroom Sector | West |

農曆五月 (June 6th - July 6th) 戊午

This is a good month to make financial gains from the property sale, but it will take its toll on your stress levels. You will have to be constantly engaged and may feel pressured from the intensity of it all. Those of you involved in religious pursuits or gaining spiritual knowledge should use this bedroom, as the outcome is likely to be good. Be forewarned that using this bedroom may bring about depression or mood swings as well.

農曆六月 (July 7th - August 6th) 己未

Any business issues that arise this month should be dealt with after careful consideration or even after obtaining some help from lawyers. There is a chance of great fortune and financial gain, but you will need to know what you are doing to realise these gains. You may find your relationship under severe stress this month and you will need to be patient and understanding towards your partner or spouse to prevent unnecessary fights.

農曆七月 (August 7th - September 7th) 庚申

This is a good time for self-cultivation and if the opportunity arises, you should take the opportunity to indulge in activities or courses for the improvement of the self. Academics and scholars will benefit from the good energies of this bedroom this month, especially if you are facing important examinations. If you're trying to make a property-related investment work, you will find that the results are likely to be profitable.

農曆八月 (September 8th - October 7th) 辛酉

Ensure that all traffic fines and outstanding taxes are up to date, as you will be plagued by the revenue offices throughout the rest of the month otherwise. This is a good sector for those who wish to become involved in religious or spiritual endeavours. If you're a parent with a son using this bedroom, you will have to be prepared for him to be more difficult and argumentative this month.

農曆九月 (October 8th - November 6th) 壬戌

This is a chance to make financial gains from property-related fields, so long as the deals have been carefully thought through. If you're a woman, using this bedroom might make you more authoritative, but on the flip side you may also suffer from slight ill-health – particularly in the form of stomach trouble. Couples will find that they get into a rut this month, so they should spend time on their own so that there is minimal upheaval and tension.

農曆十月 (November 7th - December 6th) 癸亥

Envious parties will threaten to undermine or sabotage whatever good efforts you've put in at work – consider yourself warned. Do your best to resist any attempts by such malicious people to provoke you into an argument or dispute, which will only take away all the good work you've done so far. There is, however, some extra cash to be made from side investments. Doctors and physicians will also find their skills much sought-after, thanks to their reputation and good name, rather than the incidence of more people falling ill this month.

農曆十一月 (December 7th 2018 - January 4th 2019) 甲子

The affluent and wealthy will find life to be a breeze and hassle-free this month. So, make the most out of this opportunity to prepare for the inevitable rainy day. On the other hand, salaried employees will find it difficult to make money, as the going will be tough regardless of how much effort they put into their work. Don't give up easily, but instead, work hard and smart. Meanwhile, those who're already prone to mental disorders may want to consider using a sector other than this bedroom, this month, as you could find yourself 'spiritually disturbed' by ignoring this advisory.

農曆十二月 (January 5th - February 3rd 2019) 乙丑

Those expecting to be promoted to positions of authority and high social status could find these desires being fulfilled this month. People using this bedroom sector may be more inclined towards spiritual and religious pursuits. Opportunities will present themselves this month resulting in an upturn in fortunes and an increased financial income for those involved.

| Main Door | Southeast | Bedroom Sector | Southwest |

SE | S | SW

8 | 4 | 6

E 7 | **9** | 2 W

3 | 5 | 1

NE | N | NW

農曆正月 (February 4th - March 4th) 甲寅

With the added complication of negative environmental forms, arguments could break out at work if the situation is not well-controlled. Diffuse the tension by refusing to join in the petty backbiting. Politicians will find that they are able to promote their policies this month and end up with support from those around them. This should be a good month for those in the legal fields with strong demand for their skills, but you need to be careful of unwanted gossip.

農曆二月 (March 5th - April 4th) 乙卯

Business owners should stay away from wheeling and dealing this month and those who are employed should not change jobs as well. There may be some tension between fathers and sons this time around, especially if either is using this bedroom.

農曆三月 (April 5th - May 4th) 丙辰

Property investments will yield good gains this month and those in the real estate industry will also have a fruitful month as well. If there are negative forms outside this sector, be careful of heart attacks or heart problems within this period.

農曆四月 (May 5th - June 5th) 丁巳

Those in speculative investments or stocks and equities will make good profits this month, especially if they use this bedroom. If you are looking to improve either your personal or professional relationships, you will find this to be a good month to do so. It also bodes well for travel in both leisure and business environment, especially if you are doing a fact-finding mission or are involved in research and development.

| Main Door | Southeast | Bedroom Sector | Southwest |

農曆五月 (June 6th - July 6th) 戊午

Be aware of travel-related problems this month that could result in injury to the limbs. The elderly should take care of their health this month and see a doctor rather than dismiss minor ailments as unimportant. Prevention is always better than cure! Parents of teenagers might find this a difficult month to deal with their offspring if they are using this bedroom.

農曆六月 (July 7th - August 6th) 己未

Those using this bedroom are particularly susceptible to head and brain problems, so consider relocating yourself from this sector this month. Ladies should not be tempted to indulge in illicit or scandalous affairs, as these will only sully their reputation when what they previously thought they could hide becomes public knowledge! That aside, real estate and property developers stand to reap great wealth from their investments this month.

農曆七月 (August 7th - September 7th) 庚申

There will be those who are jealous of you at work and they will try their best to sabotage your reputation. Resist getting involved in their petty games because it will only take away from what you've achieved at work so far. There will be extra income to be made from investments on the side. Doctors and physicians will also find their skills much sought-after, thanks to their reputation and good name, rather than the incidence of more people falling ill this month.

農曆八月 (September 8th - October 7th) 辛酉

Couples should be tolerant of each other and will need to put extra effort into their relationships. Exercise tolerance and patience as it will help to dispel any potential tension. Avoid putting children in this bedroom this month, as they will be rebellious and difficult to control. Employers should be careful with labour relations this month, as workers will challenge authority and become difficult to manage.

農曆九月 (October 8th - November 6th) 壬戌

Employers should monitor their staff closely and beware of dishonest and disloyal employees, who are out to defraud or steal from them this month. Couples using this sector will also find their relationship tense and strained. Exercise patience and tact in dealing with each other, as much as possible. Athletes and professional sportspersons will also need to be extra careful in training or while competing because they risk serious injuries to their head!

農曆十月 (November 7th - December 6th) 癸亥

In regards to love, individuals in this room, this month, will find the results to be satisfying. This is especially true for individuals who are single – since they are more likely to meet their soulmates. If you're a metaphysics student, this auspicious sector will also help extend your knowledge in your chosen field of study. In terms of investments, this is the time diversify and invest in other markets.

農曆十一月 (December 7th 2018 - January 4th 2019) 甲子

There will be great profits to be made from equities and financial investments this month, especially if the energies are being tapped and utilised by the individuals. In terms of career, this is the month to strengthen the ties you have with people – be it professional or personal. For those who are travelling this month, it'll be fruitful, especially if there's a trip related to scholarly pursuits and self-development.

農曆十二月 (January 5th - February 3rd 2019) 乙丑

Individuals in this room, this month, will need to remember that prevention is always better than cure – health-wise. Elders should definitely monitor their health closely, this month, and go for regular check-ups – no matter how minor or major the situation is. When travelling, be careful, as there could be an injury to the limbs occurring. Parents who have teenage children using this room, you will need to be able to practice patience when handling them.

Main Door	Southeast	Bedroom Sector	South

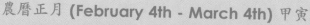
農曆正月 (February 4th - March 4th) 甲寅

Refrain from travelling this month, especially if you're a business owner. This is because your competitors will get busy! In general, the month does not bode well for flirtation and dating, and even simple socialising could lead to problems with your reputation. If you're a parent, you may well find your children to be rebellious and difficult to handle this month. See if you can relocate them from this bedroom, if the situation threatens to get out of hand.

農曆二月 (March 5th - April 4th) 乙卯

There is a good opportunity this month to make favourable financial gains from property located overseas – this is where you will need to travel in order to sign the deal. If it is a relationship that you are looking for, then this is the month to look for a new partner. Children using this room will become more aggressive than ever and they will also be competitive with each other more than usual – consider yourself warned!

農曆三月 (April 5th - May 4th) 丙辰

This is a good month to build alliance with your partners abroad or to embark on business expansion. In terms of relationships, you'll find it to be a good time to progress with new romantic endeavours but you will need to be careful of water outside this room, as it could have negative consequences. Pregnant women will also need to beware of certain irregularities to their condition if they're using this room.

農曆四月 (May 5th - June 5th) 丁巳

If you're concluding or closing financial investments this month, you will find that the outcomes will benefit you and negotiations will be in your favour. Joint ventures in the financial world are productive this month, so you will need to use this opportunity to consolidate the alliance. This is a good month for romantic endeavours and if you're keen to put a ring on it, let your partner know!

Southeast Sector Main Door

農曆五月 (June 6th - July 6th) 戊午

If you're in agriculture, forestry or dairy farming industries, you can expect to have a bumper month. You should use this month to further your name in your particular field of choice, as you are likely to receive the proper recognition you deserve. If you have written a book, you should try to find a publisher this month as it will bring good reputation and financial gain – there will be some success to be expected as well.

農曆六月 (July 7th - August 6th) 己未

If you're engaged in academic or scholarly activities, the East room will prove to be a boon for you this month. And if you're an entrepreneur, you should try to venture abroad to secure your deals. The results will be profitable to you. If you use this bedroom, asthma, bronchitis and other health problems affecting the lungs and respiratory system may well be your bane this month.

農曆七月 (August 7th - September 7th) 庚申

For those who work in the mining industry, the stock exchange or trade in financial information will find this is to be a good month in financial terms. Travelling will bring about an improvement in your stature, reputation or name in your industry or field this month as well. You'll also find yourself expanding your network of business contacts. This is a good month to consolidate both personal and professional relationships or possibly even discuss a long-term future together with your partner.

農曆八月 (September 8th - October 7th) 辛酉

Avoid gambling or dabbling in speculative investments particularly in property, as the outcomes will not be in your favour and you may sustain some losses. Steer clear of illegal or under the table deals, especially if you're an entrepreneur or a business owner. In terms of health, if you're a woman, skin problems or breast malignancies may plague you this month, so take extra care and refer to the doctor as necessary.

農曆九月 (October 8th - November 6th) 壬戌

If you're in the marketing and consulting field, you will have the opportunity to excel and make a name yourself this month by publishing papers and presenting your research. Female business owners travelling to conclude deals abroad will bring good financial gains to their businesses this month. However, female entrepreneurs will need to exercise some caution. There is a likelihood that plenty of no-good sweet-talking people will show up in their paths this month.

農曆十月 (November 7th - December 6th) 癸亥

For those in the services and property industries, they will find this time of the year appropriate for requesting the promotion and recognition they've worked so hard for all along. The fact that their relationships will also be thriving and smooth-sailing this month, only augurs well for all efforts that require networking and the support of others. So, if you're looking to embark on a joint venture, go for it, as you stand to give your enterprise a good start! Another plus: any deal concluded this month will also be beneficial in terms of the lucrative investment potential it presents.

農曆十一月 (December 7th 2018 - January 4th 2019) 甲子

Seeking the fame, promotion, recognition and advancement you've toiled for all this while? Then tap into the energies of the Southwest this month. Similarly, management consultants and professionals in the real estate and property fields will find the energies of this sector conducive towards generating revenue from their businesses. You need to know, though, that this sector is also the harbinger of health issues such as back and spinal problems!

農曆十二月 (January 5th - February 3rd 2019) 乙丑

Serious disputes and misunderstandings threaten to flare up between couples, so be mindful of your partner's feelings to prevent your relationship from falling apart. You're also advised to scrutinize all legal documents carefully before committing yourself to them, and to sidestep the possibility of any legal complications later on. Also, those working on industrial or construction sites should prioritise safety and guard against injuring their limbs at work.

Northwest Sector
Main Door

This section contains the monthly outlook for all 12 months of the year for different bedroom sectors, in a property with a Northwest Sector Main Door.

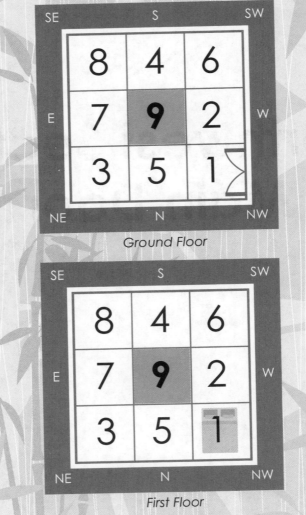

Ground Floor

First Floor

農曆正月 (February 4th - March 4th) 甲寅

Businesses like health centres, clubs, spas and discos will do well financially this month, and if you're in these industries, you need to take advantage of this favourable time to close or negotiate all the good deals that crop up. This is a good month to ask for a promotion, as your superiors notice your talent and abilities in the business. Don't be afraid of basking in the limelight and receiving the recognition, because you've certainly earned it. Couples using this bedroom this month will see an improvement in marital relationships, signifying greater harmony and an increased intimacy.

農曆二月 (March 5th - April 4th) 乙卯

Those among you in the oil and gas industries will have a financially favourable month, especially if you're bold enough to grab the bull by the horns and make full use of all the opportunities that crop up. You should be alert and quick enough to capitalise on these chances, as they may not always come twice! Those who wish to be in the literary world should use this bedroom this month, as you might find that doors are beginning to open where they were previously shut. If you're a salaried employee working on special projects, you will have a chance to shine, as there are a lot of good outcomes expected with what you're working on. Be prepared the accolades that are bound to come forth!

農曆三月 (April 5th - May 4th) 丙辰

Get ready to enjoy warm and cozy ties with your family members this month. Bear in mind, however, that travel will bring about injuries for people using this room. It will be a good idea to invest in some form of travel insurance before embarking on any trip. Academics and those in the research and development fields should market your research this month, but you should also be mindful of those who will take advantage of your ideas and discoveries. Be circumspect about the people with whom you share your work, and don't reveal more than is necessary.

農曆四月 (May 5th - June 5th) 丁巳

Those of you involved in politics will find it a very good month, as you do seem to be blessed with the Midas touch! It will be a favourable time for you to push forward with your new policies and strategies, as you'll be able to garner good, solid support from among the grassroots and your constituents. As your people skills start to pick up, you'll find it a good month in general to form bonds and alliances with other people and forge networking ties.

Main Door	Northwest	Bedroom Sector	Northwest

農曆五月 (June 6th - July 6th) 戊午

Couples who use this bedroom for the month should make an effort to communicate with each other more, do not let jealousy get the best of you, until it hurts the relationship you have with your partner. If you're so consumed by jealousy, it could result in great unhappiness and a lot of arguments. You will need to make a conscious effort to stem your insecurities this month, as it arises largely out of nothing. Avoid indulging in all forms of risky investments.

農曆六月 (July 7th - August 6th) 己未

This is a favourable room for students and scholars facing important examinations this month. It will work well during the preparations for the exams, leading to much favourable results. Any deals involving asset acquisitions concluded this month should do very well, especially if these are overseas investments or if you're dealing with contacts abroad. You'll find yourself being drawn into good relationships with others this month, and both your personal and professional ties will enjoy a nice boost.

農曆七月 (August 7th - September 7th) 庚申

People who work in the furniture industry will find this to be a rather good month, as you will be able to enjoy significant profits that will give your business a boost. However, be on the alert for anyone who might potentially be a backstabber, as betrayals will cause a loss of wealth and result in legal problems this month. Don't trust too easily, especially those who are keen to help you sell the moon – but at a cost. Partnerships and new alliances should be avoided this month, as they will result in a financial loss for you that will be hard to overturn.

農曆八月 (September 8th - October 7th) 辛酉

Older women who are sick, or feeling frail of health, should avoid using this room, this month if possible. It might be better to move them into another room for the meantime, as otherwise the possibilities of ill health are strong. Avoid picking fights over small things this month, or it could result in serious arguments for couples using this room. Where possible, let the small things blow over or else it could turn into something serious. The energies of this sector are favourable for those in the real estate business, as deals are likely to be quite profitable this month.

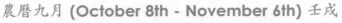

農曆九月 (October 8th - November 6th) 壬戌

Those of you who are using this room for the month need to be prepared to receive lots of media attention, publicity and recognition. Put on your best face forward, as you may have to get used to being in the spotlight! In general, this will prove to be a month to make changes for the better and begin anew on certain matters, as there will be substantial rewards awaiting you. This is also a good month to take on an ambitious endeavour, as success is practically certain. There are many mentors who will be around to help and guide you and they will be instrumental in making your ideas a reality.

農曆十月 (November 7th - December 6th) 癸亥

Your passion and excitement abound this month, much like the last, and it should be channelled into opportunities for career advancement, especially if you are in the entertainment industry. Don't put a lid on your enthusiasm or you might limit the opportunities available to you. You will find that others, especially your bosses and colleagues, start to sit up and take notice of your talents and capabilities.

農曆十一月 (December 7th 2018 - January 4th 2019) 甲子

If you work in engineering, or even in the mining or metals industries, using this bedroom will be a boon to your business this month. Both health and relationships are in good shape this month, so you'll be able to enjoy a good quality of life. This is a good month to cash in on conservative investments, so you may expect small financial gains or returns.

農曆十二月 (January 5th - February 3rd 2019) 乙丑

Academics and researchers using this room will make inroads this month, but be careful who you share your work with. Interpersonal relationships amongst family members should improve this month and you should be able to enjoy closer ties. You should also make sure that your health and travel insurance is up to date if you're intending to go on a trip. There is a chance of mishap during travel, resulting in possible injuries to the limbs.

Main Door	Northwest	Bedroom Sector	West

農曆正月 (February 4th - March 4th) 甲寅

Be careful in your business dealings this month, as things are not what they seem and rivals are out to deceive you. Don't be easily misled by being overly trusting. Remain doubtful of the person or circumstance that seems to be too good to be true! Academic Luck is not good this month and if you're a student, you may find that your thought processes lack clarity and your work might be muddled as a result. There is a possibility of discord, arguments and family disharmony for people who use this bedroom, this month – so pay more attention to your communication and ties with each other.

農曆二月 (March 5th - April 4th) 乙卯

Paranoia and superstition may set in this month, resulting in emotional setbacks for those of you who succumb to the worries and excessive agitation. The key thing is to maintain some form of emotional strength despite the negative feelings and possibly share your worries with a trusted friend. Gastric and intestinal problems will plague those using this bedroom, this month, so those who are prone to these issues should take care. Older people in politics will find that you make good headway in the political field and you will receive recognition for your work in the community.

農曆三月 (April 5th - May 4th) 丙辰

Couples using this room will be distracted at work as a result of their romantic involvement, so they shouldn't allow their relationship to affect their professional life. It is just a rough patch that will soon return to normal, so in the meantime, concentrate on your career instead of blowing it off. Investment in gold mines this month will return good profits for you, so if you've always wanted to invest in gold mines, this is the time to do so! Ill health is also a problem this month, with head and brain problems coming to the fore. Take note of any sudden headaches and it will be best to go for an early medical check-up if it troubles you.

農曆四月 (May 5th - June 5th) 丁巳

Those of you who have property portfolios to divest should do so this month, as you are likely to gain some very pretty profits from it! The name of the game this month is work, work, and more work – and this is especially true for salaried employees. Don't be disheartened if the benefits of hard work are not yet forthcoming at this point in time, because it will come soon enough.

| Main Door | Northwest | Bedroom Sector | West |

農曆五月 (June 6th - July 6th) 戊午

Financial loss as a result of negligence or disputes is possible, especially for those of you directly involved in the world of finance. You will need to step up your vigilance and be more aware of the trends around you. This is not the right time to take it easy or slacken your grip on things. Where health is concerned, abdominal illness is a problem this month for people using this room. However, it will most likely affect the older women in the home more than anyone else.

農曆六月 (July 7th - August 6th) 己未

Mothers and daughters in law will have tense relations this month, so if you're either one of the above, it will be best to exercise tact and diplomacy in your dealings with each other! Women in the literary field will have a time to shine this month, as they will receive awards and achievements for all their creative labours, thus far. This is a time for self-cultivation and if the opportunity arises, you should take a self-development course. It is a good month to work on improving yourself and you're likely to feel a lot better about your life in general.

農曆七月 (August 7th - September 7th) 庚申

Make sure that all taxes and fines are up to date this month or you may find yourself in trouble with the law otherwise! Getting yourself extricated out of that mess might require all of your creativity and ingenuity. Couples should make sure that they spend as little time together as possible, as they will end up with tense and stressful situations, especially if they share this room, this month. It will be better instead to give each other some much needed space. This is a good sector for those who wish to become involved in religious or spiritual endeavours.

農曆八月 (September 8th - October 7th) 辛酉

If you're in the medical field, you will find that your skills are in great demand this month, and you can expect to enjoy an increase in profits. Those of you wishing to invest in property will find that this to be a good month to get involved in the venture, as the returns will be quick and profitable. Get the advice of the experts for guidance if you need it. Women who are pregnant should avoid this sector this month, as the chance of miscarriage is possible or some other complications could crop up as well.

農曆九月 (October 8th - November 6th) 壬戌

While your Financial Luck is still somewhat good, you will need to exercise some caution and not get too carried away. Don't spend too much of your money too soon or else you'll be left with nothing. Maintain good ties with your friends and family, and don't let any arguments escalate out of control this month, as you'll have a hard time putting the pieces back together otherwise. Don't be too gullible this month, as people may tend to take advantage of you.

農曆十月 (November 7th - December 6th) 癸亥

It is important not to make any important business decisions this month, as confusion will play into the decision-making process. This could cloud your judgement in the entire process, resulting in some bad choices being made. Arguments and family disharmony will be a problem for you this year, so you will need to be mindful of the way you interact with your family members. There is a possibility of miscarriage this month for pregnant women who use this sector, so move to another room if possible. At the very least, take all proper precautions to prevent any complications from occurring.

農曆十一月 (December 7th 2018 - January 4th 2019) 甲子

You may have to deal with quite a bit of emotional turbulence this month, including feeling somewhat anxious and paranoid. The key thing is to maintain some form of emotional strength despite the negative feelings. Health-wise, you will have to deal with gastric and stomach troubles, if you're using this bedroom, so be cautious with your health habits.

農曆十二月 (January 5th - February 3rd 2019) 乙丑

There is a possibility for you to make money this month from side investments that will return good profits. If you make smart decisions, you can expect to enjoy a well-padded wallet! If you're a doctor, you will find that you have increased business. This is not because more people are ill, but because there is a demand for your skills in many sectors. Couples in this house may find that they are unable to have children, and using this bedroom, this month will complicate things further – if possible, you should try shifting to another room.

農曆正月 (February 4th - March 4th) 甲寅

Family relations are strained and tense this month, but it is better just to keep the peace, as this is not a good time to thrash it out with the family. It's best to save the emotional probing to a more conducive time in the future. There are opportunities to make money from property investments this month, but you will need to have a good knowledge of the market to be successful in this venture. In other words, study the property market inside out before attempting anything in it - or at the very least, consult an expert!

農曆二月 (March 5th - April 4th) 乙卯

Those in the academic and literary fields will benefit from new ideas and inspiration that are likely to bring favourable financial gains this month. Don't ignore an idea even if it seems crazy, as that just might be the ticket! If you are in metal trading or share and equity trading, this is a month where good deals will be concluded and financial gains are made. Scholars and students who are facing important examinations should make use of this room for their study preparations, as academic results are likely to be favourable.

農曆三月 (April 5th - May 4th) 丙辰

Professional sportspeople should be careful of leg injuries, or accidentally hurting themselves if they use this room this month. Don't neglect these injuries if they occur, and get medical treatment. There is an increased risk of car accidents and injuries this month, so be especially cautious if you're on the road. There will be increased tension between father and son this month as well, especially if there are negative structures located outside this sector.

農曆四月 (May 5th - June 5th) 丁巳

Salaried employees may find that they face obstructions in career prospects this month, but they will need to be patient and wait it out, as this is only temporary. Continue to put in good effort and don't skimp on the quality of your work. Women may experience gynecological problems this month, if they use this bedroom, so any complications or troubles should be checked out immediately by a medical professional.

Main Door	Northwest	Bedroom Sector	Southwest

農曆五月 (June 6th - July 6th) 戊午

Entrepreneurs and those wishing to start new ventures should use the good energies of the Southwest bedroom to go out and make a start. It will provide auspicious vibes for new beginnings. A rocky relationship or business partnership that is on the verge of a break up will be exacerbated if this room is used this month. If you're facing any troubles in your romantic or professional relationships, you may want to take extra care in your dealings with the other party. Be careful of what you say, especially in moments of stress and anger.

農曆六月 (July 7th - August 6th) 己未

Parents should avoid putting children in this bedroom, this month if it can be helped, as they will be rebellious and difficult to control. Otherwise, a potentially tiring month is in store for you! There may be internal bickering this month, so you will need to keep a low profile at work and make sure that you keep out of the office politics. Avoid taking sides and playing the blame game. Older males using this room should take care of their health, especially with regards to high blood pressure or lung disease.

農曆七月 (August 7th - September 7th) 庚申

A change in career, a pay raise, or some form of career advancement is likely this month, and this could result in financial rewards that could make you very happy! This is not a month to be afraid of new things. Investment and merchant bankers who engage in stock and corporate deals will make good financial profits this month. Most of them in general, will find that there are coaches and mentors around to offer good advice, so take heed of their suggestions. They are able to achieve financial success if they consider their suggestions wisely.

農曆八月 (September 8th - October 7th) 辛酉

Senior personnel in communications industry will be able to see an increase in profits this month. It might be a month of physical aggression for males, as jealousy and rivalry amongst them could result in fights. These could likely end up in the law courts. Therefore, it might be good to put the bravado aside and consider the situation using reason instead of brawn and ugly legal wrangles can be avoided. This is a month for short-term flings rather than long-term relationships and if you're comfortable with that then you should be able to enjoy it - just don't put all your expectations into one basket and you should be fine!

農曆九月 (October 8th - November 6th) 壬戌

Employees may become rebellious this month, and superiors will find them difficult to handle. General tact and diplomacy will be needed to ensure that situation does not explode out of control. Good profits can be realised this month, but a more hands-on approach is required to maximise profits – so you should not be hesitant to get your hands dirty! This bedroom will benefit you, if you're into professional sports and are participating in any competitive events this month, as you're likely to see more victories than losses.

農曆十月 (November 7th - December 6th) 癸亥

Family ties will be tested this month, therefore it's better for you to keep the peace and this is not a good time to bring up matters that could rub others the wrong way. The family's situation is already tense and strained – so thread with caution. One-on-one conversations with others might get a little emotional, it is probably best you save it for some other time. This month will not be the month for confrontations. Legal issues could crop up as well, if you're an employer. This could happen due to the sacking of staff and employees, as industrial labour are likely to play a big role this month. There are opportunities to make money from the property market this month. But be sure you're equipped with enough knowledge before making any investments or decisions.

農曆十一月 (December 7th 2018 - January 4th 2019) 甲子

For those of you in the academic and literary fields, you will be rewarded for your new ideas. Your talents will only bring about financial gains for you this month. For children who may be sitting for important examinations, they should make full use of this room to prepare, as all signs point to favourable outcomes. And for individuals in the psychology, counselling or mentoring fields, they will be able to gain the respect and recognition they crave for, this month. This is largely due to their services and expertise that are on high demand. This is also a good month for those who happen to travel to earn money.

農曆十二月 (January 5th - February 3rd 2019) 乙丑

Travel-related problems could result in leg injuries this month, so be especially careful on any of your trips. Minor health issues could be a problem as well, but do not think that these are unimportant or it could end up becoming serious issues later on, which would cost you a lot of money. So, get issues checked out with a professional, no matter how minor they may be. There is also an increased risk of car accidents and injuries this month, so be careful when driving and out and about. Employees in the engineering field will benefit from the support of superiors, which could result in financial reward and recognition.

| Main Door | Northwest | Bedroom Sector | South |

農曆正月 (February 4th - March 4th) 甲寅

Those of you who are artistically creative should make an effort to approach the international market, as the demand for quality work is high and you're likely to receive creative support for your work in addition to acclaim. Those travelling this month should expect some sudden changes or last-minute problems. It would be best for you to invest in some good travel insurance. Children using this sector could be encouraged by peer pressure to get involved in rebellious activities. If you're a parent, it pays to be more aware of your children's friends and their social activities.

農曆二月 (March 5th - April 4th) 乙卯

Female employees will have an excellent month, especially for those of you who work in the real estate industry. Profits will literally be pouring in for you! However, as competition amongst women employees intensify, there will be little progress made on the actual work projects for those of you in the other industries. Try not to get caught in the middle of professional rivalries. This is a good month to invest in self-cultivation, either by attending new courses or learning a new trade. Consider taking a class in something that you've always wanted to try.

農曆三月 (April 5th - May 4th) 丙辰

There will be harmonious relations for those who use this bedroom, this month, but they have to be careful if there's no water features outside this sector. Those of you working in the arts and culture industry will be able to gain good exposure from the media this month, leading to increased recognition for your work. You can also expect to prepare for your moment to shine bright in the spotlight! This is a good month to build alliance partners abroad, or embark on business expansion, so think about focusing your endeavours on the international arena at this point in time.

農曆四月 (May 5th - June 5th) 丁巳

Relationships are generally on the upswing this month and those using this bedroom should take full advantage of them. Make an effort to reconnect with old friends, spend more time with the family and strengthen your marriage and relationships further. All your endeavours in this particular area of your life are likely to go down well, giving you favourable results. However, this is not a good time to travel, as your rivals will make inroads into your client base while you're gone. It will be best to stay closer to home and keep an eye on your business proceedings – you can always take that break some other time.

Main Door	Northwest	Bedroom Sector	South

農曆五月 (June 6th - July 6th) 戊午

Health issues may arise in the form of back and spine injuries this month, so take extra care when performing physical activities. This also applies for those of you who exercise frequently and play sports, or those of you who dabble in extreme sports. Where finances are concerned, this is the month to get involved in joint ventures. If this is in your line, then it is suitable to get involved in gilt bonds or shares, as the profits are likely to be significant.

農曆六月 (July 7th - August 6th) 己未

Words need to be used with care this month, as there is a tendency for misunderstandings arising out of words misconstrued. Therefore, think carefully before saying anything this month, as you might find yourself having to eat quite a lot of your words otherwise! Those of you in the furniture business will have a good month, but you will need to be careful when signing any legal documents. Double-check everything at least once. If your work involves being at construction and work sites, then be careful while using sharp metal objects.

農曆七月 (August 7th - September 7th) 庚申

It's a good month for both personal and professional relationships, so if you want to cultivate closer ties – this would be the ideal time to do it. This is especially the case in communication, as the more you work on making it better, the greater the results will be! As much as possible, though, avoid dabbling in speculative investments – especially in equities, shares and futures. Losses can be quite huge, so it would be best to avoid it altogether. Your stature, reputation and name will improve if you travel to conduct business this month, so strive to make as many business opportunities abroad!

農曆八月 (September 8th - October 7th) 辛酉

This is not a month for gambling, because financial losses are the only thing looming on the horizon. In that vein, those among you who have dabbled in speculative investments – particularly involving property or real estate – should withdraw from these deals or divest their investments before they endure any significant losses. Ladies using this room are likely to run into some serious health problems this month, so to be safe, it would be best to schedule a mammogram to rule out possibilities of breast cancer.

農曆九月 (October 8th - November 6th) 壬戌

Health problems continue into the month, with asthma and bronchitis being some of the major ones plaguing people using this room. If you show symptoms of these illnesses, get medical treatment so as not to worsen your situation. Gambling activities should be avoided this month at all costs. Ladies who own businesses will find that travels abroad to conclude deals will ultimately lead to good financial gains. Make the most of the travelling for work opportunities that crop up this month!

農曆十月 (November 7th - December 6th) 癸亥

You'll be feeling ambitious and raring to go this month and this is definitely something admirable – but beware of jealous rivals who may dog your path. And as for those who happen to dabble in the metals and equities markets, now is a good time to use your experience and expertise to your advantage. Health problems in the form of gastrointestinal ailments and limb injuries could prove to be the bane of those using this bedroom in this month.

農曆十一月 (December 7th 2018 - January 4th 2019) 甲子

Your friendships may be tense over a power struggle this month and this could lead to the end of their friendship. If things get out of hand, legal problems are also liable to occur. Unfortunately, you may also need to ensure that all security procedures are in place, as your employees or even family members may defraud or steal from you – particularly if you own a business or run a family's business.

農曆十二月 (January 5th - February 3rd 2019) 乙丑

Feeling stressed and lonely lately? Then moving out of the South bedroom for the time being may do you a world of good. This is a month where subordinates will challenge their superiors, and in the family, children will challenge their parents – particularly where sons and fathers are concerned. Elderly males are advised to go for a full medical check-up, to minimise the risk of suffering from an internal injury or bleeding.

農曆正月 (February 4th - March 4th) 甲寅

There is a good possibility of financial gains this month, so look to realise these profits in your portfolio. It's also a good month for networking and developing new client and business relationships. You will need to engage your diplomatic skills and put your best foot forward, but the results will be good and probably better than what you expected. Children using this room, this month will be more independent and autonomous, which benefits their parents.

農曆二月 (March 5th - April 4th) 乙卯

Business deals that require you travel to close them, will be especially profitable for you. Therefore, always persist in finalising the deal abroad, if possible. And if you're in the banking industry, you can look forward to a promotion or advancement in your career, this month. Mentors, life coaches and those in the self-help and motivational industries will see success in their endeavours this month, especially if they make changes in their personal lives that reflect their advice. In other words, all you need to do is practice what you preach for success!

農曆三月 (April 5th - May 4th) 丙辰

This is a good month for those in the property development and real estate industries, as speculative investments made now will only bring good profits in the future. Let relationships take a back seat this month, so don't focus on the partnership so much, but rather, concentrate on your career and spend more time developing that aspect of your life. In terms of health, you may have experience pain or encounter issues with bone and joints this month, if you use this room – so, always take extra precautions!

農曆四月 (May 5th - June 5th) 丁巳

This is a good month to unbundle your property portfolios (if you have them), as there are generous profits to be made. Overseas business opportunities will become more lucrative for those using this bedroom this month, as profits and new clients abound for those involved. If you're a student or in academia, using the Southeast bedroom this month will be beneficial in terms of ensuring success – particularly in examinations.

| Main Door | **Northwest** | Bedroom Sector | **Southeast** |

農曆五月 **(June 6th - July 6th)** 戊午

This is a difficult month generally but by making key changes, this can be turned around into a positive situation. Don't be blown about by every wind with regards to your emotions. It would be best to keep young kids out of this room, this month, as they may be prone to injury from sharp metal objects. At best, keep sharp implements out of their reach, just to be safe.

農曆六月 **(July 7th - August 6th)** 己未

Speculative investments in real estate will provide handsome profits this month, but make sure that the details have been taken care of by lawyers. Those who are in high authority or of high social status will find that things are in their favour this month, so they should take advantage of any opportunity that comes their way. In your personal life, your relationships will be a smooth-sailing ride and you'll have no problems communicating with each other.

農曆七月 **(August 7th - September 7th)** 庚申

Marital relationships proved to be harmonious and rewarding this month for those in this bedroom. Couples can expect to enjoy closer ties and lesser squabbles. They're also able to talk to each other with greater clarity and less friction and tension. Love is well and truly in the air!

農曆八月 **(September 8th - October 7th)** 辛酉

If you're in the construction industry, you will be happy to know that this month brings about some improvement. As there will be profits to be made, you will have to keep your eye on the ball. Good news and celebrations await those using this bedroom this month, especially if they want to start a family. If this is something they've discussed in length with their partners, then this will be the auspicious month to take that appropriate next step.

農曆九月 (October 8th - November 6th) 壬戌

Romance blooms for you this month, so if you're single and searching, then this will be a good month to put yourself out there. Be ready to explore different avenues and people, and remember that staying at home as a homebody won't bring you a lot of opportunities! If you're a salaried employee, identify some of the things standing in your way to success – this will be a good month to overcome them.

農曆十月 (November 7th - December 6th) 癸亥

If you are in the share and equity markets, this month should show good profits, if you decide to cash in your shares. It is important to put the money in the bank, rather than let it slip through your fingers. Children sitting for important examinations this month will find positive support from the good energies in this bedroom. This will also be a happy and harmonious month for couples using this bedroom. Windfall gains are possible this month, so look to realise these profits in your portfolio. Additionally, this is a good month for networking and developing new client and business relationships. You will need to utilise your diplomatic skills wisely and put your best foot forward – the results will be good and better than you expected.

農曆十一月 (December 7th 2018 - January 4th 2019) 甲子

If there are business deals that requires travelling to be sorted out – get on that plane and make your presence felt. Close the deals and you'll be rewarded handsomely. Remember to always insist to finalise deals abroad, if you can. As for those of you in the banking industry, you can be prepared for a career advancement or well-deserved promotion this month. For those in futures, share and equity trading, and property and real estate industries – you will do well this month. Family-owned businesses will also make good returns this month and any form of travels will bring about new businesses and increased profits for the company.

農曆十二月 (January 5th - February 3rd 2019) 乙丑

Wealth Luck is generally favourable for those using this sector's bedroom in this month. Couples using this bedroom will find that this is a good room to be in this month, as the quality of the relationships can be expected to increase and you are able to derive fulfilment from your ties to each other. Employees may find that they are more stressed this month as superiors step up the pressure for them to perform. Expectations are rather high and this may increase your stress levels, so you will need to learn how to manage anxiety and turn it into useful energy – this will be beneficial for you in the long run.

Main Door	Northwest	Bedroom Sector	East

SE | S | SW

8	4	6
7	**9**	2
3	5	1

E ... W

NE | N | NW

農曆正月 (February 4th - March 4th) 甲寅

Elderly women who use this bedroom should be careful of their health, especially where stomach ailments are concerned. This is especially true if there are negative structures located outside this sector. In general, professional rivalry and competition starts to heat up this month – resulting in possible physical violence, especially if the arguments become explosive! Try not to add to the problem, but seek to calm the situation instead. Those in the legal and judicial fields will do well this month, as the demand for their services increases.

農曆二月 (March 5th - April 4th) 乙卯

All business deals that are undertaken this month should be concluded in writing, otherwise miscommunication is rife and it will lead to more troubles. In general, you should avoid making decisions in both professional and personal capacities, because the outcome might not be good. Couples will find misunderstandings on the rise this month, so both partners should make the effort to communicate openly with each other. Work a little bit harder to stabilise your relationship and things are likely to progress well.

農曆三月 (April 5th - May 4th) 丙辰

For females, things are not so smooth on the domestic front, or at work. There could be some tense relations or full-blown disagreements that could cause stress for the people around them. Health-wise, those of you with respiratory problems should be extra careful this month, as it may worsen and exacerbate other health issues. Leisure travel bodes well for you this month, but be sure that you are alert to times of departure, otherwise you could find yourself in a last-minute fix!

農曆四月 (May 5th - June 5th) 丁巳

Those who work in dangerous and hazardous jobs should be extra careful, as there is a risk of occupational injury this month. This will most likely be to the limbs, so don't be negligent when working with heavy machinery or sharp implements. There is little prospect of making financial profits this month and if you own or manage a company – you must be careful of employees defrauding the company. Keep an eagle eye on your staff, but don't succumb to mindless suspicion as you could alienate the trustworthy ones.

| Main Door | Northwest | Bedroom Sector | East |

農曆五月 (June 6th - July 6th) 戊午

Those who are employed should look for opportunities to make some side income this month, as there are good profits to be made from sound opportunities. You'll have to work a little bit harder and maybe sacrifice a bit more sleep than necessary, but you'll be plenty pleased when you look at your bank account balance at the end of the month! This is a good month in general for doctors who use this room, as people will make an effort to seek out your expertise. You'll be able to build on your patient base.

農曆六月 (July 7th - August 6th) 己未

People who work in the entertainment business, or who run bars, pubs, and nightclubs, will find that there is no such thing as bad publicity this month! Even if it seems like the only thing that comes about is notoriety, you should ride out the publicity wave and try to gather some good business gains! However, politicians, or those of you in public service, should try to keep a low profile and avoid attracting attention this month. Otherwise, your reputation will suffer.

農曆七月 (August 7th - September 7th) 庚申

Professionals will gain an increase in publicity and fame this month, so don't be shy and don't hide from the limelight! It'll be exactly what you need to give your career a good boost and in no time, the accolades will come pouring in. There will be problems in the office involving female colleagues, as they try to show off their abilities and compete with one another. Your public image and status also stands to improve from increased travelling this month, but bear in mind that your stress levels will also increase, thus resulting in unstable emotions.

農曆八月 (September 8th - October 7th) 辛酉

Word-of-mouth deals within the property industry can result in financial gains for you, so you need to keep your ears to the ground and cultivate your network of contacts. In general, most of you will be able to take on your competitors this month, equipped with renewed zeal and energy. Go full steam ahead, as you're likely to attract new customers by doing so, as well. Teenagers using this room will be subject to a whirlwind of emotions and feelings. They should be careful not to be swept away by their feelings, otherwise it could result in haphazard decisions and actions.

農曆九月 (October 8th - November 6th) 壬戌

Males will need to be on their guard this month, because there will be females about with the gift of gab who will prove to be extremely tempting to you – but in all the wrong ways! Tread with caution or you could find yourself caught in an embarrassing situation. Be on guard where your personal safety is concerned, as robbery and theft are serious threats as well. Those of you involved in businesses like reflexology or massage should avoid starting new ventures, as these are unlikely to turn out well for you.

農曆十月 (November 7th - December 6th) 癸亥

You may need to watch out for arguments becoming violent and physical as competition and rivalry increases this month. As much as possible, you will need to keep a lid on the rising tension. If you're a lawyer or in legal service, you will find that demand for your service increases this month. Elderly women who have stomach ailments should avoid using this bedroom this month. This is especially true if there are negative structures outside of this room's sector.

農曆十一月 (December 7th 2018 - January 4th 2019) 甲子

Couples will be faced with communication issues this month. Therefore, if your communication with each other is already on rocky ground, as the other half, you will need to work harder to stabilise your relationship. All business deals should be concluded in writing this month, as miscommunication may cause headaches or troubles in the long run. This is a very unfavourable month for important decisions to made – be it both personal and professional, so hold off on making them for the time being.

農曆十二月 (January 5th - February 3rd 2019) 乙丑

Domestically, there is competition and conflict between women of the house or at work this month. This could result in frosty and tense relations. This is also a good month to embark on leisure travel but make sure that you check the times of departure to alleviate trivial problems and any last-minute hindrances. In terms of health, if you have respiratory problems you should be especially careful this month, as it may exacerbate other health issues.

農曆正月 (February 4th - March 4th) 甲寅

Marriages are likely to come under fire this month, as both partners will be especially tense and stressed out. Instead of taking out their frustration on each other, they should address the situation promptly, and with tolerance, before the outcome ends in a divorce. Those of you working in advertising and event management will have a particularly profitable month, especially if you consider making timely changes to your business plan. Where your professional life is concerned, you need to address the arguments, quarrels and gossip that crop up in a diplomatic and thoughtful manner, otherwise it could result in legal issues.

農曆二月 (March 5th - April 4th) 乙卯

Individuals involved in the legal field will find this to be a good month for increased business. This is because there is a demand for your expertise and skills. You will have your hands full, but this will be a good thing! If you're a senior personnel at work, be prepared for possible theft and fraud, as there are unscrupulous third parties waiting for the perfect opportunity to extort large sums of money from you. Those among you working as mentors or counsellors will also be inundated with new clients this month.

農曆三月 (April 5th - May 4th) 丙辰

The situation on the domestic front starts to get a little harried this month, as parents whose children use this room will find them a little hard to tame! Getting angry or impatient won't help matters, so try to be use more guile and tact in trying to impose some form of order. Avoid meddling in other people's affairs this month, because they are not going to be grateful. Individuals involved in business dealings should not expand at this point in time. Instead, they should consolidate their position for future and be focused long-term gains.

農曆四月 (May 5th - June 5th) 丁巳

People involved in the fashion business, or in fashion retail, will find this to be a month of excellent gains. Make full use of the opportunities that come up to widen or expand your business. In general, it's also a favourable month to make a fair amount of money from property and real estate. Use your past experiences and in-depth knowledge to great advantage!

| Main Door | Northwest | Bedroom Sector | Northeast |

農曆五月 (June 6th - July 6th) 戊午

People using this room who are already in weak or frail health should exercise greater caution. This is because internal injuries are a possibility. As such, one should be particularly careful when performing any heavy manual labour or activity, or when indulging in sports. Don't ignore any injuries if the signs indicate that something is amiss – seek professional medical treatment immediately! This is a good month to gain good financial profits from deals that are conducted with international partners and contacts.

農曆六月 (July 7th - August 6th) 己未

Individuals using this room should prepare for a new position that affords them more power and authority, especially if they've been long due for a career advancement. But do bear in mind that with more authority (and a higher pay!) comes greater responsibilities, so ensure that your expectations are moderate to avoid disappointment. There will be strange power disputes between friends this month, so if there is tension imminent – try to diffuse it before it gets out of hand. Parents with teenage sons using this room will find them to be more hardheaded and rebellious this month.

農曆七月 (August 7th - September 7th) 庚申

This is not the month to dabble in speculative financial investments, as losses are possible – and in worst-case scenarios, lawsuits and legal entanglements. Avoid spending all your hard-earned money on gambling, because the losses may be greater than what you expect. Be careful of potential health problems that come in the form of ulcers, gallstones, and liver troubles. Get a professional medical opinion if it's needed.

農曆八月 (September 8th - October 7th) 辛酉

Romance issues come to the forefront this month, and those of you who are in relationships should put in more effort. There is competition looming on the horizon and if you take your partner for granted, you are likely to be left licking your wounds! People using this room will have to battle some emotional and psychological problems this month. Those among you who work in research and development are likely to get noticed for your abilities this month, and this is especially true if you are dealing with companies and associates abroad.

農曆九月 (October 8th - November 6th) 壬戌

Be wary of road trips this month, as those of you using this room are prone to getting into car accidents. If you drive, be especially careful with how you conduct yourself on the road. People who are involved in politics and who rely heavily on their oratory skills, will find it to be a very good month to perform well and obtain favourable results. Those among you who work in the analytic or scientific fields will find this to be a good month, as well, and are likely to achieve a breakthrough in your line of work.

農曆十月 (November 7th - December 6th) 癸亥

This is not the month to play with the law, so any outstanding taxes, fines, and payments should be cleared immediately. Property deals that come out of the blue this month should do well, but be very specific on the details, as legal issues may arise if you are not careful. Relationships are on a downturn; so no important decisions should be made this month as the outcome will be less than pleasing.

農曆十一月 (December 7th 2018 - January 4th 2019) 甲子

Lawyers and those of you who work in the legal field, you will find this to be a good month for your business as the demand for your services grows. And if you're a senior personnel at work, you should be on guard against thieves and shady individuals who will end up extorting large sums of money from you. Those of you who are mentors and counsellors will find that you are blessed with new clients – who are looking for help, support and needing quite a bit of guidance.

農曆十二月 (January 5th - February 3rd 2019) 乙丑

This is not the month to offer your advice to others or meddle in things that do not involve you. This will be especially true if the advice is unsolicited. If you're in business, you should consolidate or strategise for the future rather than try to expand the business, as losses and fraud will be prevalent.

| Main Door | Northwest | Bedroom Sector | North |

農曆正月 (February 4th - March 4th) 甲寅

Speculative investments and gambling should be resisted this month, as it is likely to bring financial losses. You'll do well to curb all your instincts to gamble and take a risk! Problems arising this month will be difficult to solve as the cause is not easily evident, and your rivals will take quick advantage of this factor. It is imperative that you keep your guard up. Stay away from casual relationships this month, as it is likely to result in sexually-transmitted diseases and will be more trouble than it's worth – both psychologically and physically.

農曆二月 (March 5th - April 4th) 乙卯

Those involved in labour negotiations or in the legal field will find this to be a good month, as the outcomes are generally promising and you are likely to gain victory. This month as well, you'll need to pay close attention to your behaviour, as unwise remarks and a lack of common sense will give rise to problems that will be hard to shrug off in the future. You'll be a magnet for bad investment advice this month, so you will need to double check all tips that you receive as deals signed this month may well turn sour.

農曆三月 (April 5th - May 4th) 丙辰

Mothers and older women who use this bedroom for the month will find an increased risk of kidney problems and kidney-related ailments. If possible, you might want to move them to another room to lessen the impact. In general, bad external formations outside this sector can lead to an increase in accidents and illnesses for the occupants, so ensure that there are no negative structures outside this sector. Do not try to make property acquisitions this month, as this will likely end in failure.

農曆四月 (May 5th - June 5th) 丁巳

Those among you who are entangled in sticky lawsuits should just cut to the chase and avoid getting involved in a long and messy drama. Try to settle the case out of court, because if you don't, it's likely to cost more time, money and energy for everyone involved. Bladder and kidney problems are key health concerns that come up for the occupants of this room this month.

農曆五月 (June 6th - July 6th) 戊午

Romantic relationships will come under pressure for those of you using this bedroom, this month. You're likely to feel like you're in a pressure cooker as stress and anxiety build up, causing you to take it out on those who are nearest and dearest to you. Hence, arguments and general unpleasantness will plague couples, so both partners will need to make a conscious and concentrated effort to be more patient with, and forgiving of, each other. Health problems continue to be a problem this month and you're likely to battle kidney and ear problems.

農曆六月 (July 7th - August 6th) 己未

Business owners should avoid any expansion this month and should instead focus on consolidating their current position. It will be best in the long run to pay extra attention and care to customers and clients, as disloyalty amongst employees is rife, and they will seek to undermine you through your most sensitive point – your clientele. Keep in mind that conservative property-related deals will bring good financial gains this month, but those of you who own a business will lack the leverage to benefit from positive investment outcomes.

農曆七月 (August 7th - September 7th) 庚申

Competition and rivalry, especially from competitors, will affect the people using this room for the month. If you're not careful, this could digress into a very emotional issue that could result in acute psychological warfare. You will need to be on guard, but don't overreact and resort to petty responses. Lawyers will have a tough time putting their case across this month and may need to use every ounce of strength to fight. In general, people using this room should be careful as accidents could be caused by mishaps with other people, resulting in muscle and tendon injuries.

農曆八月 (September 8th - October 7th) 辛酉

Those among you who play sports for a living and compete professionally will find the competitions to be an uphill battle this month. Instead, they should use the time for some physical improvements that could bring future benefits. Stress and depression may end in mental instability or neurosis this month, especially if there are negative external forms located outside this sector. Health issues may also arise in the form of migraines or headaches this month, so try to relax more and not let worries and anxieties get to you. Sometimes, it's just not worth it to sweat the small things!

農曆九月 (October 8th - November 6th) 壬戌

Stay away from the fashion and apparel industries, as the outcomes for those industries are likely to be quite disastrous this month. If you're working in those industries, it will be best to lay low and postpone any plans for expansion. For business owners this month, everything that can go wrong, will, and even those things that usually run smoothly will cause trouble and obstruction. You will need to be prepared and have a backup plan. Pregnant women should be careful when using this bedroom, this month, as there is a risk of complications and troubles. If possible, switch to another room for the duration.

農曆十月 (November 7th - December 6th) 癸亥

If you're in top-level management or in managerial positions, you will find your wisdom and intelligence bringing about positive outcomes for the company. Others will demonstrate their approval by showing you greater respect. Kidney stones are amongst the variety of health issues that could plague those using this room this month. Stay away from unhealthy activities such as gambling and drinking, as these will have negative consequences on your health, and your health is weak this month.

農曆十一月 (December 7th 2018 - January 4th 2019) 甲子

If you work in the IT industry, you will do well this month. This is thanks to your network of contacts and recommendations from satisfied, existing clients. Bear in mind that strokes or internal bleeding could pose a serious threat to the individuals (including elders) using this sector's bedroom, this month – especially if they've already been feeling poorly of late. Couples using this bedroom will also find their relationship to be more strained and tense than usual. Give each other space and don't place too much pressure on each other.

農曆十二月 (January 5th - February 3rd 2019) 乙丑

There will be money to be made from conservative property-related deals this month, but if you're a business owner you may find yourself lacking the leverage to benefit from their positive investment outcomes. Relationships won't exactly be your forte this month, and those using this bedroom need to be a little more patient in dealing with their loved ones. It's also a risky month for pregnant women using this room.

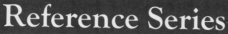

JOEY YAP'S
QI MEN DUN JIA MASTERY PROGRAM

This is the world's most comprehensive training program on the subject of Qi Men Dun Jia. Joey Yap is the Qi Men Strategist for some of Asia's wealthiest tycoons. This program is modelled after Joey Yap's personal application methods, covering techniques and strategies he applies for his high net worth clients. There is a huge difference between studying the subject as a scholar and learning how to use it successfully as a Qi Men strategist. In this program, Joey Yap shares with you what he personally uses to transform his own life and the lives of million others. In other words, he shares with his students what actually works and not just what looks good in theory with no real practical value. This means that the program covers his personal trade secrets in using the art of Qi Men Dun Jia.

There are five unique programs, with each of them covering one specific application aspect of the Joey Yap's Qi Men Dun Jia system.

Joey Yap's training program focuses on getting results. Theories and formulas are provided in the course workbook so that valuable class time are not wasted dwelling on formulas. Each course comes with its own comprehensive 400-plus pages workbook. Taught once a year exclusively by Joey Yap, seats to these programs are extremely limited.

Getting Whatever You Want from Whatever You've Got™ Spiritual Qi Men™

Qi Men Forecasting Methods™

Qi Men Destiny & Life Transformation™

Qi Men Feng Shui™

Qi Men Strategic Execution™

Qi Men Warcraft™

JOEY YAP CONSULTING GROUP

Pioneering Metaphysics-Centric Personal and Corporate Consultations

Founded in 2002, the Joey Yap Consulting Group is the pioneer in the provision of metaphysics-driven coaching and consultation services for professionals and individuals alike. Under the leadership of the renowned international Chinese Metaphysics consultant, author and trainer, Dato' Joey Yap, it has become a world-class specialised metaphysics consulting firm with a strong presence in four continents, meeting the metaphysics-centric needs of its A-list clientele, ranging from celebrities to multinational corporations.

The Group's core consultation practice areas include Feng Shui, BaZi and Qi Men Dun Jia, which are complemented by ancillary services such as Date Selection, Face Reading and Yi Jing. Its team of highly trained professional consultants, led by its Chief Consultant, Dato' Joey Yap, is well-equipped with unparalleled knowledge and experience to help clients achieve their ultimate potentials in various fields and specialisations. Given its credentials, the Group is certainly the firm of choice across the globe for metaphysics-related consultations.

The Peerless Industry Expert

Benchmarked against the standards of top international consulting firms, our consultants work closely with our clients to achieve the best possible outcomes. The possibilities are infinite as our expertise extends from consultations related to the forces of nature under the subject of Feng Shui, to those related to Destiny Analysis and effective strategising under BaZi and Qi Men Dun Jia respectively.

To date, we have consulted a great diversity of clients, ranging from corporate clients – from various industries such as real estate, finance and telecommunication, amongst others – to the hundreds of thousands of individuals in their key life aspects. Adopting up-to-date and pragmatic approaches, we provide comprehensive services while upholding the importance of clients' priorities and effective outcomes. Recognised as the epitome of Chinese Metaphysics, we possess significant testimonies from worldwide clients as a trusted Brand.

Feng Shui Consultation

Residential Properties
- Initial Land/Property Assessment
- Residential Feng Shui Consultation
- Residential Land Selection
- End-to-End Residential Consultation

Commercial Properties
- Initial Land/Property Assessment
- Commercial Feng Shui Consultation
- Commercial Land Selection
- End-to-End Commercial Consultation

Property Developers
- End-to-End Consultation
- Post-Consultation Advisory Services
- Panel Feng Shui Consultant

Property Investors
- Your Personal Feng Shui Consultant
- Tailor-Made Packages

Memorial Parks & Burial Sites
- Yin House Feng Shui

BaZi Consultation

Personal Destiny Analysis
- Individual BaZi Analysis
- BaZi Analysis for Families

Strategic Analysis for Corporate Organizations
- BaZi Consultations for Corporations
- BaZi Analysis for Human Resource Management

Entrepreneurs and Business Owners
- BaZi Analysis for Entrepreneurs

Career Pursuits
- BaZi Career Analysis

Relationships
- Marriage and Compatibility Analysis
- Partnership Analysis

General Public
- Annual BaZi Forecast
- Your Personal BaZi Coach

Date Selection Consultation

- **Marriage Date Selection**
- **Caesarean Birth Date Selection**
- **House-Moving Date Selection**

- **Renovation and Groundbreaking Dates**
- **Signing of Contracts**
- **O icial Openings**
- **Product Launches**

Qi Men Dun Jia Consultation

Strategic Execution
- Business and Investment Prospects

Forecasting
- Wealth and Life Pursuits
- People and Environmental Matters

Feng Shui
- Residential Properties
- Commercial Properties

Speaking Engagement

Many reputable organisations and institutions have worked closely with Joey Yap Consulting Group to build a synergistic business relationship by engaging our team of consultants, which are led by Joey Yap, as speakers at their corporate events.

We tailor our seminars and talks to suit the anticipated or pertinent group of audience. Be it department subsidiary, your clients or even the entire corporation, we aim to fit your requirements in delivering the intended message(s) across.

CHINESE METAPHYSICS REFERENCE SERIES

The Chinese Metaphysics Reference Series is a collection of reference texts, source material, and educational textbooks to be used as supplementary guides by scholars, students, researchers, teachers and practitioners of Chinese Metaphysics.

These comprehensive and structured books provide fast, easy reference to aid in the study and practice of various Chinese Metaphysics subjects including Feng Shui, BaZi, Yi Jing, Zi Wei, Liu Ren, Ze Ri, Ta Yi, Qi Men Dun Jia and Mian Xiang.

The Chinese Metaphysics Compendium

At over 1,000 pages, the Chinese Metaphysics Compendium is a unique one-volume reference book that compiles ALL the formulas relating to Feng Shui, BaZi (Four Pillars of Destiny), Zi Wei (Purple Star Astrology), Yi Jing (I-Ching), Qi Men (Mystical Doorways), Ze Ri (Date Selection), Mian Xiang (Face Reading) and other sources of Chinese Metaphysics.

It is presented in the form of easy-to-read tables, diagrams and reference charts, all of which are compiled into one handy book. This first-of-its-kind compendium is presented in both English and its original Chinese language, so that none of the meanings and contexts of the technical terminologies are lost.

The only essential and comprehensive reference on Chinese Metaphysics, and an absolute must-have for all students, scholars, and practitioners of Chinese Metaphysics.

| The Ten Thousand Year Calendar (Pocket Edition) | The Ten Thousand Year Calendar | Dong Gong Date Selection | The Date Selection Compendium | Plum Blossoms Divination Reference Book | Xuan Kong Da Gua Ten Thousand Year Calendar | San Yuan Dragon Gate Eight Formations Water Method |

| BaZi Hour Pillar Useful Gods - Wood | BaZi Hour Pillar Useful Gods - Fire | BaZi Hour Pillar Useful Gods - Earth | BaZi Hour Pillar Useful Gods - Metal | BaZi Hour Pillar Useful Gods - Water | Xuan Kong Da Gua Structures Reference Book | Xuan Kong Da Gua 64 Gua Transformation Analysis |

| BaZi Structures and Structural Useful Gods - Wood | BaZi Structures and Structural Useful Gods - Fire | BaZi Structures and Structural Useful Gods - Earth | BaZi Structures and Structural Useful Gods - Metal | BaZi Structures and Structural Useful Gods - Water | Earth Study Discern Truth Second Edition | Eight Mansions Bright Mirror |

| Secret of Xuan Kong | Ode to Flying Stars | Xuan Kong Purple White Script | Ode to Mysticism | The Yin House Handbook | Water Water Everywhere | Xuan Kong Da Gua Not Exactly For Dummies |

Joey Yap's BaZi Profiling System

Three Levels of BaZi Profiling (English & Chinese versions)

In BaZi Profiling, there are three levels that reflect three different stages of a person's personal nature and character structure.

Level 1 – The Day Master

The Day Master in a nutshell is the basic you. The inborn personality. It is your essential character. It answers the basic question "who am I". There are ten basic personality profiles – the ten Day Masters – each with its unique set of personality traits, likes and dislikes.

Level 2 – The Structure

The Structure is your behavior and attitude – in other words, it is about how you use your personality. It expands on the Day Master (Level 1). The structure reveals your natural tendencies in life – are you a controller, creator, supporter, thinker or connector? Each of the Ten Day Masters express themselves differently through the five Structures. Why do we do the things we do? Why do we like the things we like? The answers are in our BaZi Structure.

Level 3 – The Profile

The Profile depicts your role in your life. There are ten roles (Ten BaZi Profiles) related to us. As to each to his or her own - the roles we play are different from one another and it is unique to each Profile.

What success means to you, for instance, differs from your friends – this is similar to your sense of achievement or whatever you think of your purpose in life is.

Through the BaZi Profile, you will learn the deeper level of your personality. It helps you become aware of your personal strengths and works as a trigger for you to make all the positive changes to be a better version of you.

Keep in mind, only through awareness that you will be able to maximise your natural talents, abilities and skills. Only then, ultimately, you will get to enter into what we refer as 'flow' of life – a state where you have the powerful force to naturally succeed in life.

www.BaZiprofiling.com

THE BaZi
60 PILLARS SERIES

The BaZi 60 Pillars Series is a collection of ten volumes focusing on each of the Pillars or Jia Zi in BaZi Astrology. Learn how to see BaZi Chart in a new light through the Pictorial Method of BaZi analysis and elevate your proficiency in BaZi studies through this new understanding. Joey Yap's 60 Pillars Life Analysis Method is a refined and enhanced technique that is based on the fundamentals set by the true masters of olden times, and modified to fit to the sophistication of current times.

BaZi Collection

With these books, leading Chinese Astrology Master Trainer Joey Yap makes it easy to learn how to unlock your Destiny through your BaZi. BaZi or Four Pillars of Destiny is an ancient Chinese science which enables individuals to understand their personality, hidden talents and abilities, as well as their luck cycle - by examining the information contained within their birth data.

Understand and learn more about this accurate ancient science with this BaZi Collection.

BOOK 1   BOOK 2   BOOK 3   BOOK 4   BOOK 5   The 10 Gods

(Available in English & Chinese)

Feng Shui Collection

Design Your Legacy

Design Your Legacy is Joey Yap's first book on the profound subject of Yin House Feng Shui, which is the study Feng Shui for burials and tombs. Although it is still pretty much a hidden practice that is largely unexplored by modern literature, the significance of Yin House Feng Shui has permeated through the centuries – from the creation of the imperial lineage of emperors in ancient times to the iconic leaders who founded modern China.

This book unveils the true essence of Yin House Feng Shui with its significant applications that are unlike the myths and superstition which have for years, overshadowed the genuine practice itself. Discover how Yin House Feng Shui – the true precursor to all modern Feng Shui practice, can be used to safeguard the future of your descendants and create a lasting legacy.

Must-Haves for Property Analysis!

For homeowners, those looking to build their own home or even investors who are looking to apply Feng Shui to their homes, these series of books provides valuable information from the classical Feng Shui therioes and applications.

In his trademark straight-to-the-point manner, Joey shares with you the Feng Shui do's and dont's when it comes to finding a property with favorable Feng Shui, which is condusive for home living.

Stories and Lessons on Feng Shui Series

All in all, this series is a delightful chronicle of Joey's articles, thoughts and vast experience - as a professional Feng Shui consultant and instructor - that have been purposely refined, edited and expanded upon to make for a light-hearted, interesting yet educational read. And with Feng Shui, BaZi, Mian Xiang and Yi Jing all thrown into this one dish, there's something for everyone.

(Available in English & Chinese)

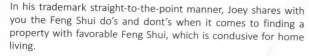

More Titles under Joey Yap Books

Pure Feng Shui

Pure Feng Shui is Joey Yap's debut with an international publisher, CICO Books. It is a refreshing and elegant look at the intricacies of Classical Feng Shui - now compiled in a useful manner for modern day readers. This book is a comprehensive introduction to all the important precepts and techniques of Feng Shui practices.

Your Aquarium Here

This book is the first in Fengshuilogy Series, which is a series of matter-of-fact and useful Feng Shui books designed for the person who wants to do a fuss-free Feng Shui.

More Titles under Joey Yap Books

Walking the Dragons

Compiled in one book for the first time from Joey Yap's Feng Shui Mastery Excursion Series, the book highlights China's extensive, vibrant history with astute observations on the Feng Shui of important sites and places. Learn the landform formations of Yin Houses (tombs and burial places), as well as mountains, temples, castles and villages.

Walking the Dragons : Taiwan Excursion

A Guide to Classical Landform Feng Shui of Taiwan

From China to Tibet, Joey Yap turns his analytical eye towards Taiwan in this extensive Walking the Dragons series. Combined with beautiful images and detailed information about an island once known as Formosa, or "Beautiful Island" in Portuguese, this compelling series of essays highlights the colourful history and wonders of Taiwan. It also provides readers with fascinating insights into the living science of Feng Shui.

The Art of Date Selection: Personal Date Selection (Available in English & Chinese)

With the Art of Date Selection: Personal Date Selection, you can learn simple, practical methods to select not just good dates, but personalised good dates as well. Whether it is a personal activity such as a marriage or professional endeavour, such as launching a business - signing a contract or even acquiring assets, this book will show you how to pick the good dates and tailor them to suit the activity in question, and to avoid the negative ones too!

Your Head Here

Your Head Here is the first book by Sherwin Ng. She is an accomplished student of Joey Yap, and an experienced Feng Shui consultant and instructor with Joey Yap Consulting Group and Mastery Academy respectively. It is the second book under the Fengshuilogy series, which focuses on Bedroom Feng Shui, a specific topic dedicated to optimum bed location and placement.

If the Shoe Fits

This book is for those who want to make the effort to enhance their relationship.

In her debut release, Jessie Lee humbly shares with you the classical BaZi method of the Ten Day Masters and the combination of a new profiling system developed by Joey Yap, to understand and deal with the people around you.

Being Happy and Successful at Work and in your Career

Have you ever wondered why some of us are so successful in our careers while others are dragging their feet to work or switching from one job to another? Janet Yung hopes to answer this question by helping others through the knowledge and application of BaZi and Chinese Astrology. In her debut release, she shares with the readers the right way of using BaZi to understand themselves: their inborn talents, motivations, skills, and passions, to find their own place in the path of professional development.

Being Happy & Successful - Managing Yourself & Others

Manage Your Talent & Have Effective Relationships at the Workplace

While many strive for efficiency in the workplace, it is vital to know how to utilize your talents. In this book, Janet Yung will take you further on how to use the BaZi profiling system as a tool to assess your personality and understanding your approach to the job. From ways in communicating with your colleagues to understanding your boss, you will be astounded by what this ancient system can reveal about you and the people in your life. Tips and guidance will also be given in this book so that you will make better decisions for your next step in advancing in your career.

Face Reading Collection

The Chinese Art of Face Reading: The Book of Moles

The Book of Moles by Joey Yap delves into the inner meanings of moles and what they reveal about the personality and destiny of an individual. Complemented by fascinating illustrations and Joey Yap's easy-to-understand commentaries and guides, this book takes a deeper focus into a Face Reading subject, which can be used for everyday decisions — from personal relationships to professional dealings and many others.

Discover Face Reading (Available in English & Chinese)

This is a comprehensive book on all areas of Face Reading, covering some of the most important facial features, including the forehead, mouth, ears and even philtrum above your lips. This book will help you analyse not just your Destiny but also help you achieve your full potential and achieve life fulfillment.

Joey Yap's Art of Face Reading

The Art of Face Reading is Joey Yap's second effort with CICO Books, and it takes a lighter, more practical approach to Face Reading. This book does not focus on the individual features as it does on reading the entire face. It is about identifying common personality types and characters.

Faces of Fortune: The 20 Tycoons to bet on over the next 10 years

Faces of Fortune is Tee Lin Say's first book on the subject of Mian Xiang or Chinese Face Reading. As an accomplished Face Reading student of Joey Yap and an experienced business journalist, Lin Say merged both her knowledge into this volume, profiling twenty prominent tycoons in Asia based on the Art of Face Reading.

Easy Guide on Face Reading (Available in English & Chinese)

The Face Reading Essentials series of books comprises of five individual books on the key features of the face — the Eyes, the Eyebrows, the Ears, the Nose, and the Mouth. Each book provides a detailed illustration and a simple yet descriptive explanation on the individual types of the features.

The books are equally useful and effective for beginners, enthusiasts and those who are curious. The series is designed to enable people who are new to Face Reading to make the most out of first impressions and learn to apply Face Reading skills to understand the personality and character of their friends, family, co-workers and business associates.

2018 Annual Releases

| Chinese Astrology for 2018 | Feng Shui for 2018 | Tong Shu Desktop Calendar 2018 | Qi Men Desktop Calendar 2018 | Professional Tong Shu Diary 2018 | Tong Shu Monthly Planner 2018 | Weekly Tong Shu Diary 2018 |

Discover the True Significance of the Ancient Art of Lion Dance

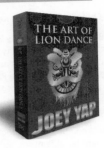

The Lion has long been a symbol of power and strength. That powerful symbol has evolved into an incredible display of a mixture of martial arts and ritualism that is the Lion Dance. Throughout ancient and modern times, the Lion Dance has stamped itself as a popular part of culture, but is there a meaning lost behind this magnificent spectacle?

The Art of Lion Dance written by the world's number one man in Chinese Metaphysics, Dato' Joey Yap, explains the history and origins of the art and its connection to Qi Men Dun Jia. By creating that bridge with Qi Men, the Lion Dance is able to ritualise any type of ceremony, celebrations and mourning alike.

The book is the perfect companion to the modern interpretation of the art as it reveals the significance behind each part of the Lion costume, as well as rituals that are put in place to bring the costume and its spectacle to life.

Educational Tools and Software

Joey Yap's Feng Shui Template Set

Directions are the cornerstone of any successful Feng Shui audit or application. The Joey Yap Feng Shui Template Set is a set of three templates to simplify the process of taking directions and determining locations and positions, whether it is for a building, a house, or an open area such as a plot of land - all of it done with just a floor plan or area map.

The Set comprises three basic templates: The Basic Feng Shui Template, Eight Mansions Feng Shui Template, and the Flying Stars Feng Shui Template.

Mini Feng Shui Compass

The Mini Feng Shui Compass is a self-aligning compass that is not only light at 100gms but also built sturdily to ensure it will be convenient to use anywhere. The rings on the Mini Feng Shui Compass are bilingual and incorporate the 24 Mountain Rings that is used in your traditional Luo Pan.

The comprehensive booklet included with this, will guide you in applying the 24 Mountain Directions on your Mini Feng Shui Compass effectively and the Eight Mansions Feng Shui to locate the most auspicious locations within your home, office and surroundings. You can also use the Mini Feng Shui Compass when measuring the direction of your property for the purpose of applying Flying Stars Feng Shui.

MASTERY ACADEMY
OF CHINESE METAPHYSICS
Your **Preferred** Choice to the Art & Science of
Classical Chinese Metaphysics Studies

Bringing **innovative** techniques and **creative** teaching methods to an ancient study.

Mastery Academy of Chinese Metaphysics was established by Joey Yap to play the role of disseminating this Eastern knowledge to the modern world with the belief that this valuable knowledge should be accessible to everyone and everywhere.

Its goal is to enrich people's lives through accurate, professional teaching and practice of Chinese Metaphysics knowledge globally. It is the first academic institution of its kind in the world to adopt the tradition of Western institutions of higher learning - where students are encouraged to explore, question and challenge themselves, as well as to respect different fields and branches of studies. This is done together with the appreciation and respect of classical ideas and applications that have stood the test of time.

The Art and Science of Chinese Metaphysics – be it Feng Shui, BaZi (Astrology), Qi Men Dun Jia, Mian Xiang (Face Reading), ZeRi (Date Selection) or Yi Jing – is no longer a field shrouded with mystery and superstition. In light of new technology, fresher interpretations and innovative methods, as well as modern teaching tools like the Internet, interactive learning, e-learning and distance learning, anyone from virtually any corner of the globe, who is keen to master these disciplines can do so with ease and confidence under the guidance and support of the Academy.

It has indeed proven to be a centre of educational excellence for thousands of students from over thirty countries across the world; many of whom have moved on to practice classical Chinese Metaphysics professionally in their home countries.

At the Academy, we believe in enriching people's lives by empowering their destinies through the disciplines of Chinese Metaphysics. Learning is not an option - it is a way of life!

MASTERY ACADEMY
OF CHINESE METAPHYSICS™

MALAYSIA
19-3, The Boulevard, Mid Valley City, 59200 Kuala Lumpur, Malaysia
Tel : +6(03)-2284 8080 | Fax : +6(03)-2284 1218
Email : info@masteryacademy.com
Website : www.masteryacademy.com

Australia, Austria, Canada, China, Croatia, Cyprus, Czech Republic, Denmark, France, Germany, Greece, Hungary, India, Italy, Kazakhstan, Malaysia, Netherlands (Holland), New Zealand, Philippines, Poland, Russian Federation, Singapore, Slovenia, South Africa, Switzerland, Turkey, United States of America, Ukraine, United Kingdom

The Mastery Academy around the world!

United States of America
Canada
United Kingdom
France
Netherlands
Denmark
Switzerland
Czech Republic
Austria
Poland
Germany
Slovenia
Italy
Cyprus
Croatia
Hungary
Greece
Turkey
Russian Federation
Ukraine
Kazakhstan
India
South Africa
China
Philippines
Kuala Lumpur
Malaysia
Singapore
Australia
New Zealand

Feng Shui Mastery™
LIVE COURSES (MODULES ONE TO FOUR)

This an ideal program for those who wants to achieve mastery in Feng Shui from the comfort of their homes. This comprehensive program covers the foundation up to the advanced practitioner levels, touching upon the important theories from various classical Feng Shui systems including Ba Zhai, San Yuan, San He and Xuan Kong.

Module One:
Beginners
Course

Module Two:
Practitioners
Course

Module Three:
Advanced
Practitioners Course

Module Four:
Master Course

BaZi Mastery™
LIVE COURSES (MODULES ONE TO FOUR)

This lesson-based program brings a thorough introduction to BaZi and guides the student step-by-step, all the way to the professional practitioner level. From the theories to the practical, BaZi students along with serious Feng Shui practitioners, can master its application with accuracy and confidence.

Module One:
Intensive
Foundation Course

Module Two:
Practitioners
Course

Module Three:
Advanced
Practitioners Course

Module Four:
Master Course in BaZi

Xuan Kong Mastery™
LIVE COURSES (MODULES ONE TO THREE)
* Advanced Courses For Master Practitioners

Xuan Kong is a sophisticated branch of Feng Shui, replete with many techniques and formulae, which encompass numerology, symbology and the science of the Ba Gua, along with the mathematics of time. This program is ideal for practitioners looking to bring their practice to a more in-depth level.

Module One:
Advanced
Foundation Course

Module Two A:
Advanced Xuan
Kong Methodologies

Module Two B:
Purple White

Module Three:
Advanced Xuan Kong
Da Gua

Mian Xiang Mastery™
LIVE COURSES (MODULES ONE AND TWO)

This program comprises of two modules, each carefully developed to allow students to familiarise with the fundamentals of Mian Xiang or Face Reading and the intricacies of its theories and principles. With lessons guided by video lectures, presentations and notes, students are able to understand and practice Mian Xiang with greater depth.

Module One:
Basic Face
Reading

Module Two:
Practical Face
Reading

Yi Jing Mastery™
LIVE COURSES (MODULES ONE AND TWO)

Whether you are a casual or serious Yi Jing enthusiast, this lesson-based program contains two modules that brings students deeper into the Chinese science of divination. The lessons will guide students on the mastery of its sophisticated formulas and calculations to derive answers to questions we pose.

Module One:
Traditional Yi Jing

Module Two:
Plum Blossom
Numerology

Ze Ri Mastery™
LIVE COURSES (MODULES ONE AND TWO)

In two modules, students will undergo a thorough instruction on the fundamentals of ZeRi or Date Selection. The comprehensive program covers Date Selection for both Personal and Feng Shui purposes to Xuan Kong Da Gua Date Selection.

Module One:
Personal and
Feng Shui Date
Selection

Module Two:
Xuan Kong
Da Gua Date
Selection

Joey Yap's
SAN YUAN QI MEN XUAN KONG DA GUA™

This is an advanced level program which can be summed up as the Integral Vision of San Yuan studies — an integration of the ancient potent discipline of Qi Men Dun Jia and the highly popular Xuan Kong 64 Hexagrams. Often regarded as two independent systems, San Yuan Qi Men and San Yuan Xuan Kong Da Gua can trace their origins to the same source and were actually used together in ancient times by great Chinese sages.

This method enables practitioners to harness the Qi of time and space, and predict the outcomes through a highly-detailed analysis of landforms, places and sites.

BaZi 10X

Emphasising on the practical aspects of BaZi, this programme is rich with numerous applications and techniques pertaining to the pursuit of wealth, health, relationship and career, all of which constitute the formula of success. This programme is designed for all levels of practitioners and is supplemented with innovative learning materials to enable easy learning. Discover the different layers of BaZi from a brand new perspective with BaZi 10X.

Feng Shui for Life

This is an entry-level five-day course designed for the Feng Shui beginner to learn the application of practical Feng Shui in day-to-day living. Lessons include quick tips on analysing the BaZi chart, simple Feng Shui solutions for the home, basic Date Selection, useful Face Reading techniques and practical Water formulas. A great introduction course on Chinese Metaphysics studies for beginners.

Joey Yap's
Design Your Destiny

This is a three-day life transformation program designed to inspire awareness and action for you to create a better quality of life. It introduces the DRT™ (Decision Referential Technology) method, which utilises the BaZi Personality Profiling system to determine the right version of you, and serves as a tool to help you make better decisions and achieve a better life in the least resistant way possible, based on your Personality Profile Type.

Millionaire Feng Shui Secrets Programme

This program is geared towards maximising your financial goals and dreams through the use of Feng Shui. Focusing mainly on the execution of Wealth Feng Shui techniques such as Luo Shu sectors and more, it is perfect for boosting careers, businesses and investment opportunities.

Grow Rich With BaZi Programme

This comprehensive programme covers the foundation of BaZi studies and presents information from the career, wealth and business standpoint. This course is ideal for those who want to maximise their wealth potential and live the life they deserve. Knowledge gained in this course will be used as driving factors to encourage personal development towards a better future.

Walk the Mountains!
Learn Feng Shui in a Practical and Hands-on Program

 Feng Shui Mastery Excursion™

Learn landform (Luan Tou) Feng Shui by walking the mountains and chasing the Dragon's vein in China. This program takes the students in a study tour to examine notable Feng Shui landmarks, mountains, hills, valleys, ancient palaces, famous mansions, houses and tombs in China. The excursion is a practical hands-on course where students are shown to perform readings using the formulas they have learnt and to recognise and read Feng Shui Landform (Luan Tou) formations.

Read about the China Excursion here:
http://www.fengshuiexcursion.com

Mastery Academy courses are conducted around the world. Find out when will Joey Yap be in your area by visiting
www.masteryacademy.com
or call our offices at **+6(03)-2284 8080**.

Online Home Study Courses

Gain Valuable Knowledge from the Comfort of Your Home

Now, armed with your trusty computer or laptop and Internet access, the knowledge of Chinese Metaphysics is just a click away!

3 Easy Steps to Activate Your Home Study Course:

Step 1:
Go to the URL as indicated on the Activation Card and key in your Activation Code

Step 2:
At the Registration page, fill in the details accordingly to enable us to generate your Student Identification (Student ID).

Step 3:
Upon successful registration, you may begin your lessons immediately.

Joey Yap's Feng Shui Mastery HomeStudy Course

Module 1: Empowering Your Home
Module 2: Master Practitioner Program

Learn how easy it is to harness the power of the environment to promote health, wealth and prosperity in your life. The knowledge and applications of Feng Shui will not be a mystery but a valuable tool you can master on your own.

Joey Yap's BaZi Mastery HomeStudy Course

Module 1: Mapping Your Life
Module 2: Mastering Your Future

Discover your path of least resistance to success with insights about your personality and capabilities, and what strengths you can tap on to maximise your potential for success and happiness by mastering BaZi (Chinese Astrology). This course will teach you all the essentials you need to interpret a BaZi chart and more.

Joey Yap's Mian Xiang Mastery HomeStudy Course

Module 1: Face Reading
Module 2: Advanced Face Reading

A face can reveal so much about a person. Now, you can learn the Art and Science of Mian Xiang (Chinese Face Reading) to understand a person's character based on his or her facial features, with ease and confidence.